The Making of a
Homegrown Terrorist

The Making of a Homegrown Terrorist

Brainwashing Rebels in Search of a Cause

Peter A. Olsson, MD

PRAEGER

AN IMPRINT OF ABC-CLIO, LLC
Santa Barbara, California • Denver, Colorado • Oxford, England

Library of Congress Cataloging-in-Publication Data

Olsson, Peter Alan, 1941–
    The making of a homegrown terrorist : brainwashing rebels in search of a cause / Peter A. Olsson, MD.
        pages cm
    Includes bibliographical references and index.
    ISBN 978-1-4408-3101-0 (hardcopy : alk. paper) —
ISBN 978-1-4408-3102-7 (e-book)
1. Domestic terrorism. 2. Terrorism—Religious aspects—Islam. 3. Hate groups—Computer network resources. 4. Terrorists—Biography. I. Title.
    HV6431.O5587   2014
    363.325—dc23   2013046085

ISBN: 978-1-4408-3101-0
EISBN: 978-1-4408-3102-7

18 17 16 15 14   1 2 3 4 5

This book is also available on the World Wide Web as an eBook.
Visit www.abc-clio.com for details.

Praeger
An Imprint of ABC-CLIO, LLC

ABC-CLIO, LLC
130 Cremona Drive, P.O. Box 1911
Santa Barbara, California 93116-1911

This book is printed on acid-free paper ∞

Manufactured in the United States of America

9|14

I dedicate this book to Vamik Volkan, MD, my mentor, colleague, and friend. Vamik has taught me about applied psychoanalytic approaches to psychohistory, international relations, and psycho-biography. His work is alive with the application of empathy and good-humored curiosity toward complex and difficult people and situations, such as homegrown terrorists and terrorism.

Adolescents and young adults will live and die for worthy causes and leaders. Thus, youths need mature adult leaders who provide noble ideals, goals, and spiritual values. An important corollary is . . . adults value being admired by youths. It helps them to imagine and create good things for their personal legacy, and the future of their community. Such adult leadership is predominantly spiritual in nature. For authentic ideals and values to endure, they must be taught by example . . . not preached. They best transcend the importance of leaders' personal wealth, power, or prestige. These are crucial forms of the power, mystery and vulnerability of love as leadership.

—Peter A. Olsson, MD

Contents

Preface

It is unethical for a psychiatrist and psychoanalyst to make a medical psychiatric diagnosis or recommend treatment without face-to-face consultation meetings with, and examination of, his or her patient. The limitations of the author's psycho biographical approach in this book need to be noted at the outset, because he has not personally examined nor treated any of the homegrown terrorist subjects discussed in this study.

The psychodynamic formulations presented, however, reflect the opinions of, and informed speculations of, the author after his study of biographical materials, recorded professional journalistic interviews, and journalists' or learned biographers' observations of homegrown terrorists.

Osama bin Laden and the other homegrown terrorists discussed in this study would shun knocking on the door of a psychoanalyst's or psychotherapist's office. Although we do not have data obtained from the analytic couch or consulting room about these homegrown terrorists, we do have books about Osama bin Laden, his videotaped statements, and his writings. There are perceptive journalistic writings that describe the observations of family, friends, neighbors, teachers, and coaches of our homegrown terrorist subjects. They can be used to make inferences and speculate about homegrown terrorists' minds and motives. Of particular **applied psychoanalytic** interest in this respect is the poignant poetry that Osama has written (Olsson 2005, 140–42). In addition, there are articles and biographies written about Osama and his radical Islamist colleagues. They offer some convergence of psychobiographical data that allow psychodynamically informed inferences about Al Qaeda leaders, their recruits, and followers. Understanding the minds and the conscious and unconscious motives of homegrown terrorists and suicide bombers has obvious heuristic and possible preventative importance.

It is, of course, fascinating for a psychiatrist, psychotherapist, or psychoanalyst to imagine how Osama bin Laden, Ayman al-Zawahiri, or other Islamist terrorists would react to a well-documented and well-timed interpretation of their destructive acting-out behavior. We can assume that their well-fortified narcissistic defenses and religious rationalizations/delusions would provide them with staunch protection at such a hypothetical confrontation. Osama bin Laden rejected even his own mother's effort to reason with him about his violent terrorist path (Bergen 2006, 151).

NOTE

Terms highlighted in **bold** throughout the text are defined in the Glossary at the back of the book.

Acknowledgments

I am indebted to, and appreciative of, Dr. Allen Sapp's Consultation to a Group for the Advancement of Psychiatry (GAP)'s May 1997 Think Tank Presentation and discussion that occurred at the GAP Committee on International Relations. The notes from our discussions were helpful in preparation of Chapter 13, "Right Wing Ideology and Its Violent Fringe." Dr. Sapp is professor emeritus at the University of Central Missouri.

Significant portions of material about a number of the homegrown terrorists discussed in this book appeared as an article titled "Homegrown Terrorists, Rebels in Search of a Cause: Understanding the Psychological Roots of Domestic Terrorism," which appeared in the summer 2013 issue of *Middle East Quarterly*, 20(3): 3–10.

I appreciate and value the concise contributions of Andrew T. Olsson who prepared the cogent and concise historical background sections about Pakistan in Chapter 12 and Chechnya in Chapter 15. Andrew also provided valuable editorial help on the manuscript.

I also appreciate the helpful consultation and editorial help provided by Robert E. White, MD, of Houston, a valued friend and colleague of over four decades.

C. F. Kendall II and Nathaniel J. Olsson provided valuable legal perspectives, for which I am grateful.

As always, I am grateful to Debbie Carvalko for her clear, practical, and knowledgeable editorial help. Her good sense of humor and encouragement are always appreciated.

Pam Olsson, MD, the love of my life and respected colleague, has been of enormous support and encouragement throughout this project.

Introduction

I don't have a single American friend, I don't understand them.
—Tamerlan Tsarnaev, the older Boston Marathon bomber,
to a photographer in 2009 (Remick 2013, 19)

The Boston Marathon bombing has refocused public attention on a steadily growing phenomenon the Obama administration has been trying to minimize: homegrown, domestic Islamist terrorists whose familiarity with American culture makes them more difficult to detect prior to their acts of terror. The two Boston Marathon bomber brothers are of Chechnyan descent but can be considered homegrown terrorists. A question is, In what home was their terror grown and nurtured? In the Tsarnaev home in Chechnya? Dagestan? Russia? Boston? Was there additional thought reform or brainwashing done via an Internet self-radicalization process? What is self-radicalization? The Internet's world of jihadist websites has blurred the boundary of whether radicalization occurs via personal contacts with radical charismatic Islamist recruiters, purely by lone wolf or wolf-pack activities, self or group self-radicalization, or, all three. The FBI investigation will likely reveal the extent that Tamerlan Tsarnaev was influenced by radical jihadists during his six-month stay in Russia and Chechnya/Dagestan (see Chapter 15).

By way of preventing similar attacks in the future, it is necessary not only to monitor terror networks but also to understand the psychodynamics of the creation of homegrown terrorists in general? What is the appeal of radical Islam to "in-betweeners" in particular, that is, young persons in a transitional phase in one or more key aspects of their lives?

DEFINITIONS

Terrorism is an act or threat of violent action against noncombatants with the objective of exacting revenge, or intimidating/influencing/ shocking an audience. It is an assault on the individual self and the group self of a people. Fear and intimidation are powerful political tools. A terror event is threatened or executed in order to threaten a society, a political hierarchy, an economy, a peace initiative, or an international agreement. One objective is the shock value of an action that is novel, symbolic, unsuspected, and strategically damaging in its pragmatic scope and painful victimization. Modern TV media provides a unique worldwide cybernetic reverberating psychodrama stage of frightening visual imagery and a powerful propaganda platform for terror events.

Homegrown terrorism constitutes terrorist attacks from within the target nation, often Western. The controversial and failed (but useful, in the author's opinion) Violent Radicalization and Homegrown Terrorism Prevention Act of 2007 defines homegrown terrorism as the "use, planned use, or threatened use of force or violence by a group or individual born, raised, or based and operating primarily within the United States or any possession of the United States to intimidate or coerce the United States government, the civilian population of the United States, or any segment thereof, in furtherance of political or social objectives." The Congressional Research Service report, *American Jihadist Terrorism: Combatting a Complex Threat,* describes homegrown terrorism as a "terrorist activity or plots perpetuated within the United States or abroad by American citizens, permanent legal residents, or visitors radicalized largely within the United States." The definition of homegrown terrorism includes what is normally considered domestic terrorism, such as the Oklahoma City bombing. Since the 9/11 attacks in the United States, and U.S. military actions in Afghanistan and Iraq, the term has often been applied to terrorism perpetrated by Western-born Muslim citizens, or those who have spent a considerable part of their lives in the West. Domestic terrorists have nearly identical means of militarily and ideologically carrying on their fight without necessarily having a centralized command structure, regardless of whether the source of inspiration is domestic, foreign, or transnational (Beutel 2007).

THE MEDIA AS TERRORISTS' MESSENGER

In 1964 Marshal McLuhan wrote presciently and prophetically about media saying:

> In a culture like ours, long accustomed to splitting and dividing things as a means of control, it is sometimes a bit of a shock to be reminded that, in operation and practical fact, the medium is the message. (McLuhan 1964, 23)

In other words, TV media, the Internet, e-mail, and social media are extensions of ourselves. The multidimensional immediacy of modern electronic media also forms a potential worldwide grandiose visual mirror and screen for the terrorist and his or her act. In a confoundedly paradoxical way, the media provides an international psychodrama stage for terrorists. If a business or an organization were to purchase the television time that terrorists get for free, it would cost millions of dollars.

Social media and the Internet add exponentially to TV images toward making terrorism an uncanny sensational media event. Many Islamic terrorists and Western domestic terrorists despise and decry the evil nature of modern technology and Western technology in particular. Yet, they paradoxically and hypocritically benefit from, and skillfully use, the Internet and modern technology. Homegrown American terrorists lone wolf Ted Kaczynski and Timothy McVeigh espoused hate and disgust with modern technology and its application. Kaczynski and McVeigh hated the American "system" of authority, yet the media aided in the expression of their spurious causes. Exciting media coverage of a terror event or on an Internet website can be used to recruit vulnerable future homegrown terrorists in search of a cause.

THE PSYCHOLOGICALLY UNCANNY IMPACT OF A TELEVISED TERROR EVENT

Many people who saw the World Trade Center towers hit by airliners said things like, "It was surreal!" or "It looked like a scary Hollywood movie." In fact, successful moviemakers or horror fiction writers exploit the same experience of "the uncanny" that a terrorist also plans. Every horror movie screenwriter should read the lesser known paper by Freud titled "The Uncanny" (Freud 1919, 219–52). Stephen King breathes these concepts in his works of fiction (Olsson, 2007, 63).

The intuitive or calculated impact of the terrorist act relies on our human tendency to briefly regress into magical, black-and-white, superstitious, or primitive thinking under stress or shock (Freud 1919, 240). Our transiently shocked nervous systems and minds become more fragile and vulnerable to anxiety and fear. Osama bin Laden had issued threats and warnings months before his terror cult's actions. This gave a magical, grandiose, even prophetic quality to the 9/11 events. It was almost like Osama bin Laden had studied Freud's paper on "The Uncanny" (Olsson 2007, 63).

Profound issues are stirred up by the psychosocial and spiritual power of TV and the Internet (YouTube and social media). Good and compassionate media and Internet programs can be accomplished. Or crime, malignant social-political manipulation, and profoundly evil displays like beheadings also become possible on the Internet. The ethical and pragmatic legal structures around media and their uses require continuing study, humility, and cooperative multidisciplinary efforts to provide appropriate controls.

THE PSYCHOLOGICAL FABRIC OF A HOMEGROWN TERRORIST RECRUITER AND HIS GROUP

Freud (1921, 123) described the leader of a horde or mob as an idealized, mythical hero who symbolizes the original idealization of the Oedipal father. He reflected upon the archaic, powerful sense of closeness in crowds, and concluded that this results from their collective projection of their ego ideals onto the leader. This group regression results in diminished maturity of conscience and collective intelligence.

Freud felt that the mobilized group processes of primitive idealization, introjection, and identification were analogous to the uncanny powers of the hypnotist. The author believes that Freud's observations can be directly applied to understanding what Osama bin Laden, Awlaki, and Azzam did with terrorist recruits, and what al-Zawahiri is still trying to mobilize with video-sermonizing performances on the Internet. Freud said that group members need the feeling that they are equally and justly loved by a leader. The leader himself, however, thinks he needs no one else. The charismatic leader is absolutely narcissistic, self-confident, and independent (Freud 1921, 123).

Freud's concepts can be used to interpret the coaxing, soothing qualities of Osama bin Laden's hypnotic television efforts, which are modeled on maternal imagery (his mother/himself). The threatening aspects of terrorist leaders' messages are derived from a stern father image. Freud said the hypnotist stirs in his follower the childhood need to obey his parents and fear of the father in particular. The subject feels he can only take a passive compliant position. His will must be surrendered, or he will be in danger. Freud thought that the follower became like a member of the primal horde alone, staring in the face of the father-leader (Freud 1921, 127).

Fortunately, America has not taken a passive masochistic stance toward Osama bin Laden, Al Qaeda, and other Islamic terror groups. Unfortunately, our American leaders do not grasp or underestimate the powerful legacy of Osama bin Laden's symbolic martyrdom and its magnetism for many Muslim youths.

The best salesperson gets his or her customer to seek him or her out to buy the product or service. Terror cult recruiters from Al Qaeda and its franchises have many exciting terror group membership sales techniques. They are sophisticated brainwashers. Internet advertisement is popular, even "hip" for modern terrorist recruiters. Charismatic imams use fiery anti-American sermons on the Internet or at mosques to attract young men who are "in-betweeners"—that is, in-between jobs, in-between relationships, in-between their family homes and their own marriage, in-between schools, or, in general, in-between young adulthood and adulthood (Olsson 2005, 108; Singer 1995, 21).

Recently, terror cult recruiters, such as the now-deceased sinister American imam Anwar al-Awlaki, have mesmerized and recruited young adult Americans into the cadres of violent Islamist jihad. Jihadi Internet sites use heroic images of Osama bin Laden, Anwar al-Awlaki, Ayman Zawahiri, Feiz Mohammad, Adam Gadahn, and other Al Qaeda charismatics to peddle their distorted propagandistic theology of violent anti-American, anti-Western jihad.

These Internet sites show followers exactly how to create and trigger violence. One such site provided this when Tamerlan and Dzhokhar Tsarnaev learned how to make the pressure-cooker bombs they ignited with remote controls at the Boston Marathon. The Tsarnaev brothers killed four people and maimed hundreds—many with lost or maimed legs. This was a truly cruel symbolism at a marathon run where good legs are essential. The attack on marathoners' legs was malevolently planned either consciously or unconsciously. Both Tsarnaev brothers were accomplished athletes (Tamerlan, a boxer, and his younger brother Dzhokhar, a wrestler). Tamerlan Tsarnaev probably had contact with Islamist bomb-making mentors in Dagestan, when he spent six months there during the year before the Boston bombing.

Some lonely, disaffected, or rebellious youths search out jihadi websites on their own (**self-radicalization**). Many repeated watching of jihadist websites for hour after hour can be similar to self-hypnosis with posthypnotic suggestions toward violent action.

NORMAL AND ABNORMAL LEADERS AND GROUPS

During rapid social and economic change and stress, utopias are often sought by fearful groups and promoted by exploitive leaders. Most utopian dreams emerge out of the psychological cesspools of malignant individual and group narcissism. When merged with fundamentalist mentality, they are destined for tragedy and destruction. It does not matter if the doomed utopia is formulated in terms of religious metaphor and precepts, or political ideology and propaganda. For example, Jim Jones's "Socialist Heaven" for his People's Temple, Luc Jouret's pollution-free and spiritually liberating suicidal journey for his Solar Temple, Hitler's fascist utopia, Osama bin Laden's terror-paved Islamofascist caliphate, and Stalin's communist state were/are, all headed for tragic failure.

One way to help prevent future apocalyptic events such as a Jonestown or Waco, even a 9/11–type event, is to carefully compare destructive cults and terror groups to normal religious groups. It is also helpful to examine relatively normal religious and political leaders, again as compared and contrasted with destructive leaders. These carefully studied comparisons between normal and abnormal lead to some important observations, conclusions, and cautions.

NORMAL RELIGIOUS GROUPS VS DESTRUCTIVE CULT GROUPS

Characteristics of Normal Religious Groups

A normal religious group has centrally shared experiences of worship, wonder, reverence, and meaningful community service. The normal spiritual leader shares leadership with group members. The normal religious group gives positive support for lifelong loving connection and support for and from families of origin. A normal religious group promotes respect and support for the sanctity, fidelity, and self-respecting boundaries of couples' freely chosen marital and sexual commitments. Normal spiritual groups do not tolerate priests, imams, rabbis, or ministers who berate or flagellate their congregations with words of derision or hate toward anyone.

The normal religious congregation embraces projects that contribute to the betterment of the community at large and not just their group narcissism or the narcissism of their leader. Such altruism is regarded as evidence of spiritual growth and value. Monies raised over and above parish staff salaries and building expenses are normally used for projects to help the broader community or society. Normal religious congregations seek sacred music that promotes joy, beauty, wonder, reverence, contemplation, and worship.

Characteristics of a Destructive Cult or Terrorist Group

Exploitive-destructive cults and Islamist terror groups concentrate a large percentage of their efforts on recruiting new members and controlling the political, spiritual, financial, social, familial, and sexual or aggressive lives of their members. These groups promote isolation from the ferment of ideas abounding in the broader society and culture. They actively seek to alienate all their members from potential moderating influences found in healthy modern families, communities, and churches of origin. In fact, the cult or terror group itself is often inserted as a member's new and, by implication, "superior/holy family." The destructive cult leader becomes a father/God/prophet himself. Fund-raising and recruiting new members is a high priority and a source of status for cult leaders. The First Amendment protection and tax-exempt status in America and democratic countries can obviously aid and abet destructive-exploitive and terror cults. Freedom of religion and speech in America and Western-styled democracies can unfortunately allow safe havens for subtly, incrementally constructed Trojan-horse cults and terror cells, masquerading as old or new religious forms of expression. The sinister plans of the group often are made secretly by the leader and his lieutenants.

NORMAL RELIGIOUS LEADERS VS DESTRUCTIVE CULT LEADERS

Characteristics of a Normal Political or Religious Leader

It is helpful to outline what personality characteristics are often possessed by those who become "good" leaders. They are capable of making "good" decisions even under adverse circumstances. A normal religious group leader has similar traits. A "successful" leader must have high intelligence. Intelligence is necessary for strategic conceptual thinking and decision making. In addition, a normal religious leader must be intelligent and knowledgeable but wise and discerning enough to avoid rigidity and fundamentalist mentality. Second, the leader must have incorruptible honesty (no mean characteristic to possess)! Third, the leader's personality organization needs to be capable of establishing and maintaining good human relationships in depth. Such an ability is essential for evaluating others realistically. Fourth, the leader requires healthy narcissism, making him or her self-assertive rather than self-effacing (all exploitive cult and terror leaders have malignant narcissism). Fifth, the leader must have a sense of caution and alertness to the world for the sake of himself and his people (Kernberg 1984, 1–17). The normal leader does not use speeches to enflame his people toward hate and destructive action or to polarize his subgroups within his group against each other.

Characteristics of Destructive (Abnormal) Leaders

Exploitive and destructive leaders develop a relentless quest to become strong parents or father/mother figures to enhance their self-esteem. This lifelong search, of course, requires a ready supply of child admirers, who are found in their followers. Such *Malignant Pied Pipers* (Olsson 2005) give psychological birth to followers through an array of indoctrination and seduction techniques. Destructive leaders have experienced harsh disappointments in their own parents and often their home community via neglect, abandonment, shame, or humiliation during their childhood. As the years go by, their loneliness and their memories of empathy-starved and shame-dominated childhoods become magnified, as if these lonely, humiliating years had become a psychological deformity.

These poignant experiences of neglect, shame, psychological abandonment, and fear of being alone lead them toward advocating dramatic action. Actions provide a sense, however spurious, of inner restitution and parallel revenge. The evolving dynamic in the terror cult family group or even worldwide community is a two-way street between the members' passive or masochistic narcissism and the active, aberrant behavior advocated and orchestrated by the leader. This time the leaders feel empowered, rather than powerless as they were in childhood.

In essence, destructive leaders gain a sense of power and mastery over their own early childhood feelings of insignificance by becoming overwhelmingly significant and powerful in the lives of their followers. The followers feel fused and merged with a power they coauthor with the leader. These followers feel special and as if they have transcended the mediocrity, ordinariness, and boredom of their families of origin.

But beneath the outward confidence and swagger is an unconscious sense of shame and a fear of humiliation ready to surface when the group or leader's progressively fragile narcissism is punctured. Thus, the honeymoon is eventually over, and because of the leader's own malignant narcissism, he recapitulates the neglect, abuse, and ultimate loneliness and victimization he once experienced as a child. But this time, the cult leader is the neglecter, abandoner, and victimizer. The grand finale, as the world saw in Jonestown, 9/11, and Waco, is group suicide or homicide. For Al Qaeda, the utopian dream of a future return of a worldwide Sharia-based Caliphate makes martyrdom while fighting the West a joyful quest toward paradise.

In summary, the leader is crucial to any group. When a normal group has an ethical, rational, and caring leader, it functions smoothly. A normal and effective leader helps facilitate rational decision making within the group, exhibits incorruptible honesty, makes decisions with empathy and realism, shares leadership and cultivates it in younger members of the group, encourages individual freedom and dignity, and respects and helps the group with positive projects that help the community at large. In times of great stress, healthy leadership matters even more. Think of New York City on 9/11 when leaders and people pulled together to help victims of the terrorist attacks.

Normal individual and group action and freedom require genuine responsibility, wisdom, independent judgment, and altruism. The above effort to compare characteristics of normal leaders and groups with *abnormal* leaders and groups, hopefully, will stimulate thought and discussion of this important topic for the application of contemporary psychology and psychiatry to societies and their leaders under great stress.

DISCERNING "HEALTHY" CHARISMA IN YOUTHS

CHARISMA: A special quality conferring extraordinary powers of leadership and the ability to inspire veneration. A personal magnetism that enables an individual to attract or influence people. (*Random House Webster's* 2001, 223)

Characteristics of Healthy Charisma	Characteristics of Unhealthy Charisma
(1) Noncutting sense of humor that connects.	(1) Cutting, sarcastic, cold-aloof humor and empathizes with peers to encourage that puts down or victimizes peers, their autonomy and participation.
(2) Sanguine ability to empathize with peers in a way that helps self and other.	(2) Empathy that largely promotes the Self above others and eventually at their expense or harm.
(3) Creativity applied to leadership that promotes creativity in group projects and in individual group members.	(3) Dark creativity that promotes destructive subgroups that cause isolation or alienation from the larger group.
(4) Charismatic leader's personal needs are met by benevolent reaching-out to challenge the peer group to connect with their community via helpful projects and activities.	(4) Charismatic leader's personal needs or psychopathology is deepened by efforts to dominate the peer group.
(5) This leader reaches out to foster and mentor positive leaders in younger grade level kids. This provides future leaders ("Generativity"). Erik Erikson (1950, *Childhood and Society*)	(5) This "leader" bullies or puts-down followers. younger aspiring leaders so as to maintain his or her fiefdom.

Active, empathic engagement, teaching and counseling by parents, teachers, coaches and caring school administrators can help to shift Unhealthy Charisma to Healthy Charisma. This takes persistent, firm but caring efforts. There is no more important project as 9/11 and Osama bin Laden's Terror Cult Leadership has shown us.

So-called homegrown terrorists are the source of great concern for U.S. Homeland Security experts. These "homegrowns" are very familiar with American or their native culture. Thus they are more difficult to detect prior to their acts of terror. Other countries obviously have their own homegrown terrorists. This book will apply individual and group psychodynamic psychology toward understanding and hopefully in aiding the prevention of *homegrown terrorism*.

1

The Vulnerable In-Betweeners and the Children of Terror

Olsson (2007, 56–57) applies to terror cults Margaret Singer's cogent idea about "in-betweener" or life-transition experience(s) of individuals, and vulnerability to seduction by an exploitive cult. Singer thought and clearly described such vulnerable individuals. They are often lonely and are in life transitions. They are between high school and college or between college and a job or graduate school. Some might be traveling away from home and unsettled in a new location or country. Other in-betweeners might have been recently jilted, divorced, or have lost a job. In-betweeners feel overwhelmed about how things are going and do not know what to do next. Singer felt, and the author agrees, that at such times all persons are more open to persuasion and are more suggestible to accepting things, ideas, and new behaviors. An **in-betweener** is less likely to consider that such offerings might have strings attached (Singer 1995, 21).

Some exploitive cults have training manuals and training programs for their cult recruiters. Such training manuals saturated with Islamist religious dogma were found in Al Qaeda training camps in Afghanistan, Yemen, Iraq, and, recently, on the Internet. They are designed, among other things, to exploit in-betweeners.

Not surprisingly, similar materials have been burgeoning in the camps and meetings of neo-Nazi groups, white supremacists, survivalists, Aryan Nations, and some radical religious conservative militant antiabortion groups. Right wing terror groups often use the so-called Christian Identity Theologies of Wesley Swift, William Gale, and Richard Butler to advance their violent antigovernment authority agendas.

Others like the recent homegrown Norwegian bomber/assassin, Anders Behring Breivik, claim to be completely radical secular "social

Darwinians" or "true" patriots not unlike Ted Kaczynski, the Unabomber, or Timothy McVeigh, the antigovernment bomber of the Oklahoma City federal building (Sapp 1997). (See Chapter 13.)

THE CHILDREN OF TERROR AND MARTYRDOM: LOCATING THE SELF-PSYCHOLOGICAL SOIL AND ROOTS OF SOME FUTURE TERRORISTS

The Dedicated Work of Dr. Rona Fields

Children who are exposed constantly to terror and death show per-
sisting impact on their mental and emotional life. Psychologist Rona
Fields has studied the cognitive, affective, and moral development
of children in Northern Ireland, the Middle East, and Africa in situations where they have grown up amid constant violence and terrorism. Fields's psychological testing and empirical study of children 6 to
16 years old reveals that these children show an intense concern about
right and wrong. The traumatized children of terror become stuck at
the stage of moral development where right and wrong are viewed in
the context of their identity group (**group self**). The threatened minority group grasps the situation in terms of righteous indignation about
the wrongs and feels entitled for vendetta (Fields 1986, 5–6).

Fields observed that these children have available a narrow range of
role models and a continuing sense of helplessness that is not corrected
by observing parental effectiveness in dealing with the terror. There is
no feeling of hope that they will ever get out of this powerlessness.
Fields reported that personality testing showed that these children and
adolescents were psychodynamically fixated at a phase of infantile impotent rage. Their raw anxiety was in response to stress based on the
perceived threat of annihilation. This developmental position is very
hard to shift because the threats persist and are reinforced over time
(Fields 1986, 6).

It is fascinating but chilling that Fields found that both Protestant
and Catholic youths in Northern Ireland had nearly identical psychodynamics and stunted moral development. Fields concluded
that in such circumstances the children have been socialized in a cli-
mate of constant intergroup violence, fear, and anger about potential annihilation. But they have low anxiety about their anger and a
higher-than-average curiosity about violence. They are more likely
to become terrorists. In fact, Fields's studies of adult terrorist groups

from Northern Ireland, members of the Palestine Liberation Organization (PLO), and South African paramilitary terrorist groups all show a State-Trait Personality Inventory that is essentially the same for all terrorists! These otherwise normal personalities have a readiness to commit violence without remorse. Their elevated scores on trait and state anger are matched by their low scores on state and trait anxiety. There is no emotional conflict about expressing or experiencing their anger through violence. Says Fields, "It is the anger of which righteous indignation is construed" (Fields 1986, 7).

It is likely that homegrown terrorists like the Boston Marathon bombers are able to split their minds in a way that they have no empathy for their victims. "**Splitting** is a mental mechanism in which the self or others are viewed as all good or all bad, with failure to integrate both the positive and negative qualities of self and others into cohesive images. Often the person alternately idealizes and devalues the same person (or the self)" (Gabbard, Litowitz, and Williams 2011, 96). Homegrown terrorists have been brain washed through repetitive exposure to radical Islamist dogma and propaganda. Over time, they vicariously identify with killed and wounded Muslim brothers and sisters who they vividly perceive as victims of American and Western invasions and violent attacks. Their split-off feelings and blunted consciences resemble Rona Fields's traumatized and terrorized child subjects. Their minds have been blurred, split, distorted, and corrupted through brainwashing, radicalization, and self-reinforcing radicalization via the *jihadi* Internet websites. Often, both the radical Internet websites and personal contact with radical imams and peer *jihadis* are involved. Prison settings or ghetto community situations are also often involved.

Some of the children Fields originally examined were later retested by her when they were jailed as young, adult terrorists. Again, she found that "these individuals will seek novel and adventurous means for experiencing and expressing their anger." In other words, it is a fearsome personality dynamic involving righteously indignant, angry violence devoid of empathy. This personality dynamic is established over childhood and exists concomitantly and secretly alongside benign-appearing "normal" day-to-day social behavior. The accumulating unconscious mandate, however, involves an inexorable "conversion of the terrorized into the terrorist" (Fields 1986, 7).

This pattern is frighteningly similar to the multigenerational patterns of child abuse and sexual abuse in many societies. An abused

child so very often becomes an abusing parent as the sad cycle is perpetuated. Mental health clinicians and researchers have observed this
consistent pattern (Engel 2005, Intro). The future homegrown terrorist
often grows up around terror events and a family or community that
positively sanctions terrorist acts or bombing as a tactic of revenge for
shared traumas while also seeking triumph over the group's fear and
anxiety.

INDOCTRINATING FATHERS IN GAZA

Jeffrey Goldberg presents cogent findings in his article entitled, "Letter from Gaza," published in *The New Yorker* on September 11, 2006.
Goldberg provides good descriptions of the imminent dangers of war
between Israel and the Palestinians in Gaza, as well as between Israel
and the Hezbollah in Lebanon. (In the author's opinion, only Israeli
and American cocoons of **denial and rationalization** protect us from
constant reality-based tension and anxiety about Gaza.)

Pertinent to this study of homegrown terrorists are Goldberg's poignant interviews with Abu Obeidah (Abu Nasser) and other Hamas
militant, rocket-firing leaders. He describes his visit to Gaza as "like
breaking into a large beachfront prison." At times, Goldberg portrays
a grim rivalry Hamas leaders feel for the media attention that Hezbollah has received. Abu Obeidah brags in an odd, surrealistic way that
Hamas is at the vanguard of the anti-Zionist Muslim revolution (Goldberg 2006, 43).

A psychological picture of the sad and defective role models that
Hamas leaders provide for their own sons emerges in Goldberg's interview with Abu Hussein, a leader of the Qassam Brigades in Gaza. During the interview, Goldberg poignantly describes the following tragic
scene: Abu Hussein pulled his young son close. Hussein wanted the
ninth grader to finish his studies but if the boy dies a martyr and takes
Jews with him, that is fine with Hussein! The boy showed Goldberg
his martyr picture with him holding an AK-47. The picture would be
posted among the Gaza martyr posters. The boy, who is Abu Hussein's
only son, hugged his father saying that all his schoolmates have martyr photos, so when they get killed they will have the best pictures.
Then the boy laughed.

Such profound sadness surrounds this scene of profound child
abuse and related masochism (Goldberg 2006, 45). At the close of his

article, Goldberg interviews Rafiq Hamdouna, a former Fatah leader, who talks about the temptations of violent death and Palestinian father–son relationships. Hamdouna said to Goldberg that every devoted Muslim father in Gaza faces this issue (Goldberg 2006, 47).

What is astounding is that these spiritually masochistic fathers have not found ways to get their rigid, stubborn Hamas leaders to compromise with, and live in peace with, Israel so that their sons could then possibly move beyond ignorant, rigid, and violent positions. The child abuse of these pathologically narcissistic Palestinian fathers is truly sad. Allah must weep at their folly! Goldberg observed the youngsters playing martyr bomber games with their play bomb vests while Goldberg interviewed their fathers. It must be assumed that the mothers of Gaza were ignorant of, intimidated by, or in agreement with these father–son death pacts and games. Father hunger, father longing, and mother longing are powerful forces for children of terror and their communities.

2

Basic Techniques of Terrorists' Brainwashing and Indoctrination

Al Qaeda training camps, some radical American mosques, right wing survivalists' camps, and even cleverly designed Internet websites for rebellious loners provide ideal climates to satisfy Singer's five conditions to put thought-reform ("Brainwashing") processes into action (Singer 1995, 64–69):

1. Keep the person unaware that there is an agenda to control or change the person. [The terrorist training camps use peer-modeling, peer pressure, and the military, weapons, and explosives training provided to excite and dazzle angry young men in search of an identity. The radical Islamist theology of jihad is presented as normal extensions of the recruits' Koranic study and memorization.]
2. Control time and the physical environment (restrict contacts, information, etc.). [This is easily accomplished in Al Qaeda Yemen camps where U.S. recruits are often sent or willingly travel.]
3. Create a sense of fear or dependency. [The charismatic leaders hold forth a fantasy of shared grandiose power and merger with their visions of victorious jihad. Fort Hood shooter psychiatrist Dr. Hassan was seduced via the Internet and personal contacts with Al-Awlaki's propaganda via e-mails! Often young people adrift are looking for an exciting and noble cause that goes beyond the humdrum boring trade or profession of their fathers.]
4. Suppress old behavior and attitudes. Manipulate a system of reward and punishments. Promised rewards from Allah in heaven and for families left behind after martyrdom are offered by Al Qaeda's distorted theology. Al Qaeda instills new behavior and attitudes. [Terror groups manipulate by a system of financial rewards and rewards of social prestige for the new terrorist identity and ideology they proffer.]
5. Put forth a closed system of logic. [Us versus Them, In-group (True believers) versus Out-group (Infidels). Imbed the system in black-and-white thinking.]

Lifton (1989, 420–37) has identified eight psychological themes central to totalistic environments. Terror cult recruiters use these themes in promoting radical behavioral and attitudinal changes in Muslim youth as they convoy them toward terrorism and martyrdom. The parallels to Singer's five conditions are self-evident.

1. *Milieu Control.* Gossip, disagreements or expressed doubts are negatively sanctioned. Rarely do young men stand up in mosques to challenge the hate-filled sermons at Friday prayers.
2. *Loading the Language.* The leaders insist on the jargon of radical Islamist theology and the "group-speak" and "groupthink" of Jihad or, in the case of right wing terrorists, Christian Identity theology concepts are used for this purpose.
3. *Demand for Purity.* The "us versus them" orientation in the camps is promoted by an all-or-nothing, black vs. white concepts . . . "our Islamist way, or the highway" belief system. There is a blurring of the Koran and radical interpretations thereof.
4. *Cult of Confession.* This is not necessary in Al Qaeda camps because the recruit has no doubts about the evil nature of Jews, Christians and infidels as radical Islamist ideology asserts.
5. *Mystical Manipulation.* A sense of the "higher purpose" of Allah becomes equated with Al Qaeda leader gurus' pronouncements as they deem themselves to be Allah's spokespersons.

Lifton thinks that such manipulated individuals develop what he calls the *psychology of the pawn.* They are unable to escape from forces that they feel are more powerful than themselves. They subordinate everything in order to adapt themselves to the imperatives created by the manipulator (1989, 423). They come to define the words' complete dedication.

6. *Doctrine over Person.* The all-encompassing doctrines of the vibrant theology and ideology of radical violent jihad are center stage. Dr. Hasan, for example, felt divinely called and justified as he killed Americans at Fort Hood! The homegrown terrorist envisions an idealized sacred utopian result for his brutal act . . . a perfect and just future world based on Sharia law.
7. *Sacred Science.* Intellectual and scientific creativity is cleverly focused on weapons training, explosives handling, chemical and biological weapons, and computer proficiency for the terror cult recruits. As our daily TV news documents, Al Qaeda operatives become exponentially more skilled in the science of death devices and bombs via the internet.
8. *Dispensing of Existence.* The elite, special, and Allah-blessed status of Jihadis as a superior group is held dear. Rich rewards for them personally are assured in paradise . . . and even for their family after they are martyred; such are frequent teachings.

The intense power of thought reform/brainwashing/mind control, described by Singer and Lifton, is made even more profound when Islamism's spiritual aura is entwined with the anti-Western, antimodernity ideology/theology of Al Qaeda and its franchises.

THE OFTEN-UNDERESTIMATED POWER OF RELIGION IN THE WAR ON ISLAMIC TERROR AND TERROR RECRUITMENT PREVENTION

Counterterrorism experts need to be reminded that the war against terrorism is often a religious, spiritual, and theological war for the so-called hearts and minds even souls of individuals and groups. Many future homegrown terrorists are torn by existing personal, family, or marital conflicts, and are very primed to project hate onto America as a negative parental **transference object**; that is, the father who disappointed them or did not protect them, or the mother who worshipped them, didn't nurture them, or neglected them.

Muslim versus Christian versus Jewish theological ideas are often used for verbal religious combat on *jihadi* Internet websites. According to a neighbor of Tamerlan Tsarnaev, the Boston bomber, Tamerlan said that the Bible was an inferior book to the holy Koran, and the Bible's ideas were merely used to excuse invasions and attacks of Muslim lands by Christians and Jews (I Don't Understand Them 2013, 1–2). This flawed dualistic thinking and fundamentalist mentality in Tamerlan Tsarnaev is right out of the **rationalizations** and writings of Osama bin Laden (Olsson 2007, 8–11; Lawrence 2005, 24–30).

Mr. Albrecht Ammon, the 18-year-old neighbor of Tamerlan Tsarnaev, reported that Tamerlan idolized the Koran and talked down the Christian Bible, which he said was being used as an excuse to invade other countries (I Don't Understand Them 2013, 2). Tamerlan, according to Mr. Ammon, said that the United States was a colonial power trying to take over the Middle East and Africa. Tamerlan also took the position that in the wars in Afghanistan and Iraq, most casualties were innocent people gunned down by American soldiers (I Don't Understand Them 2013, 2). Homegrown terrorist recruiters use such exaggerations and blurring of religious ideas with political ideas in their propaganda of hate of America and the West.

Andrew Sullivan (2001), in an elegantly written, scholarly and prescient article, supports the thesis that the war on Islamic terrorism is definitely a religious war, a war not of Islam versus Christianity and Judaism, but a war of fundamentalist mentality against faiths of all kinds that are at peace with freedom and modernity (Sullivan 2001, 1). Sullivan aptly observes that Islamic terrorism is a part of Islam not shared by most Muslims but one that cannot be ignored, minimized, or denied.

Sullivan also notes the parallel in America between aggressive violent forms of Christian fundamentalism and mainstream Protestantism and Catholicism. The author (Olsson) would note a corollary found in angry, resentful atheistic groups who confuse Christian symbols and loving traditions with destructive Christian fundamentalism and fundamentalists. In a sense, their atheistic religion compels them toward removing loving symbols of spiritual comfort, hope, and consolation from communities. They seek to detract from healthy religious traditions out of a distorted sense of "equal rights": really legalism.

TYPES OF ATHEISM

Silver and Coleman have very recently completed an evocative and interesting study about *non-belief in America*. They found six types of atheists or agnostics. (1) *Intellectual Atheists/Agnostics (IAA):* They enjoy reading and seeking open discussions, debates, and arguments about the nonexistence of God on Internet sites (Silver 2013, 3). (2) *Activist Atheists (AAA):* They want to tell others why they reject religion and why society would be better off if we all believed likewise. They are very vocal and active about other social causes like humanism, feminism, lesbian/gay/bisexual/transgender human rights, environmental concerns, animal rights, and separation of church and state (Silver 2013, 3). (3) *Seekers/Agnostics (SA):* They embrace uncertainty. They keep an open mind about their uncertainty about God's existence. Some actually miss being a believer because of the reduced social benefits and emotional or family connections (Silver 2013, 3–4). (4) *Anti-Theists:* They are assertively and diametrically opposed to religious ideology. They see religion as ignorant, backward, and socially detrimental. They are compelled to share and educate others with what they see as their superior understanding of the detrimental, even antievolutionary and antiprogressive, aspects of religion. They are outspoken, devoted, and, at times, confrontational (Silver 2013, 4). (5) *Non-Theists:* This smallest group in the study can be described as apathetic and disinterested, and they live their lives with no conscious concern about religion or the consequence of its absence in their lives (Silver 2013, 4). (6) *Ritual Atheists/Agnostics* (*RAA*): They do not believe in God or an afterlife. They attend to some religious wisdom teachings, rituals, musical opportunities, and traditions. They, in some instances, identify with Judaism, Paganism, Buddhism, or LaVeyan Satanism (Silver 2013, 4–5).

DESTRUCTIVE ATHEISM AND AMERICA'S REDUCED RESISTANCE TO HOMEGROWN TERRORIST RECRUITMENT

The destructive atheists referred to by the author earlier seem to fall into numbers 2 and 4 in Silver and Coleman's typology. Silver and Coleman's further detailed study will be of great heuristic value. It is the author's opinion that destructive, narrow-minded atheism erodes America and the West's ability to prevent the recruitment of home-grown terrorists. A parallel study of the various forms and types of theism would be of considerable value. The author's exploration of destructive **fundamentalist mentality** as found in Islamism would be informed and forwarded by such an additional study.

Lively, articulate, well-reasoned, philosophically well-founded Judeo-Christian apologetics courses and compassionate teaching of Judeo-Christian values and traditions are valuable assets in home-grown terror prevention. The author believes that if Ted Kaczynski, Adam Gadahn, Omar Hammami, Colleen LaRose, and Richard Reid had the availability of such materials and particularly if shared with them by steady, loving father figures, it could have helped forestall their radicalization. Bill Ayers acknowledged at times the impact of authentic Christian imagery on his thought and feelings (Ayers 2001, 107). Ayers clearly had benevolent, moral, and altruistic intentions even in the midst of his radicalization (Ayers 2001, 62).

See the work of Dinesh D'Souza as a good example of thought-ful, reasoned, and lively presentations of Christianity that is not off-putting to thoughtful youths (D'Souza 2009). Such books, websites, and courses available to high school, college, and graduate students help prevent the nihilism and situations like "Harvard's Culture of Despair" that Alston Chase thought had such a profoundly negative effect on Ted Kaczynski, the Unabomber, during his Harvard years.

Atheism in some of its forms can clearly be as destructive as fundamentalist mentality. Many of the young homegrown terrorists discussed in this book like John Walker Lindh (The American Taliban) and Adam Gadahn found the Koran and Islam more meaningful than the tepid, uninspiring Judeo-Christian commitments of their disappointing parents. Radical Islam is often perceived by youths as strong compared to the weak agnosticism, atheism, or tepid Judeo-Christian stances of their parents.

I'm not an atheist. The problem involved is too vast for our limited minds. We are in the position of a little child entering a huge library filled with books in many languages. The child knows someone must have written these books. It does not know how. It does not understand the languages in which they are written. The child dimly suspects a mysterious order in the arrangement of the books but doesn't know what it is. That, it seems to me, is the attitude of even the most intelligent human being toward God. (Einstein's statement cited in Isaacson 2007, 386)

3

In-Betweener Countries and Communities

Like "in-betweener" individuals, countries and communities can sometimes become large-group "in-betweeners." They are vulnerable on a larger scale than individuals to terror cult recruitment efforts. This is particularly true for late adolescent and disaffected young adult populations in countries or population groups in transition such as Afghanistan after the Soviet occupation, Iraq after the defeat of Saddam or the American departure, among immigrant Muslim youth rioting in France, in politically unsettled Lebanon after the departure of Syrian armed forces, and unstable Somalia, Sudan, and Yemen. In such social, political, and cultural transitions, there are extended periods of vulnerability to the recruitment efforts of terror cults like Al Qaeda. "Arab Springs" can be fertile recruitment grounds for Salafi Jihad. The social context that rewards the emerging jihadi is in a kind of reverberating cybernetic equilibrium with his or her internal identity and self-formation.

Stern (2003, 220–22) describes in detail the Madrassah schools in Pakistan. She offers a poignant interview with Syed Qurban Hussain, a traditional doctor of herbal medicine and father of seven sons, all of whom were trained as mujahideen fighters in Afghanistan. One son died a martyr in the jihad. He had been educated through the eighth grade, learning the Koran by heart in a Madrassah. Stern reports that Hussain felt happy to have given a son to the cause of Jihad. Hussain is convinced that his dead son who gave his life to Allah will live forever. They earn 70 places for family members in heaven. The martyr apparently picks these people after he arrives in paradise. What a powerful motivator for *jihadi* membership and martyrdom! Certainly so in an in-betweener community.

Hussain told Stern that everyone in his village treats him with more respect for having a martyred son. Martyrs in a village stimulate more youths to join the jihad. The spirit of the whole village soars (Stern 2003, 220–21).

Thus, whole communities can be in-betweeners and are capable of being seduced and recruited by Islamists of Al Qaeda and their allies. The Al Qaeda cult is built on a pied piper *jihadi* theology that declares a "just cause" for the terror group's actions. The "cause" is posited by the self-appointed malignant messiah. Radical Islamic terror groups like Al Qaeda use and twist Muslim teachings and the Koran to suit their own ends in recruiting and indoctrinating recruits. Many Madrassah schools are like prep schools for *jihad*! These recruits to terror cults come to understand death by martyrdom as a desirable end that brings respect to the martyr's family. The spiritual/religious sermonizing and discussions draw many young people toward the idealistic pursuit of social justice or the utopian causes embedded in jihadist propaganda. The exciting study of weapons, military tactics, physical fitness, and bomb-making technology appeals to young people. They prefer jihadism to the mundane vocations of their own fathers. Jobs are scarce in most countries because of global economic problems. Al Qaeda's affiliates like the Muslim Brotherhood in Egypt and the Taliban in Afghanistan have political and public service arms that help provide housing, water, sanitation, and electricity. These projects project credibility and apparent genuine goodwill.

Like other malignant pied pipers, Al Qaeda's now-martyred bin Laden's appeal has a unique "fit" or appeal to magnify and expand normal adolescent rebelliousness and search for independent identity. Anna Freud (1936, 13–14) observed that adolescents become enthusiastic about community activities at times and at others they long for solitude. They can be submissive to a chosen leader or defiant to any authority. They can be extremely self-absorbed or materialistic, and simultaneously very idealistic. What would be "normal" adolescent rebellion and protest for some adolescents become terrorist identity, actually negative identity and actions—all via the tutelage of a malignant leader like al-Awlaki. In other words, Al Qaeda recruiters, by intuition, design, or mere favorable location, take advantage of a normal adolescent stage. Adolescents in transition are typically characterized by independent strivings, rebellion, and searching for identity. The turmoil and joblessness in the Middle East and many parts of the Muslim world create many young adults who are in the phase of what psychoanalysts call "prolonged adolescence." Bernfeld (1923, ix) describes this specific kind of male adolescent development as "the protracted type." Osama bin Laden himself seemed stuck in a protracted destructive adolescent acting-out pattern of behavior until his death. Protracted adolescence extends far beyond the usual time frame of adolescent characteristics. It is epitomized by intensely creative work that is bent toward idealistic aims and assertion of intense moral and spiritual values. It can also lead to what Erikson called **negative identity formation**.

There are uncanny similarities in "follower psychology" between Al Qaeda recruits and recruits in destructive cults. The followers are not all poor or uneducated young people. Osama bin Laden's lieutenants and Al Qaeda leader colleagues are well educated and collectively dedicated to the ideal of jihad. Radical Islamists like bin Laden and al-Awlaki seem to recruit by using personal charisma and manipulating the Koran. These manipulations of the Koran form exciting mixtures of theology turned into starkly articulated radical political action ideology. In fact, Osama and company's followers often seek the Islamists out via their own adolescent identity searching, rebellion, or idealism! All good salespersons savor customers who seek them out, rather than having to canvas mosque attendees or make cold-calls on the Internet.

Marc Sageman (2004, 82–91) emphasizes the importance of *social networks* in the origins and development of what he calls "the Global Salafi Jihad." His careful and detailed study of 175 jihadi participants is valuable in its social psychological explanatory power. Sageman emphasizes the important motivational power of the support for future jihadis found in social networks. It is complementary with the intrapsychic/psychodynamic approaches used in this book. Social terror networks are the external side of the inner personal identity coin of the jihadis. In other words, external experiences in jihadis' social networks are powerful influences in intrapsychic identity formation and, therefore, homegrown terrorist formation. (There are no Robinson Crusoes without men Fridays.) In addition to his ideas about motivation, Sageman makes astute practical recommendations of importance for informed law enforcement and policy makers.

THE INDIVIDUAL SELF AND THE GROUP SELF

Individual Self-Formation

Every young child experiences two basic forms of self-love during his or her first three years. At times there is a sense of grandioseexhibitionistic self-delight, and at other moments, an admiration and resonance with the idealized image of the parent or their surrogate childhood hero. The smooth, steady, and healthy integration of the self is facilitated by responsive, empathic, and confidently affirming participation by parents or their surrogates. Empathic parenting helps modify the child's early grandiose fantasies of undue power, ambition, and significance in interaction with the strength of parental heroes. This socialization process provides gradually internalized realizable goals, values, and guiding principles for the young individual. These early, crucial, and transitional self-other experiences with parents or role models provide models in the young mind for self-love, self-esteem, intimate relationships, and confidant, responsible actions (Kohut 1971, 70–71).

Group Self-Formation

There is a parallel process by which an individual's sense of himself or herself as part of a group is formed during his or her personality development (Kohut 1978, 837–38). In essence, inner representations of our self and our self-in-a-group are parallel and conjoined during very early developmental and maturational processes. A group can become greater or lesser than the sum of its members in terms of morality, compassion, or evil.

LEADERS, SELF-EXTENSIONS, AND GROUP POWER

Volkan (1986, 27–34) has observed that children often experience angry or destructive feelings as dangerous and alien. These dangerous impulses are often displaced onto the external world of "others." This externalizing process is the way we all form a concept of 'the enemy," really a projected part of our own feelings. As our sense of self and self-in-a-group is forming, there are other influences besides our parents. These have been called "extensions of the self," extensions of the group-self experience, or "cultural amplifiers" (Volkan 1986, 31–34). These self-extensions include the national geography or terrain and symbols and monuments such as flags, churches, mosques, or synagogues. They also often include charismatic political figures from outside the family. Fiery and grandiose hate speeches can stir the rebellion or idealism of youth, as can dramatic Internet presentations.

GROUP PSYCHOLOGY AND COMMUNITIES
WHERE TERRORISTS RECRUIT

It is important to understand the uniquely chilling social-psychological fit between the religiously flavored charismatic leadership of Al Qaeda recruiters and the large group psychology of communities where they recruit devoted terrorists. It was a serious mistake to glibly label and dismiss Osama bin Laden as simply a mass murderer, psychotic, thug, or criminal. Al Qaeda and others are not merely problem groups for law enforcement officials' attention. In fact, Osama bin Laden was and still is a Robin Hood–like figure and a spiritual hero for many people in the Muslim world. Al Qaeda gurus and Internet propaganda are often sought out by "homegrown" aspiring American *Jihadis*. Some of the power of Al Qaeda's attacks has involved psychological power domains. It is thus important for us to understand the intrapsychic dynamics as well as the group psychology behind Al Qaeda's power. This can help in our recovery from post-9/11 trauma, in the prevention of future attacks, and in spotting future homegrown terrorists early in their negative identity searches.

HOMEGROWN SUICIDE BOMBERS

Homegrown suicide bombers have found fertile psychological soil and roots in in-betweener countries like Iraq, Afghanistan, Pakistan, and other unstable Arab and Muslim communities. Among leaders and organizers of suicide bomber groups, a state of low self-esteem is converted to a sense of unusual self-importance. The leaders come to think they have special abilities; they are convinced that they have special abilities in reasoning and judgment. Such a superiority complex leads to a sense of entitlement about dominating and controlling other people. The terrorist convinces himself that he acts for the benefit of others in his community, even if it entails extremes of abuse and violence. Black-and-white thinking prevails. This feeling of special status, in fact, reflects a sluggish self, a self that is unable to feel its genuine significance because of the psychological neglect or distortions via rigid, narrow dogmatic moral teaching during its early development (Olsson 2007, 80–88).

TECHNIQUES AND CIRCUMSTANCES OF TERROR CULT RECRUITMENT

What kind of ideology or approach do terror cult leaders use to attract followers? In regressed communities that feel victimized, a rigid, moralistic, and fundamentalist ideology is provided to bolster group self-confidence. The unconscious aim of the leader may be to rebel against the early disappointments in his life, but on the surface he becomes a strong and charismatic leader. This dramatic terror-group leadership experience and identity compensates for his inner weakened or injured self. He might have otherwise gone unnoticed by others. This need for a feeling of strength is evidenced by Osama bin Laden's continuous search for strong father figures among men like Azzam, al-Zawahiri, and Turabi. It is also found in his effort to be a great warrior father figure himself (Olsson 2007, 136–41). This rebellion and revolutionary attitude gets expressed in dramatic suicide bombing operations and giant explosions.

SUICIDE CULT FOLLOWERS AND PERFORMERS

The narcissistic injuries to followers in adolescence result in low self-esteem. This affects the developmental processes through which these individuals pass. According to Erik Erikson's psychosocial (epigenetic) model of personality development, individuals develop an ego identity by late adolescence. This identity is assimilated from the emotional, intellectual, and moral standards in the family and community. If this stage of identity formation is passed through successfully, the individual will have a clear identity, that is, a sense of who he is and where he comes from, as well as his role in society and in life in general.

In other words, the lack of feelings of basic trust (Erikson) and lost self, fragmented self, or false self (Kohut 1971, 70–71), caused by unresolved early life adversities, results in failure to develop a solid identity. Instead, a diffused identity is formed, a vague identity that does not grasp an authentic meaning of existence. This vague identity continues to create cravings for clearer definition and meaning. These individuals may become susceptible to recruitment and brainwashing by charismatic leaders. The low self-esteem of some potential followers leads to them to identify with the strong outlook of the leaders. In this way, a spontaneously organized network is formed with strong bonds and destructive plans.

Olsson (2005, 20–22) uses the analogy of the Pied Piper of a German myth to describe the operations of a terror cult leader. In the story, the Pied Piper used his music to lead away the rats and mice that had infested a village. When the villagers did not pay the Piper for his services as they had originally agreed, the Piper got revenge by leading off the village children. They were never returned. The villagers grieved deeply.

A recently deceased malignant pied piper is the terror cult leader in Iraq, Zarqawi. He sought recruits among Iraqi children as potential future terror performers. The pipers of terror try to convince Iraqi children that their death in a terror bombing gives them immortality and God's smile of greeting them in heaven. The mass media provides free publicity for the terror cult and leader, and their grandiose narcissistic affirmation via the terrorist event.

SOCIAL PSYCHOLOGY OF SUICIDE BOMBERS

Against expectations, it was found that most suicide bombers do not come from low socioeconomic status families. Most come from upper middle-class families. Most have high educational achievement, and a large proportion of them had the opportunity to travel to the West to further their education. Problems begin for young immigrants. These individuals start to feel marginalized in the new Western cultures. They feel lonely and devalued. They seek companionship and support at mosques, where the charisma of radical Islamist clerics turns them into followers in terrorist cells. The comfort and power found in these groups is accompanied by anger toward Western ways and standards. The domineering leader's charisma draws them into the radical fundamentalist mentality of hate. Western civilization becomes the target of their hatred. Even innocent children and civilians become targets of homicidal bombings.

THE PEER PRESSURE POWER OF VICARIOUS ADMIRERS

Another aspect of the phenomenon of suicide killing is the presence of a number of populations that consider these acts heroic and sacrificial. The suicide bomber may be motivated by the desire to have the attention of his people, an attention that was not available when he was a growing child or an adolescent. If his countrymen do not encourage such a maladaptive way of behavior, the potential bomber may use other, less destructive, ways of being admired by his people. These new ways can even be of benefit to society. If the Arab and Muslim populations do not send messages of acceptance for terrorist acts, then very few individuals will commit them. This point underlines the need for vigorous and ubiquitous political participation by as many Iraqis as possible.

Here we can apply ideas about societal regression in Islamic and Arab countries. These countries and cultures have been suffering continuous turmoil and instability for centuries. Regression, with all its consequences, is usual in such circumstances. One of the consequences is the need for a strong leader to satisfy needs for dependency and protection. Enter the dictators who make the situation worse by directly preventing societal progression in many Arab/Muslim countries. Individual rights are suppressed to secure "protection," women's rights are ignored, and productive activities of individuation are inhibited. Individual identities are diffused in order to maintain "safe" societal regression and dependency. A rigid fundamentalist religious identity is fostered. Empty rituals are rewarded, while inner values and identity are lost or weak.

Even words describing values are emptied of their meaning by continuous abuse. Rigid rules judge intimate interactions, even marital relations. "Big Brother" is watching. Primitive defenses such as **projection** are commonplace as a result. Conspiratorial thinking ensues. Polarized ideas—"us" vs. "them"—are encouraged, and nations in the West easily become their enemies. Such in-betweener states of social psychology have begun to arise more virulently in Iraq after the U.S. haste to leave without insisting on a status of forces agreement.

But what makes individuals involve themselves as performers in regressed malignant groups such as suicide bombing terror cults? The regressive processes discussed earlier and especially those directed toward women in such countries affect the quality of care given to children in these cultures. Early developmental emotional disturbances, including narcissistic injuries and defective character structure, are inevitable in such an environment. A constant atmosphere pervaded by the fear of sudden death from a suicide bomb blast is in itself eroding of basic trust and healthy morality and narcissism. These circumstances result in defective identity formation. The group identity based on such regressed societal states will inevitably be marred by the presence of grudges, paranoia, and dishonesty. It can be expected that simplistic and violent solutions will prevail, which are occurring again in Iraq, in escalated fashion.

The process of identity formation depends on a society or culture's avenues of educational and vocational pursuits for its young people. If a culture is able to present youth with these opportunities, then young people do not need to turn to radical causes or fundamentalism for their identity formation.

THE WEST AS FATHER FIGURE (LARGE-GROUP TRANSFERENCE)

The West (i.e., Western Europe and the United States) is a pioneering location in most fields of endeavor: science, education, and political organization. In addition, the West was involved directly in the modern history of most Islamic countries through long years of occupation, rule setting, and the establishment of systems of government, administration, and leadership. It is interesting that bin Laden strove to attract the attention of the "Western" media for his purposes. Osama scoffed at modernity but did not mind using modern TV and media for his propaganda. The West, with its democracy and encouragement of human rights, becomes a father figure, the target/victim of displaced narcissistic aggression and explosive, rebellious rage.

Volkan traces the powerful connections between a hurt and victimized country and the spiritual warrior-leader who himself feels personally victimized. A large group or country thus claims a leader to focus its collective hate, revenge, and hoped-for triumph.

Volkan also asks an important question:

> But how does a pathologically vengeful individual such as Osama bin Laden [or Mullah Omar], persuade other individuals to die intentionally for his politico-religious cause? (Volkan 2004, 157)

In essence, Volkan's answer is through charismatically applied, religiously saturated indoctrination, education, and social approval; a person's large-group identity/group self is made to trump his individual identity. Volkan concludes:

> Thus, future suicide bombers feel normal, and often experience an enhanced self-esteem. They become, in a sense, a spokesperson for the traumatized community and assume that they, at least temporarily, can

reverse the shared sense of victimization and helplessness by expressing the community's rage. (Volkan 2004, 159)

Many experts underestimate the power of the religious imagery and loyalty that Al Qaeda and its franchises use and abuse. In the process of their terror cult's Pied Piper music, Osama bin Laden, Ayman Zawahiri, and others seem to be seeking a sense of inner restitution and revenge as they lead their followers away from their families and countries of origin. Recruits join Al Qaeda's *jihad* of **acting out**. Al Qaeda's Robin Hood–like heroes are the ultimate malignant pied pipers. Osama bin Laden sought payback from his disappointing Saudi father and father figures among contemporary Saudi leaders–and their Western friends! Ayman Zawahiri seeks similar revenge against Egyptian father figures like the now-defeated Mubarak.

The West was and is a negative collective father figure for Al Qaeda. Osama bin Laden was/is an idealized hero for many Muslim youths. Despite our American administration's downplaying of it, we are in one key respect fighting a religious war. We are in a religious/theological/ philosophical war of ideas against Al Qaeda's version of Islam. One can argue that fundamentalist mentality poses grave dangers, whether it is Christian, Jewish, or Muslim. So, when it comes to social justice, it is often Al Qaeda or Sharia's way or the highway, Timothy McVeigh's way or a bomb, Ted Kaczynski's way or a bomb, and so on.

4

The Personal Pathway Model of Terrorist Development

Eric Shaw (1986, 188–89) has presented a pragmatic model by which the development of homegrown terrorists can be understood. Shaw calls it "the Personal Pathway Model." It can be usefully applied to understanding homegrown terrorists. We use it here in combination with the in-betweener concept mentioned earlier in this book. Shaw's ideas are cogent and complementary with the intrapsychic psychodynamic concepts in the fabric of our study.

Shaw found four dynamics that help make terrorists: (1) Their identity is solidified through the group cohesion and personal connection instilled in them through shared experiences of harsh treatment they receive from security forces and prison experiences. (2) narcissistic injuries during childhood and adolescence. (3) A telling contradiction in future terrorists' experiences occurs when they realize that there are glaring inconsistencies between their parents and/or families of origins' political philosophies and beliefs and their parents' actual impotence in terms of effective social or moral action. In modern vernacular, "They talk the talk but they don't walk the walk"! (4) Young nascent terrorists are frustrated about failure to achieve a traditional professional, marital, or vocational place in society, even though they often have had adequate educations. Prison can provide a personal connection, spiritual inspiration, and group identity for a future terrorist. Al Qaeda and its franchises implement a comparable but calculated psycho-inspirational charismatic mystical indoctrination and group connection in their training camps. The Internet serves as a homeschooling or virtual Al Qaeda training camp. The recent homegrown terrorist brothers in Boston apparently participated in this virtual world extensively. (See Chapter 15.)

OSAMA BIN LADEN—PROTOTYPE OF THE PERSONAL PATHWAY TO TERRORISM

We can see in bin Laden's life trajectory evidence of what Olsson calls dark epiphanies in destructive cult leaders (Olsson 2005, 34–35). These later life experiences reify and magnify their earlier molding experiences of disappointment, neglect, shame, or humiliation experienced toward parents and other childhood role models. In adolescent or young adult life phases, parental surrogate heroes are often chosen to counteract disappointment or humiliation/shame experiences with parental figures. Osama bin Laden had many such father and brother replacement heroes on his road to being a homegrown Saudi terrorist.

Osama bin Laden's Life Pathway toward Homegrown Terror

Osama bin Laden's father, Mohammad, was born in about 1930, and immigrated as a laborer from a poor Yemeni family to Saudi Arabia in the late 1950s. His son Osama was born in Saudi Arabia on March 10, 1957, in Riyadh. *Osama* means "young lion" in Arabic. Mohammad bin Laden became a skilled engineer, started a construction company, and gained the enduring respect and favor of both King Saud and his successor, King Faisal. Mohammad was a trusted confidant of King Saud. King Faisal gave Mohammad bin Laden the lucrative contract to rebuild the Islamic holy sites at Mecca and Medina in 1973 (Bergen 2001, 47–48).

Mohammad bin Laden had 11 wives during his lifetime; Osama had more than 50 siblings. Osama's mother, Hamida, is a Syrian, and Osama was the only son of her marriage to Mohammed bin Laden. Hamida refused to accept the traditionally passive female role in the marriage. Sharp conflicts over this issue led Mohammed to banish Hamida to another town (Tabuk). Osama, already of low family rank as the 17th son, was separated from his mother (Robinson 2001, 39).

Some "quality time" for Osama and his father occurred during an annual weeklong "male-bonding" winter hunting vacation in the wild desert regions of the Saudi kingdom. Osama blossomed during these brief trips with his father and his royal friends. Mohammed was very impressed with Osama's prowess in the desert, and probably recalled his own boyhood adventures in the Yemeni desert. Osama also excelled in Islamic studies, which drew positive attention and praise from his father (Bergen 2006, 16–18).

Osama bin Laden's Father's Death as Psychological Wound and Profound Narcissistic Injury

Though a multimillionaire, Mohammad bin Laden was poverty stricken when it came to paying the Piper of parenthood. It was impossible for him to spend quality time with each of his 50 children, particularly his bright and perceptive son of the "lesser" Syrian wife. He espoused religious piety but also worshipped the accumulation of money. Osama was 10 when his father died. Mohammad bin Laden was traveling home when his helicopter crashed in the desert. Observers reported that 10,000 men gathered for his funeral. Osama seemed deeply affected. Robinson says:

> His grief was deeper than simply the loss of a loved one. Beneath the surface, he had long repressed a deep gouge in his psyche caused by the partial loss of his mother (via divorce) and a relationship with his father shared with so many siblings, a handful of wives, and the pressure of a vast business empire. (Robinson 2001, 54–55)

We know that since his boyhood and early school years, Osama bin Laden had been deeply devoted and committed to Wahhabism (Coll 2005, 50–61). Robinson observes that before his father's death Osama and his father were drawn closer because of their mutual embracing of conservative Islam. The paternal relationship Osama craved was dashed by Mohammad Bin Laden's sudden death. Family members recall him reeling emotionally and withdrawing into himself (Robinson 2001, 55).

OSAMA'S SHAME, PAIN, AND HUMILIATION AS "SON OF THE SLAVE"

Another source of narcissistic wounds in Osama's childhood is found in the way he was treated by his half-siblings in the household. Osama's banished birth-mother, Hamida, was spitefully referred to as *Al Abeda* (the slave). Osama was cruelly labeled *Iban Al Abeda* (son of the slave). This constant teasing and devaluation of Osama by his half-siblings hurt him deeply and festered in his heart (Robinson 2001, 39).

The Painful Loss of Osama's Best Friend

During his preadolescence and early adolescence, Osama had one best friend. This friendship with Abdul Aziz Fahd began during the annual father–son desert camping trips with their fathers. They enjoyed frequent visits because their fathers were close. They also spoke on the phone frequently. But when Mohammad bin Laden died, the two families' relationship changed. The bin Laden family remained respected by the Fahd family, but the closeness between the two families ceased (Robinson 2001, 59).

Shortly after Osama returned to Jeddah from Tabuk, he was delighted to learn that Prince Fahd was soon coming to Jeddah for a visit. His best friend Abdul Aziz would be with the prince. During Abdul's visit, Osama tried dozens of times to contact his friend by phone but was rebuffed. Osama was even turned away from the door of the house where Abdul was staying. Osama never heard from or seen his friend again. This was the source of Osama's intense and relentless search for friends and brothers.

OSAMA'S SEARCH FOR FATHER FIGURES, MENTORS, AND BROTHERS IN TERROR

Peter Bergen (2001, 55) documents the notion that, consciously, bin Laden idealized his father. Osama said that his father was eager that one of his sons would fight against the enemies of Islam, and it is clear that Osama saw himself as that chosen son. According to Bergen, Osama told a Pakistani journalist, "My father is very keen that one of his sons should fight against the enemies of Islam. So I am the one son who is acting according to the wishes of his father" (Bergen 2001, 55).

Thus began Osama's hungry search for father figures. Let us examine several of these men in depth.

Azzam

During his college years, Osama began to show intense interest in Islamic studies. One of his mentors was Sheik Yussuf Abdallah Azzam, who was born in a village near Jenin, Palestine, in 1941. Sixteen years older than Osama, he graduated with a degree in theology from Damascus University in 1966. Assam hated Israel, which he blamed for taking Palestinian land. Azzam fought against Israel in the 1967 war. He got a master's degree and doctorate in Islamic jurisprudence at al-Azhar University in Cairo by 1973 (Bergen 2001, 55). He was extremely charismatic. The eloquent Azzam established the worldwide network of *jihad* that won the Afghan war against the Russian communists.

Osama and Azzam believed fanatically in the need for Khalifa, the dream that Muslims around the world could be united under one devout Islamist ruler (Bergen 2001, 55).

Qutb and Rahman

Azzam was a friend of the famous *jihad* ideologue Sayyid Qutb and the Egyptian sheik Omar Abdel Rahman (who inspired the 1993 bombing of the World Trade Center towers). All three were heroes and mentors of Osama. They were leaders in the formation of an Internet network of holy warriors in the 1980s (Bergen 2001, 55).

Sayyid Qutb was executed in 1966, but his writings in prison led him to be called the Karl Marx of Islamist global *jihad.* Qutb wrote his masterwork, *In the Shade of the Quran.* Qutb's work has inspired Al Qaeda, Egyptian Islamic Jihad, the Islamic Group (Egypt), and the Muslim Brotherhood.

Qutb's ideas are sophisticated and powerful. He went to college in Cairo. He wrote novels, poems, and a book that is still well regarded, called *Literary Criticism: Its Principles and Methodology.* Qutb traveled to the United States in the 1940s and studied education administration at Colorado State College of Education (Bergen 2001, 203).

Qutb's Muslim youth–inspiring prose comes not from an academic ivory tower, but from prison, where anti-Western hatreds find their spiritual headwaters. Qutb thought the human race had lost touch with human nature. Man's inspiration, intelligence, and morality were degenerating. Sexual relations were deteriorating "to a level lower than the beasts." Man was miserable, anxious, and sinking into insanity and crime. People were turning, in their unhappiness, to drugs, alcohol, and existentialism. Qutb admired economic productivity and scientific knowledge. But he did not think that wealth and science were rescuing the human race. He thought that the richest countries were the unhappiest of all (Berman 2001, 203).

Abu Musab al-Suri: Theorist of Jihad

Al-Suri was a brilliant Islamist brother who not only inspired Osama bin Laden but also criticized him extensively. In the long run, he has been in many ways more dangerous and subtle than Osama. Al-Suri is theoretician and theologian of the death politics of Islamofascism. He was born into a middle-class family in Aleppo, Syria, in 1958. He is described as red-haired and sturdily built. He has a black belt in judo and his real name is said to be Mustafa Setmariam Nasar. Al-Suri studied engineering at the University of Aleppo, where, like many jihadists, he got involved in politics. He moved to Jordan where he joined the Muslim Brotherhood that opposed the Syrian dictator Hafez al-Assad. In 1982, Assad killed about 30,000 people in the city of Hama, a Muslim Brotherhood base. Al-Suri was shocked by such violent action, renounced the Brotherhood, and moved to Europe for several years.

After his marriage and Spanish citizenship, al-Suri moved to Afghanistan, where he met Osama bin Laden. He was greatly critical of Osama's training camps because they were disorganized and taught no ideology or Islamist doctrine (Wright 2006, 48). Al-Suri moved back to Spain in 1992, where he established a terrorist cell and soon moved to London where he wrote articles for *al-Ansar* whose editor, Abu Qatada, the Palestinian cleric, was regarded as the spiritual guide of Al Qaeda in Europe. Al-Suri and others in their Jihadi think tank began planning to undermine the despotic regimes in the Arab world and promotion of attacks on the largely unaware West. The Saudis regarded al-Suri as far more radical than Osama in the early 1990s when Al Qaeda was largely an anticommunist organization. Al-Suri and the very puritanical Salafi jihadis used the presence of American troops in the Arabian Peninsula and the Saudi royal family's complicity in order to stoke bin Laden's anger (Wright 2006, 50).

Wright was told by Peter Bergen, who had spent time with al-Suri, that al-Suri is tough, smart, intellectual, and a serious student of history (Wright 2006, 50). Al-Suri, who greatly admired the Taliban, told Osama in 1999 that he was endangering the Taliban regime with his highly theatrical attacks on American targets! Like a tough mentor, al-Suri mocked bin Laden's narcissistic love of publicity (Wright 2006, 50).

Al-Suri saw his legacy as the codifier of doctrines that would inspire future generations of Muslim youths for religious war. In 2002, in an Iranian hideout, al-Suri began writing his 1,600-page magnum opus called "Call for Worldwide Resistance," which was published on the Internet in 2004. Al-Suri writes chilling words about creating the greatest number of casualties for America and its allies. He specifically hates Jews but he does not leave out NATO, Russia, China, atheists, pagans, and hypocrites.

Al-Suri regrets the demise of the Taliban, which he and Salafi jihadis see as the modern world's only true Islamic government. Al-Suri thinks the next stage of jihad will be carried out by small groups or individuals, which he calls "leaderless resistance." Later he predicts war on an "open front." Al-Suri cleverly supports the use of democracy to gain broader public support. Hamas in Gaza may be an example of a clever al-Suri doctrine. Al-Suri does caution against harming other Muslims, women, and children, and other noncombatants. Suri saw the American occupation of Iraq as a wonderful rescue of the Jihadi movement!

Clearly one implication and conclusion from the findings of this study is that American diplomats and politicians need to listen more carefully to our allies and enemies in the Mid-East and in the rest of the world. Al-Suri should be a must read for any U.S. security, homeland security, FBI, and military intelligence experts. Psychodynamic and group dynamic consultants would greatly benefit our policy decision makers. Often our arrogant and narcissistic-sounding American position is presented as if it were some special privilege or reward for Iran's, North Korea's, or Syria's leader to speak with our leader or his plenipotentiary. Often we demand something from a sovereign enemy country before we will even talk with them or listen to them. To talk to and listen to an enemy is not to be weak or acquiescent.

The psychologically fatherless Osama bin Laden was deeply impressed and brainwashed by his conservative Islamist professors who taught that only a return to strict Islamism could protect Muslims from the sins and materialism of the "Satanic West" (Bodansky 1999, 3).

ZAWAHIRI

Ayman al Zawahiri, the Egyptian physician-turned-radical Islamist, and Mullah Mohammed Omar, leader of Afghanistan's Taliban, became Osama's "brother" in rebellion and rage. They also served as a replacement for Osama's Saudi half-brothers, who had disowned him.

Dr. Ayman al-Zawahiri was born in Egypt in 1951, six years before Osama bin Laden. He comes from an aristocratic, affluent Egyptian family. He was educated as a pediatrician. In 1973, as a medical student, he joined an electrical engineer and an army officer in forming the Egyptian Islamic Group that dedicated itself to the violent overthrow of the Egyptian state. He served as a medical officer in Afghanistan, where he was regarded as a hero along with bin Laden in the jihad against the

Soviet Union. In prison, Zawahiri met and became very close to Egyptian sheik Omar Abdel Rahman, the so-called blind sheik behind the 1993 bombing of the World Trade Center towers, and the assassination of Egyptian president Anwar Sadat in 1981 (Robinson 2001, 210–12).

Zawahiri grew very close to Osama (an older brother/father figure) over the years of their alliance in building what Bergen calls "Holy War Inc." Zawahiri psychologically replaced and compensated for Osama's painful loss of his best friend, Abdul Aziz Fahd, in his childhood (Robinson 2001, 210–12).

Osama was a heroic military leader in Afghanistan's successful war against the Soviet Union. For bin Laden, the Afghanistan war was a profoundly spiritual experience (Bergen 2001, 61). This enabled him to be both an admired warrior son of radical terrorist state leaders and a legendary hero/older brother/mentor for millions of angry, young Muslims. Money was never able to compensate for Osama's grief over, and ambivalence about, a father who was not around when the adolescent Osama needed his guidance most. But beneath this surface of rebellion in the service of fledgling independence and identity searching was a desperate need for a father/older brother with apparent (though spurious) moral strength and spiritual dignity. Osama hungered for bold and strong father and brother figures.

BIN LADEN'S LOYAL FRIEND/"BROTHER" AMONG THE TALIBAN—MULLAH OMAR

Ahmed Rashid in his brilliant book *Taliban: Militant Islam, Oil and Fundamentalism in Central Asia* (2001) says that Mullah Omar is surrounded by extreme secrecy but does provide some information about Osama's pious, powerful, and loyal brother figure. Rashid (2001, 23–25) documents Mullah Omar's elemental, but impressive, political leadership skills and effective grasp of stark religious symbolism. Located in Kandahar is the tomb of Ahmad Shah Durrani, the founder of the Durrani dynasty. Next to the tomb is the holy shrine of the Cloak of the Prophet Mohammad. Rashid describes how Mullah Omar, in order to legitimize his role as Afghanistan's leader in 1996, took out the cloak in front of a large crowd of Taliban who named him Amir-ul Momineen, which means Leader of the Faithful (Rashid 2001, 20).

Mullah Mohammed Omar was born around 1959 in Nodeh, a village near Kandahar. His family were poor and landless peasants of the Hotak tribe of the Ghilzai branch of Pashtuns. Like Osama and many of Osama's colleagues in terror, Omar's father died while he was a young man, which left him to fend for his mother, himself, and extended family. Omar's madrassah studies were interrupted by the war with the Soviets and he was wounded four times, with his right eye being permanently damaged by an exploding rocket. He had achieved status as a village mullah at a young age. He has three wives who live in his home village. Omar has five children (Rashid 2001, 23–24).

Mullah Omar is described as tall, well built, and has a long black beard. He usually wears a black turban. Despite having a dry and sarcastic wit, he is shy and retiring. However, he is clearly brilliant in his capacity to assess and lead people (Rashid 2001, 24). I have presented my formulations about pseudohomosexual issues, rigid sexual attitudes, and unconscious gynophobia among Christian, Jewish, and Muslim radical fundamentalist men. In this light, it is interesting that under Mullah Omar's intense leadership, the Taliban clamped down on homosexuality (**reaction formation?/denial?**). Rashid observed that Kandahar's Pashtuns were notorious for the rape of young boys by warlords. In addition to the drug trade, such predatory pedophilia Pashtun warlords were a key motive for Mullah Omar's mobilization of the Taliban in Afghanistan. The punishments for homosexuality were bizarre and were the source of endless debates and ruminations by Taliban scholars. Singing, dancing, and TV were banned because they allegedly prevented the proper study and implementation of Islam (Rashid 2001, 115).

Like other colleagues and mentors of Osama bin Laden, Mullah Omar has a deformity (loss of an eye). Omar fought with Commander Nek Mohammed of Khalis's Hizb-e-Islami against the Najibullah regime between 1989 and 1992. Omar has profoundly strong religious convictions and charisma. And he, like his soul brother Osama, has no hesitancy to defy authority and act as a powerful father figure toward recruits.

MULLAH OMAR: BIN LADEN'S DEFIANT FRIEND

After the 1998 U.S. embassy bombings in Africa, the United States increased pressure on Saudi Arabia for extraditing Osama bin Laden from Afghanistan to the United States. Prince Turki went to Afghanistan to persuade the Taliban to hand over bin Laden. Mullah Omar refused and in essence called the Saudis pawns of the United States.

The angry Saudi government suspended diplomatic relations with, and cut off aid to, the Taliban (Rashid 2001, 138–39).

After the August 1998 U.S. cruise missile attack on Osama's Afghan training camp, the Taliban was enraged and organized anti-U.S. and anti-UN demonstrations. Mullah Omar verbally attacked and insulted President Clinton, saying:

> If the attack on Afghanistan is Clinton's personal decision, then he has done it to divert the world and the American peoples' attention from that shameful White House affair [Monica Lewinsky] that has proved Clinton is a liar and a man devoid of decency and honor. (Rashid 2001, 75)

Omar further accused the United States of being the biggest terrorist in the world. He said that Osama was the guest of the Taliban and the Afghan people, and that Osama would never be handed over to the United States. Such bold, bombastic, iconoclastic, and defiant statements to the Western father/authority figures really appeal to the adolescent rebellion simmering in the disaffected psyches of many homegrown terrorists in search of a cause. Osama glowed with affection for Mullah Omar and took one of Omar's daughters as a wife.

SUMMARY: OSAMA BIN LADEN'S PERSONAL PATHWAY TO HOMEGROWN TERRORIST

Osama bin Laden ambivalently idealized his father who, as we noted, died when Osama was 10. The loss of his father itself was a crushing narcissistic injury (producing father hunger and longing). Osama's later rejection by Saudi father-figure leaders was also a further narcissistic injury (Olsson 2007, 55–56). Osama bin Laden died a disgraced outcast of his homeland, but a hero among many openly or secretly admiring Muslims particularly disaffected youths (Olsson 2007). His legacy as hero martyr lives on.

> I am telling you, and God is my witness, whether America escalates or de-escalates this conflict, we will reply to it in kind, God willing. God is my witness; the youth of Islam are preparing things that will fill your hearts with tears.
>
> —(Osama bin Laden, October 6, 2002, via
> Al Jazeera satellite TV, quoted in Gunaratna, xxvii)

Many times a psychotherapy experience or grief counseling from an experienced clergyperson is useful in resolving intense father hunger, grief, and mourning the likes of which dominated Osama bin Laden. Hurt and loss are healed when words found in the therapy context help contain pain and promote healing. Obviously Osama bin Laden had no opportunity for an effective psychotherapy. Osama destructively acted out his inner grief and conflicts. Can America and the West find ways to therapeutically connect with potential nascent homegrown terrorists before they turn radical? Can teachers and professors spot and help in-betweeners and not just teach concepts?

In many ways, Osama bin Laden was a life-long in-betweener. He was frequently in-between homes, in-between mother and stepmother, in-between countries as a hero warrior in Afghanistan fighting the Soviets, and later as a fugitive in his beloved Tora Bora fleeing American bombs and special forces. And even in death, Osama bin Laden's image dances between a sure eternity in hell via a Western believer's view, and paradise as a martyr for true Salafi believers.

Let us examine specific personal pathways of some recent homegrown terrorists. Psychological patterns begin to emerge as we look at the adolescent identity struggles of so-called homegrown terrorists no matter from what country they hail.

5

Adam Gadahn: A Television
Voice of Al Qaeda

AN ANGRY AMERICAN TRAITOR

Adam Gadahn is a 25-year-old American raised in Orange County, California. He calls himself "Azzam the American." Gadahn is the son of psychedelic musician Phil Pearlman who changed the family name to Gadahn and dropped out of society to become a goat farmer in Winchester, South Los Angeles. Adam is one of four children who worked on the family goat farm (Adam Gadahn Fast Facts 2013, 1–2). He was homeschooled in a nominally Christian and religiously eclectic home. According to a September 13, 2005, *Herald Sun of Melbourne* article by Nick Papps, Adam had his first exposure to Islam as a boy through the family business. His father slaughtered goats according to Islamic law. As a teenager, Adam began to rebel against his family and society in general. He grew to love death metal rock music (Khatchadourian 2007, 52).

In 1993, Adam moved to live with his grandparents (Adam Gadahn Fast Facts 2013, 1–2). Significantly, his grandfather is a Jewish physician. Adam wrote articles for a "death metal" publication called *Xenophobia*. Adam learned about Islam through Internet chat rooms. Adam wrote:

> I discovered that the beliefs and practices of Islam fit my personal theology and intellect as well as basic human logic. Having been around Muslims during my formative years, I knew well that they were not the bloodthirsty, barbaric terrorists that the news media and televangelists painted them out to be. (Papps 2005, 1)

So, Adam Gadahn drifted rebelliously away from his parents' eclectic (tepid and perceived as weak?) religious tastes. (His family name had been changed from the obviously Jewish name of Pearlman to Ga-dahn.) Adam left his grandparents' Jewish home to hang out at the Islamic Center of Orange County. Adam was at that time a classic "in-betweener" who was "in-between" his parents–grandparents homes and a job or school. There at an Orange County mosque, 15-year-old Adam fell under the influence of two naturalized U.S. citizens who were also radical Muslims—Khalil Deek (a Palestinian computer ser-vice engineer) and Hisham Diab (an Egyptian accountant). These men lived in apartments in an Anaheim area called "Little Gaza." Adam met them at the mosque, and Diab's ex-wife said that Diab brought the hungry boy Adam in and asked her to feed him (Khatchadourian 2007, 53–54).

After that innocent beginning, the two Islamists began indoctri-nating Adam with their extremist views. The president of the Islamic Society of Orange County thought Adam, Deek, and Diab had such extremist views that he barred them from the mosque. They openly called Islamic Society president Haitham Bundakji an infidel because he reached out to Christians and Jews. At one point, Adam assaulted Bundakji (the imam probably attracted Adam's repressed and dis-placed rage at, and disappointment in, his grandfather and father) (Khatchadourian 2007, 52–53).

Adolescents, though they put down their fathers in their strug-gles for independence, actually need strong, caring male role mod-els to help channel their energies toward healthy vocational, ethical, and spiritual development. Even painful narcissistic wounds can be sources of wisdom, humor, and creativity if fathers and family friends, or clergy, care.

However, the recruitment process of Adam Gadahn sounds like a familiar malignant Pied Piper tune! Friends and family members of Deek and Diab say that the two were loyal and avid followers of all people, including Sheik Omar Abdel Rahman (the blind sheik asso-ciated with the first World Trade Center bombing). Diab and Deek hosted Rahman, who stayed in Deek's and Diab's apartments during a visit of Rahman to lecture at local Los Angeles mosques. Sarah Olson, who divorced Diab in 1996 and had cooked dinner for Rahman, claims that Gadahn never met the sheik. Adam certainly knew all about the cleric of terror. Rahman later would call Deek and Diab from prison so they could record his fiery sermons over the telephone (Krikorian and Reza 2006, 1) Adam Gadahn was a follower of Rahman, and in 1999, Adam was secretary for Diab's "Charity without Borders." According to its charter, "Charity without Borders" was founded to "provide for educational and humanitarian aid to poor and needy people in the U.S.A. and other countries." The $150,000 that was raised was actually sent to extremist groups in the Middle East (Krikorian and Reza 2006, 1).

In 1998 Gadahn went to Peshawar, Pakistan. Adam participated in Al Qaeda camps and met its key leaders. It has since been abundantly clear that Al Qaeda is very interested in homegrown American/Western converts as well as recruits in Arab and Muslim countries. Since 2004, Gadahn has become increasingly open with his articulate and severe threats to the United States and Australia. The detailed study of Gadahn's conversion to radical Islam reveals how vulnerable many adolescents are to the *malignant Pied Piper* music of radical Islam and other dangerous social movements.

Adam Gadahn was clearly an in-betweener at the time of his radicalization. (Adam was in between his father's home, his grandfather's home, and his new Islamist home.) He, like the homegrown terrorists in this study, had significant conflicts and disappointments in his father and grandfather. Some of the disappointment involved in Adam's conflict with his father might have been related to radical shifts in his father Phil's religious and related lifestyle. This played a part in Adam's father hunger and search for father surrogates, which he eventually found among radical Islamist recruiters. It can be said that Adam could have perceived his father and grandfather as talking the religious talk, but not walking a strong walk. Gadahn's search for fathers eventually led to his assuming a paternal role as a super father-recruiter figure as the American TV voice of Al Qaeda in the world.

6

John Walker Lindh:
The American Taliban

John Walker Lindh prefers to be called Hamza Walker Lindh, but was called Suleyman al-Faris during his time in Afghanistan. Twenty-four-year-old John Walker Lindh is currently in a medium-security federal prison with four years served of his plea-bargained 20-year prison sentence for providing services to the Taliban in Afghanistan. John's family and lawyers have understandably given out minimal or selective information about John. The information they have given makes John Walker Lindh sound like a sincere, idealistic young California dreamer in search of Islamic identity.

Lawyer Henry Mark Holzer's website provides an in-depth, meticulously chronicled account of the charges against John Walker Lindh (Holzer 2001–2002). Holzer cites data to support the notion that John Walker Lindh, in his own words, embraced the spirit and plans of Al Qaeda, and the radical Islamism of the Taliban to a greater degree than his defense lawyers would have the public believe.

In all fairness, however, John was under stressful, physically painful, and dire circumstances when he expressed devotion to Al Qaeda and criticism or disdain for America. After 9/11, our country did not seem able to accept that an ordinary U.S. kid could embrace the evil perpetrators of 9/11.

In fact, John Walker Lindh actually illustrates some of the key dynamics and vulnerabilities of young people to recruitment by terror cult leaders. He was an "in-betweener" as we have described it. Attorney Holzer represents one angle of description of John Walker Lindh. It is helpful to turn to other sources of information on John's psychological development and family history (Tyrangiel 2001, 1–3). Walker was born in Washington, D.C., to Marilyn Walker and Frank Lindh. He was the middle child of three. John's father, a Catholic, was a government lawyer. His mother was a health care aide who became a Buddhist. John was baptized as a Catholic and grew up in Silver Spring, Maryland. His family moved to San Anselmo, California, in Marin County when he was 10 years old. Walker was apparently sick as a child with an intestinal disorder.

Later when John was 12, he attended several middle schools, which did not work out for him. His family decided he would be home-schooled. He rarely left home and participated constantly in Internet chat rooms, where he became a devoted fan of hip-hop music. He used fake names and sometimes pretended to be black. John saw the Spike Lee film about Malcolm X. The movie made a big impression on him and coincided with his interest in Islam. John's health improved and he enrolled at Redwood High School. However, he apparently had trouble fitting in, so he took an independent study program and got a GED at age 16 (Tyrangiel 2001, 2).

John's father Frank Lindh is a lawyer for Pacific Gas and Electric Company and his mother Marilyn Walker is an office manager for a small Marin firm. John Walker Lindh's parents' marriage apparently had serious problems throughout his adolescent years and ended in a divorce in 1999. According to Larry Backer, in a 2005 journal article in the *San Francisco Examiner*, family friends reported that Frank Lindh was apparently a closeted homosexual. Though controversial, it is possible that discovering his father's homosexuality was confusing for the teenaged Walker. This might have been one of several causes for his disillusionment with the U.S. society and his seeking identity elsewhere. As we have discussed previously, there are often traumatic/ narcissistically wounding events in the early life history of future terrorists that often involve disappointment in parental figures. The author hypothesizes that homosexual or **pseudohomosexual dynamics** are found among many radical Islamists and their recruits (Ovesey 1969). (Pseudohomosexual behavior, according to Ovesey, is motivated not by sexual pleasure but by issues of power, submission, and dependency.)

Frank Lindh is reported to have moved in with a male lover in 1997, at which time John Walker Lindh was 16. John apparently dropped his father's name in favor of his mother's name "Walker." Walker subsequently officially converted to Islam, significantly influenced by his reading of *The Autobiography of Malcolm X* according to Josh Tyrangiel (2001, 2). Walker graduated early from Tamiscal High School and requested that his name on his diploma be Sulayman al-Lindh, though he never picked up the certificate. He began attending mosques in

Mill Valley and San Francisco. In 1998, the 18-year-old Walker traveled to Yemen for 10 months to study Arabic so he could read the Koran in its original language. He returned to live with his family in the United States for eight months in 1999. John had found out that Christmas that his parents had separated (Tyrangiel 2001, 2). John returned to Yemen in February 2000 and then left for Pakistan to study in an austere madrassa (Islamic school—al-Iman University). When the USS *Cole* was bombed in October 2000, Walker had an e-mail exchange with his father from Yemen. Frank Lindh said he felt terrible for the victims and their families. John replied that the terror attack may have been justified because the *Cole* was docked in an Islamic country (Tyrangiel 2001, 3).

Khizar Hayat, a Pakistani businessman, paid for Walker's madrassa school. It is perplexing as to why Walker did not seek financial help for the madrassa school from his parents who had encouraged both his Islamic faith and his study of Arabic. They certainly could afford to have helped him. Was Walker reluctant to reveal his new more radical Islamist leanings and mentors? Was he running away from inner conflict about his father's "coming out"? Was John ambivalent about his own sexual identity as well as his spiritual roots? Was John's turn toward Islam and subsequent radicalization partially a rebellion against, and away from, his father's Catholicism?

In October 2002, *Time* magazine reported that Khizar Hayat said that he had a homosexual relationship with Walker. Lindh's lawyers and Lindh have denied this report. *The Guardian* magazine reports that the story occurred as a result of confusion in translation of Hayat's broken English. The *Time* article had said that Hayat had a good knowledge of English and only later changed his story. The homosexual or pseudo-homosexual dynamic would be compatible with Walker's passive behavior style and his likely traumatic discovery of his father's homosexual orientation during his stressful adolescent passage. This speculation about John's sexual identity struggles is intended as an observation and not an accusation (Backer 2005, 1).

It seems likely that radical Islamist influence led Walker to join the Taliban army in 2001. He purportedly spent seven weeks in an Al Qaeda training camp near Kandahar, where he met Osama bin Laden (*Time* 2002, 1). Walker was first captured on November 25, 2001, by the Afghan Northern Alliance forces and questioned by CIA agent Mike Spann, as was repeatedly shown on national TV (Adam Gadahn Fast Facts, 3–4). After the violent prison riot and the death of Spann, Walker was eventually held by U.S, forces and eventually brought to his controversial and legally complex trial as described in vast detail by Henry Mark Holzer on his website. But again we see how vulnerable adolescents can be to radical Islamist recruiters. Father hunger/ longing runs deep. Many homegrown terrorists seem, among other issues, to be in search of fathers.

7

Nidal Malik Hasan, MD: Fort Hood's *Jihadi* Doctor of Death

Physician psychiatrist Major Nidal Malik Hasan killed 13 people and wounded 33 others with a handgun at Fort Hood Texas on November 5, 2009. The terror event occurred less than a month before he was to be deployed in Afghanistan. This 39-year-old unmarried army psychiatrist is of Jordanian descent but born and raised in a Muslim family in Virginia. Hasan showed signs of identity struggles during his training years at Walter Reed Medical Center. He enjoyed the benefits of good medical and psychiatric specialty training at U.S. government's expense. However, he showed evidence of conflicts between his Muslim faith and his duties as an army medical officer (Hasan, BBC News 2009, 1–2).

Hasan was noted to have tried to convert some of his patients to Islam. He gave a bizarre PowerPoint Grand Rounds presentation to his colleagues during his psychiatric training at Walter Reed. The title of his presentation was "The Koranic Worldview as It Relates to Muslims in the U.S. Military." Hasan made some grandiose recommendations and observations, including the notion that U.S. Army soldiers who are Muslim be allowed to be conscientious objectors. He cited many Koranic passages that could be interpreted as anti-American military efforts and, in hindsight, rationalizations for his eventual murderous terrorist behavior. Hasan concluded in his Grand Rounds talk that God expects full loyalty; Muslims might be moderate but God is not and he promises heaven and hell; and Muslim soldiers should not be forced to hurt or kill believers unjustly (Herridge and Browne 2013, 1–2; McKinley and Dao 2009, 1–2). Dr. Hasan's psychiatrist supervisors and colleagues often questioned his mental stability using terms for him like *schizoid* and *paranoid*. Hasan's family claimed that Hasan felt discriminated against as an Arab and Muslim in the military (Herridge and Browne 2013, 1–5). However, he got good fitness reports, promotions, and good officer's pay, which has continued even after his crime.

In the author's opinion, Dr. Hasan's military psychiatry superiors and colleagues somehow got caught up in some vintage of politically correct denial about Hasan's behavioral warning signs. The superior officers and physician psychiatrist colleagues of Dr. Hasan appeared to allow transfer/pre-deployment orders to be used as a solution to their wariness about Hasan. They passed the buck. The military authorities could have chosen medical boarding or processes of administrative separation "for the good of the U.S. Army" and Dr. Hasan. However, that could well have rocked political boats within the Obama administration. President Obama's speech in Cairo shortly after taking office lauded efforts to work cooperatively with the Arab and Muslim world, rather than an emphasis on counterterrorism (Levi 2004). Hasan may have continued to pursue radical Islamist terrorism but would have been relieved of his significant anxiety about deployment to Afghanistan. Hasan's superiors, by not confronting his readily apparent personality problems, played into, and encouraged his, narcissistic, entitled, and grandiose behavior and mentality.

Hasan's cousin Mohammed Hasan said that Nidal Hasan did not want to go to Afghanistan because he was a Muslim and did not want to be exposed to violence and death, particularly the killing of Muslims (McKinley 2009, 2).

Hasan had significant contacts and profound respect for Imam Anwar al-Awlaki. Awlaki progressively became a champion of violent Islamist jihad. Anwar al-Awlaki, during 2001–2002, was the imam of the Dar al-Hijrah mosque and considered to be moderate. Awlaki served as the Muslim chaplain at George Washington University. Awlaki was frequently invited to speak about Islam to audiences in Washington, including Congress and the government. In 2004 Awlaki returned to Yemen (Osama bin Laden's father's home country). He was arrested and imprisoned in Yemen, where his radicalization compounded. After prison, Awlaki went into hiding but used the Internet to encourage Muslims in the West to join violent *jihad*. Awlaki was an effective orator and glowingly charismatic.

Nidal Hasan sent Awlaki 20 e-mail messages but an expert who reviewed them felt that they were appropriate in terms of Dr. Hasan's research. Awlaki denied urging Hasan toward violence but the fine line between a psycho-inspirational charismatic leader's subliminal messaging and so-called self-radicalization is shadowy to define. In 2008 and 2009, 18 further e-mails between Hasan and Awlaki reflected a growing worshipful **doppelganger**-like perception of Awlaki by Hasan. Hasan said to Awlaki: I can't wait to join you in the afterlife" (Ross and Schwartz 2009, 1).

Hasan asked Awlaki whether it was permissible for innocents to be killed in a suicide attack. Hasan appears to have looked to al-Awlaki as a father or older brother figure. The affectionate tone of Hasan's connection with al-Awlaki seemed to progressively bolster Dr. Hasan's impulses about violence toward the U.S. military. Anwar al-Awlaki was seen as a valuable moderate Muslim spokesperson early in his ministry, but then progressed to be a giant among homegrown terrorist leaders/recruiters. Awlaki was killed by an American Hellfire missile strike in Yemen. Dr. Hasan progressed from a faux Muslim pacifist to a violent Islamist true believer and jihadist murderer at Fort Hood, Texas.

NIDAL HASAN'S CHILDHOOD

Detailed psychodynamic information about Hasan's childhood is sparse. He was born in Arlington County, Virginia. His parents were Palestinian immigrants. Hasan was raised as Muslim along with his two younger brothers. After attending Wakefield High School in Arlington for one year, the family moved to Roanoke, Virginia, where he finished high school. He and his brothers helped his parents run the family restaurant in Roanoke. Hasan's father died in 1998 and his mother in 2001.

Hasan acknowledged to the members of his sanity board hearing that his commitment to Islam began after his mother's death in May of 2001. Anwar al-Awlaki was the imam at the Dar Al-Hijrah Islamic Center, where Hasan's mother's funeral was held. Hasan referred to Awlaki as his teacher, mentor, and friend. Awlaki had called Hasan a hero on Awlaki's website after Hasan's murders at Fort Hood (Herridge 2013, 2). The author believes that Awlaki became a **linking object** and psychological parental surrogate for Hasan.

Hasan joined the army while at college and graduated from Virginia Tech in 1995 with a bachelor's degree in biochemistry. A cousin said that Hasan wanted to serve in the army because his uncle and cousin had served (McKinley 2009, 1–2). The author thinks that it is also likely that Hasan chose the financial dependency and security of the military to provide for his education and physical support. This can be seen as an institutional transference where the army becomes a perceived caretaking parent. The Army and its soldiers later became objects upon which Hasan could project his narcissistic rage, which Awlaki fed into and encouraged.

Hasan's uncle, Rafiq Hamad from Ramallah, said that Hasan was gentle and fainted while observing childbirth, which was why he chose psychiatry. Rafiq said that Hasan was so sensitive that he mourned a pet bird for months after it died. Rafiq also felt that Hasan read a lot of books, including the Koran to replace the love he lost when his parents died (McKinley 2009, 2).

It is very possible that complicated or unresolved grief may have led to depression, anxiety, and preoccupation with death that played into Hasan's acted-out anger at the U.S. Army and government. As a total institution, the Army provides food, clothing, housing, and money like a super-parent. Rather than face his own inner demons and resolve his identity searches through effective psychotherapy, Hasan chose dependency on a guru and acting out as his psychological defenses.

Hasan's level of father hunger/longing, identity confusion, and "in-betweener" phenomena is a typical pattern among homegrown terrorist recruits (i.e., in-between assignments, in-between U.S. duty and his orders to leave for Afghanistan, in-between supervised training as a psychiatrist, and actual frontline clinical work).

A subtheme also echoes among all the homegrown terrorists—an ambivalence about marriage, women, and intimacy. Boys raised in fundamentalist families (Christian, Jewish, or Muslim) are often taught to dominate women. But, at the same time, they fear a woman's rejection because their own mothers fear or idealize them as "special" sons (Olsson 2007, 20–22). Like loyal parents, Dr. Hasan's family says that he was a devout and good boy.

8

Pfc. Naser Jason Abdo: An Explosive Conscientious Objector

Twenty-one-year old Naser Jason Abdo was arrested on July 29, 2011, for planning a bomb and small arms attack on a Killeen, Texas, restaurant frequented by soldiers from nearby Fort Hood. Abdo had been pressing for conscientious objector status based upon elements of his Muslim faith and the desire not to be deployed to Afghanistan. He had gone AWOL from Fort Campbell in Kentucky and began planning the attack at Fort Hood as an apparent vengeful event. His discharge from the army had been held up due to charges of child pornography possession. At Abdo's appearance in the U.S. District Court in Waco, he vehemently spoke in favor of Major Nidal Malik Hasan, the army psychiatrist subsequently accused of killing 13 people and wounding dozens more at Fort Hood in November 2009 (Johnson 2011, 1–2).

There are hints that Abdo, like most other homegrown terrorists, has a childhood history of traumatic disappointment in his father and resultant father/older brother hunger pangs. Abdo grew up in Dallas where his parents were divorced when he was three. He spent most of his developmental years with his father, Jamal Rateb Abdo. In September 2004, the police in Garland, Texas, arrested Abdo's father for soliciting sex from a detective posing over the Internet as a teenage girl. Mr. Abdo, a Palestinian with Jordanian citizenship, received a five-year sentence in a state prison after his 2006 conviction. He served three years before discharge to federal custody and was deported to Jordan in 2010 (Fernandez and Dao 2011, 2).

During Abdo's personal life pathway, he, like other homegrown terrorists, likely experienced disappointment in his father's hypocritical, defective masculine role-modeling and immoral behavior. Keen disappointment in his father and a search for a father/big brother figure

(Dr. Hasan of Fort Hood rampage infamy) is apparent, as well as in-betweener issues. Abdo was between deployment to Afghanistan and his conscientious objections to serving at all. Implied was his being between being a U.S. soldier who is Muslim and the new conscientious objector status (Fernandez and Dao 2011, 1–2).

According to Daniel Pipes of *The Washington Times*, Abdo had the identical bomb materials in the exact ingredients specified in Al Qaeda's English-speaking magazine called *Inspire*. The article was titled "Make a Bomb in the Kitchen of Your Mom" (Pipes 2011, 1). Also present in his story is anger at authority and evidence that Abdo bought his firearm at Guns Galore, the same store where his older brother figure Nidal Malik Hasan had purchased his pistol for his terror attack at Fort Hood! Abdo also had, like the Tsarnaev brothers of the Boston Marathon bombing, planned to use pressure cooker bombs in his attack (Fernandez and Dao 2011, 1)!

DANIEL PIPES'S COGENT IDEAS ABOUT MUSLIM VIEWS OF SEXUALITY

Daniel Pipes in his perceptive book *In the Path of God: Islam and Political Power* has a fascinating section in a chapter titled "Muslim Anomie," subtitled "Male-Female Relations" (Pipes 2002, 176–82). Pipe's incisive thinking is particularly helpful in trying to understand the inner struggles with sexual identity that seem to plague many American home-grown terrorists as they idealize their new found Muslim faith. They often devalue American religious pluralism in favor of putting Islam on a strong, lofty pedestal.

Pipes points out that unlike the traditional Victorian puritanical Western view that women do not or should not enjoy sex, Muslim believers actually believe that women's sexual desires are more powerful than men's. Female sexuality is regarded in the Islamicate as so powerful that it poses a significant danger to society. This creates a pervasive sociopolitical meaning and power dilemma. Islam encourages sexual satisfaction to aid a harmonious social order and a flourishing population. At the same time, Islam regards sexually unrestrained females as the most threatening challenge to the male population. Women's strong sexual desires and their attractiveness give them a power over men that rivals God's. *Fitna* (civil disorder among believers) would happen among males if left to themselves. So, while sexual activity poses no stress, the Muslim social order is a defense against the disruptive power of female sexuality. The Islamicate's social order is thus threatened from without by the infidel and within by women's sexiness. Sexual mores for Muslims are in place to preserve the social order, not to assert moralistic concerns, thus the veil to keep powerful female sexuality invisible and no trespassing by women in male spaces where she upsets men's order and peace of mind (Pipes 2002, 176–79).

Romantic love (real, passionate love) creates not only a threat of *fitna* between an unmarried man and a woman but between married partners. A married man might be so preoccupied with passionate love for his wife that he might neglect his duties to God! Contact between spouses is reduced by men tending to religion and work, women to house and family. Strict Sharia law restricts contact even between husband and wife. Married couples do not eat together or go outside the house together even to spend time playing with the children. A man can divorce his wife at will. A wife must have a special male magistrate to undertake such legal activity. A strict Muslim man may take another wife (polygyny), and many times arranged marriages occur between older men and much younger women. Sometimes a strong bond between a Muslim mother and her son can negatively affect the intimate relationship between her son and his young wife. All these items tend to diminish the likelihood of intense passionate love and companionship (Pipes 2002, 179).

Mohammad Atta, the 9/11 attack leader, left careful notes about how his dead body should be handled. Atta rigidly stated that no woman was to touch or see him. Atta was overprotected by his mother (Sageman 2004, 86). Maternal overprotection is a factor in narcissistic grandiosity in men (see also material about Tamerlan Tzarniev—Chapter 15). Yet, if the mothers of Osama bin Laden or Mohammad Atta had begged their sons to halt their 9/11 plans, it seems unlikely that either of them would have changed their action plans.

A mature, wise, and thoughtful Western person would hold that the control of sex, love, and lust is the responsibility of each individual—man or women. Each individual when confronted by a romantic, erotic, or sexually tempting situation would be responsible for his or her own actions and the consequences. The individual's moral, ethical, marital, and religious convictions would come into play. A mature person might enjoy a pleasant sexual fantasy but stop short of sexual acting-out. Even a modern Helen of Troy could not dissolve the strength of character and ego ideal of mature men. Nor could a modern Don Juan do likewise with women of solid character and maturity.

Often young men who are recent recruits to radical Islam or young men raised with radical fundamentalist views of women turn with intense devotion (pseudohomosexuality) toward older Imams, fundamentalist Christian preachers, or rabbis for succor and direction. Pfc. Nasar Jason Abdo's father longing seemed to lead him to a father/older brother figure, Major Nidal Malik Hasan, who himself sought fathering from Anwar al-Awlaki.

In Chapter 9, we will see some similarities in the paths of Jose Padilla and Bryant Neal Vinas to homegrown terrorism, and the relevance of the issues discussed earlier to their situations.

9

Jose Padilla, Bryant Neal Vinas, and Sharif Mobley

JOSE PADILLA: THE WOULD-BE DIRTY BOMBER

Jose Padilla is a 36-year-old man who planned to explode a "dirty nuclear bomb" in Chicago. Padilla sometimes calls himself Abdullah al-Muhajir. Padilla's parents moved to the United States from Puerto Rico, and he was born in Brooklyn, New York. He became a member of the Latin Kings street gang after his family moved to Chicago. Padilla was arrested in Florida in 1991 over a road-rage shooting incident and spent a year in jail. A neighbor said that his mother was worried about him, and one source says that he was implicated in a gangland murder when he was 13 (Padilla, 2005, 1)!

Padilla was arrested several times, and after serving time for aggravated assault, he converted to Islam, and like many new converts of many religious groups, he professed a nonviolent philosophy. He participated in the Masjid al-Iman mosque in Fort Lauderdale, Florida. His colleague and friend Adham Amin Hassoun was a registered agent for Benevolence International Foundation, a charitable trust, which U.S. investigators accused of funding terrorist activities. Hassoun was accused of consorting with radical Islamic fundamentalists such as Al Qaeda. Hassoun was arrested in 2002 for overstaying his visa (Padilla 2005, 1).

Padilla traveled to Egypt, Saudi Arabia, Afghanistan, Pakistan, and Iraq. He was tracked as an Al Qaeda affiliate and arrested at Chicago's O'Hare Airport on May 8, 2002, because of significant evidence that he had been trained in the making and using of a "dirty nuclear bomb" (Padilla 2005, 1). Fortunately, Padilla never struck the United States.

Significant to this study is the theme of Padilla's prison recruitment and his prolonged adolescent acting-out and rebellious search for an exciting identity. Psychopathic and narcissistic character patterns as well as adolescent identity crises are common findings among prison populations. Prisoners are by definition in-betweeners and show other elements necessary for vulnerability to recruitment as homegrown terrorists.

POLITICAL INSPIRATION AND CHARISMA BORN IN PRISONS

Intense forms of spiritual power often emerge from preaching, writing, and letters written for followers while the writer is in prison. The reader is reminded of the apostles Paul and Silas (Acts 16: 19–40), Martin Luther King Jr.'s powerful *Letter from a Birmingham Jail*, Nelson Mandela's *Long Walk to Freedom*, Alexander Solzhenitsyn's *The Gulag Archipelago*, and even Adolph Hitler's *Mein Kampf*.

Sayyid Qutb was executed in 1966, but his inspiring writings in prison have led him to be called the Karl Marx of Islamism. Qutb wrote *Milestones* as well as his masterwork, *In the Shade of the Quran*. Qutb's work has inspired Al Qaeda, Osama bin Laden and Ayman Al-Zawahiri, Egyptian Islamic Jihad, the Islamic Group (Egypt), and the Muslim Brotherhood, Egypt's fundamentalist movement of the 1950s and 1960s.

Qutb's ideas are sophisticated and powerful. He had memorized the Koran by age 10 and went to college in Cairo. His literary pursuits included novels, poems, and a book that is still well regarded, called *Literary Criticism: Its Principles and Methodology*. Qutb traveled to the United States in the 1940s and got a master's degree in education at Colorado State College of Education. Though admiring American scientific achievements, Qutb grew disgusted with the drinking, sexual immorality, and materialism he observed on American college campuses (Olsson 2007, 32, 36–37). His observations may have been in part correct but not the basis for fomenting violent terrorism in America and the West. Even brilliant, talented men like Qutb can slip into concrete, black-and-white, and distorted fundamentalist mentality.

BRYANT NEAL VINAS: LONG ISLAND HOMEGROWN TERRORIST

Bryant Neal Vinas was born on December 4, 1983, in Queens, New York. He also has been called Ibrahim, Bashir al-Ameriki, and Ben Yameen al-Kanadeeis. Vinas is a Hispanic Muslim American. He converted to Islam in 2004 (when he was 21) and traveled to Waziristan, Pakistan, in 2007, where he joined a jihadist group fighting U.S.

soldiers in Afghanistan. He was embraced by Al Qaeda and received training in combat and military explosives (Rotella and Meyer 2009, 1).

Vinas willingly gave a senior Al Qaeda leader detailed information about the Long Island Rail Road system that helped planning of a bomb attack on a Long Island Railroad commuter train in New York's Penn Station. Vinas participated in two Al Qaeda rocket attacks on U.S. soldiers in Afghanistan in September 2008 before he was captured by Pakistani forces and transferred to FBI custody. In January 2009, Vinas pleaded guilty to all charges against him. Subsequent to Vinas's conviction in a U.S. court in New York, he had a change of mind or heart or both. (The details of such changes of Vinas's mind would be very valuable when they are available!) Vinas served as a prosecution witness in key European trials and provided highly valuable information about the intricate workings of the Al Qaeda network, including how American homegrowns are pipelined to terrorist training camps in Pakistan/Waziristan. His fluency in Arabic, Dari, and Urdu allowed him to know key details that will aid in the conviction of Belgian-French terror cells and Tunisian and Moroccan Islamist militants. Vinas is in protective custody of U.S. Marshals in New York State (Rotella 2009, 1).

Bryant Vinas grew up in Long Island with his parents and sister Lina. Bryant's mother Maria Luisa Uraga immigrated from Argentina to the United States and his father, a now-retired engineer, from Peru. Vinas was raised a Catholic and at one time was an altar boy and Boy Scout. His parents divorced in 2000 when Bryant was 17, and friends and family say he was extremely upset about the divorce (Rotella 2009, 1–2).

Vinas graduated from Longwood High School in Long Island in 2000. His best friend in high school was Alex Acevedo. Bryant, who was staying with his mother at the time, grew angry and threw frequent tantrums probably significantly related to his parents' divorce. Adolescents typically have strong reactions to a parental divorce, and certainly when the family home had a significant spiritual commitment to Catholicism. Vinas's mother could not tolerate his increasing disrespectfulness and actually gave up legal custody. He lived with his father until he joined the military in 2001. Vinas did not make it through boot camp and returned home to Long Island but was an in-betweener. He went first to his mother in 2005 but, after a dispute with her, soon went to his father. He sporadically attended technical school, worked at a car wash, and drove a truck. In that in-betweener world, he reconnected with his high school best friend Alex Acevedo.

Acevedo's half-brother Victor Kulian had converted to Islam and gave Vinas a Koran, which he began studying in earnest. Bryant Vinas converted to Islam at the Al Falah in Long Island, which greatly increased tension with his father. Bryant moved to and fro from his father and got involved in mosque activities and boxing. He even traveled with his boxing instructor to Cuba and was also dating the instructor's daughter. Vinas was upset when he could not make a third trip to Cuba and lost the girlfriend (Rotella 2009, 1–2; CNN 2000, 1).

In 2006, Vinas met Ahmad Zarinni at the Selden Mosque in Long Island. Zarinni introduced Vinas to the Islamic Thinkers Society (ITS). Though somewhat controversial, the ITS was considered protected by U.S. free speech and freedom of religion laws. The ITS was actually Al Qaeda friendly. Yousef al Khattab, a key ideologue, was instrumental to radicalizing of Vinas and jihadi websites added energy to Vinas's growing anger at America. He, like many idealistic young homegrown terrorist recruits, grew convinced that the United States was at war with Islam and was intending to put Muslims in concentration camps. Gradually, however, Vinas started to feel that the ITS was all talk and no action (CNN 2011). This **transference** phenomenon is a common finding where young homegrown terror recruits experience transference toward their own parents. They feel as the saying goes, that their parents "Talk the talk, but do not walk the walk" (see Shaw's idea in his "Personal Pathway Model" in Chapter 4). In Vinas's case, he substituted Khattab and the ITS as transference objects to replace his parents and possibly the Catholic Church to be rebelled against. In 2009, Vinas's mother Maria Luisa Uraga said after his conviction:"He's not my son no more. I don't know him if he's able to do this. He has no family no more" (Karoliszyn and Marzulli 2009).

Bryant Vinas even made an unsuccessful attempt to get his father to convert to Islam before he left his father's home in 2007. He said he wanted to study Arabic and Islam in Pakistan but clearly his father hunger and longing was leading him on a journey to Al Qaeda's highest seats of power. Friends in New York helped him set up his trip. Vinas at one point volunteered to be a suicide bomber but his Al Qaeda superiors said no, feeling that he needed more depth of religious study. He took part with other masked fighters in an Al Qaeda propaganda video featuring Abu Yahya al-Libi, who was later killed by American missiles. He was a powerful theologian and recruiter for Al Qaeda's jihad. Vinas also had contact with Rashid Rauf, a Pakistani/British member who is thought to have been involved with the 2006 transatlantic aircraft plot to bring down U.S. flights. Needless to say and repeat, Vinas's change of mind and heart would be valuable to study beyond the legal strategy implications. Did a positive element of Vinas's early experiences with the Catholic Church get involved with his change of heart? Or, is he a double agent now?

Vinas met Najibullah Zazi in Pakistan in 2008. Zazi is from Queens, Long Island, and had, like Vinas, wanted to join the Taliban to fight against U.S. forces and their allies in Afghanistan. Zazi went on to attempt to perform suicide bombings in the New York subways during rush hour. He was arrested in 2009 before he could attack successfully (Suddath 2009, 1).

The Vinas–Zazi association illustrates the importance of social networks and friendships in the whole domain of terrorist recruitment that is observed by Marc Sageman (2004, 82–91, 175–84). In many instances, the terror cult network is like a new and superior family. It can be a vehicle of adventure, rebellion, and separation-individuation from conflicts and angry disappointments in parents and families, churches, and temples of origin.

Bryant Neal Vinas illustrates many of the dynamics involved in the making of a homegrown terrorist:

(1) In-Betweener phenomena (in-between jobs, religious affiliations, home and being on his own),

(2) Anger, disappointment, and conflict with parents (it is remarkable how many homegrown terrorists-to-be like Vinas have experienced parental divorce as traumatic as he had. Even Osama bin Laden had such a narcissistically painful experience with parental divorce (Olsson 2007, 18–23),

(3) Several elements observed by Eric Shaw in his Personal Pathway Model:

   (a) resentment of parents and mentors who "talk the talk," but do not "walk the authentic walk" or take effective action,

   (b) vulnerability to charismatic gurus of jihad and the Internet forms of brainwashing or thought control,

   (c) intense bonding with *jihadi* colleagues in the midst of fear and anger at authority, and

   (d) the negative identity formation so often found among homegrown terrorists.

(4) An in-depth study of Bryant Vinas's change of heart and mind about violent jihad would be very informative from a psychodynamic point of view.

Experts can benefit by an in-depth knowledge of the how, what, and why of such conversions if they are authentic. In the author's experience, there are some rare and dramatic examples of profound life-changing experiences and events. Sometimes they occur in the contexts of a religious conversion (Saul converted to St. Paul on the road to Damascus. Acts [9:1–30]), and sometimes during Alcoholics Anonymous Twelve-Step work. The latter is comparable to personality changes experienced in a successful psychoanalysis or psychotherapy.

SHARIF MOBLEY: HOMEGROWN TERRORIST AND U.S. NUCLEAR PLANT WORKER

Sharif Mobley. was born on January 19, 1984. Mobley's claim to fame or infamy as a homegrown terrorist stems from the fact that from 2002 to 2008 he worked for contractors at five U.S. nuclear power plants in New Jersey, Pennsylvania, and Maryland. Mobley did maintenance work at Three Mile Island, three Public Service Enterprise Group nuclear power plants on Artificial Island in Lower Alloways Creek, New Jersey; the Peach Bottom, Limerick, Pennsylvania; Calvert Cliffs, Maryland; and Salem-Hope Creek, New Jersey. He has not been accused by Yemen or U.S. authorities for attempting to make a bomb or attack a nuclear plant (Kates 2010, 1–2). In fact, the Nuclear Regulatory Commission's spokesperson did acknowledge that Mobley had worked at the five plants after passing the required background checks, drug testing, and psychological tests. However, Governor Chris Christi's office stated that Mobley had always been supervised and had not caused any problems or breaches of security (Kates 2010, 1–2).

Had Mobley planned to return to attack U.S. plants after inspiration by Awlaki and bomb training in Yemen? His practical knowledge of U.S. nuclear power plants had been extensive. The Mobley situation raises the issue of the extreme importance of the careful screening and continuous supervision of nuclear power plant employees at every level of activity at nuclear and other power plants and grids!

Mobley had moved to Yemen in 2008 to study Arabic and Islam. Mobley was arrested in Yemen in March 2010 as a suspected Al Qaeda and Al-Shabab terrorist member. While in jail, he grew sick and was hospitalized for a physical exam. During an escape attempt and siege, Mobley allegedly shot two guards, one of them fatally (Kates 2010, 1–2).

MOBLEY'S LIFE PATHWAY

Sharif Mobley's parents were born in the United States and Sharif was raised in Atlantic County, New Jersey. Like Dzhokhar Tsarnaev,

Mobley had been a member of his high school wrestling team. Sharif obtained a black belt in karate before he graduated from high school in 2002. He was brought up Islamic and as a boy studied Arabic. High school classmates said that Mobley had strong religious opinions. His views had grown more radical after graduation, and Roman Castro, a high school colleague recently back from duty in Iraq, said that Mobley yelled at him, "Get the hell away from me you Muslim killer" (Kates 2010, 1). Mobley's family and imams who knew him well said that he never talked about killing anyone (Kates 2010, 1–2). There is no information about any specific conflicts Mobley had with his parents like we found among many other homegrown terrorists in this study. The author speculates that Mobley may have sought a more robust, stronger experience in radical Islam. Did such a rebellious adventure seem more exciting than a bland "Americanized" version of Islam?

According to senior U.S. security officials, Mobley left home in New Jersey to seek out al-Awlaki, hoping Awlaki would become his Al Qaeda mentor (Kates 2010, 1–2). Mobley had contact with the enormously charismatic and persuasive Awlaki who had contact with three of the 9/11 attackers, the Christmas Day Bomber (Abdulmutullab), and Nidal Malik Hasan of Fort Hood infamy. Awlaki's image as enduring father-mentor-martyr is like Osama bin Laden's, an Internet legacy for Al Qaeda and its burgeoning franchises. They have not been ended by Hellfire missiles, any more than Christianity was ended at Jesus Christ's crucifixion.

10

Richard Reid and Umar Farouk Abdulmutallab: UK and Nigeria's Homegrowns

RICHARD REID: THE SHOE BOMBER

Richard Reid unsuccessfully attempted his shoe bombing on December 22, 2001. He was indicted for attempted murder and use of a weapon of mass destruction in January 2002 and later convicted. The infamous, but thankfully unsuccessful, "shoe bomber" is the son of an English mother and a Jamaican father. Richard was born in 1973 in the London suburb of Bromley. Richard's parents divorced when he was 11 years old (Elliot 2004, 1). Richard's father Robin Reid had been in prison for most of Richard's childhood. Robin Reid has said:

> I was not there to give him the love and affection he should have had. (Reid 2001, 1)

> I was no great example to my son. (Elliot 2004, 1)

Richard left school at 16 and fell into a life of petty crime, and in the 1990s was jailed for assault and was placed several times in youth prisons. According to *Time*, after another release from prison, Richard ran into his father at a shopping mall in 1996. Richard's father Robin thought Richard was depressed and downhearted. Robin, who had converted to Islam in prison, told Richard that Muslims "treat you like a human being." Robin advised Richard to convert to Islam. Richard took his father's advice, and the next time he was incarcerated, he converted (Elliot 2004, 1).

In Feltham prison, Reid converted to Islam. After his release from prison, Richard, like many of his prison colleagues, went to the Brixton Mosque in south London. This mosque is known for attracting and helping ex-offender converts adjust to life in the world outside prison. Initially he did well, calling himself Abdel Rahim. Abdul Haqq Baker, the chairman of the Brixton Mosque, says that at some point Reid was "tempted away" by Islamist extremists (Reid 2001, 1). Baker told the BBC the extremists worked on weak characters and that Reid was "very, very impressionable" (Elliot 2004, 3).

Reid changed his dress from Western clothes to traditional Islamic robes with a khaki combat jacket on top. Reid moved to the notoriously radical Finsbury Park Mosque area of London, which French authorities call "Londonistan" (Reid 2001, 1). The Finsbury Park Mosque allowed extremists to operate and recruit more freely in those years before British authorities got stricter. For example, the fiery sermons of Abu Hamza al-Masri were often attended by a thousand young men from all over London (Reid 2001). Finsbury attracted disaffected younger Muslims from working-class backgrounds, many of whom were unemployed and unmarried. Feeling disheartened and under siege, these young men saw jihad as a salvation (Reid 2001). Richard Reid was one of those young men.

Richard probably met Zacarias Moussaoui, the 9/11 conspirator, during this his extended "father-hungry" period. Moussaoui, who attended the Brixton Mosque during the 1990s, was expelled from the mosque because of his extremist views (Elliot 2004, 3). At Finsbury Park, Reid was in a social network where Al Qaeda stalwarts like Djamel Beghal, who participated in the plot to blow up the American Embassy in Paris, held court (Elliot 2004, 3). Such father and older brother figures for young impressionable Muslims were plentiful.

Reid, after training at camps in Pakistan, apparently began travels to Egypt, Turkey, Pakistan, Belgium, the Netherlands, France, and Afghanistan to test security procedures on many airlines. On December 22, 2001, Reid was on Flight 63 from Paris to Miami. He was overpowered by passengers and crew on the flight after trying to light a fuse connected to explosives in his shoe (Reid 2001, 1). A fair question to be raised here is, Are there relatively nonintrusive ways that Western intelligence officers can engage in monitoring of groups or individuals that have the potential for recruitment of young people for their dangerous and radical causes? More importantly, can specially trained teachers, diplomats, and "peace corps" workers listen to, and dialogue with, these vulnerable young persons before they are brainwashed or seek brainwashing as a means of belonging? This is a profoundly difficult group therapy task if Al Qaeda brainwashing efforts are already in progress. Such therapy work is not unlike

Alcoholics Anonymous and Narcotics Anonymous, and treatment of severe character and personality disorders. It often takes three to five years or more, and not the brief shallow terrorist rehab programs tried in Saudi Arabia (Holliday 2007, 1–2).

Reid highlights the extreme level of susceptibility to recruitment by a radical Islamist terror cult. The common and ominous findings in the lives of future homegrown terrorists are absent or weak fathers, conflicts with authority, identity struggles, unresolved father/parent hunger, and exposure to radical Islamist imams or recruiters, often in prisons, in ghettos, and on the Internet.

UMAR FAROUK ABDULMUTALLAB: THE UNDERWEAR BOMBER

Umar Farouk Abdulmutallab, the Underwear Bomber, was home-grown in Nigeria. Some observers think the core arena of Umar's radicalization took place in London, England (Burns 2009, 1–4). Abdulmutallab's father's wealth enabled him to attend the prestigious University College in London (Burns 2009, 2).

On Christmas Day 2009, Umar carried an explosive Christmas gift from Al Qaeda to Americans in Detroit. The bomb in his underwear was intended to kill hundreds of Americans on board the plane and more on the ground. The 23-year-old Nigerian youth described himself on the Internet as lonely and never having found a true Muslim friend (Anderson 2005, 1–3; Burns 2009, 2). Umar came from a large family and his father is a wealthy banker who expressed concerns to the U.S. Embassy about his son's radical leanings. Umar had 14 siblings and, like Osama bin Laden's father Mohammad who had 40 children, it is doubtful if there was enough quality father–son time available. In an Internet posting when he was in boarding school (Burns 2009, 1–3), Umar said:

> I have no one to speak to . . . no one to consult, no one to support me and I feel depressed and lonely. I do not know what to do. And then I think this loneliness leads me to other problems. (Anderson 2005, 1–3)

Umar associated anxiously about love, marriage, college ambitions, and standardized tests. Mingled in were openly expressed conflicts about his liberalism versus extremism (Anderson 2005, 1–3).

Umar lived in a luxury apartment in London's wealthy area within walking distance of school. On the shadow side of his Pimpernel-like life in London, Umar appears to have been influenced by a London subculture of Islamist hatred of America and the West (Burns 2009, 2).

It is also apparent that Anwar al-Awlaki and his recruiter colleagues then in Yemen were asserting their nefarious talents as father substitutes for young Umar (White 2012, 1). In some of his Internet postings, Umar Abdulmutallab expressed conflicts about women, marriage, family traditions, and conflicts that a good father would have best listened to thoroughly during "quality time." Umar's father had at least tried to warn authorities about his son's signs of exponential radicalization but apparently did not enter into conversations that might have connected better with his son. Umar was a classic vulnerable father, big brother hungry "in-betweener" who almost became a successful jihadist killer of many Americans.

11

Omar Hammami of Alabama: The *Jihadi* Next Door

For a 15-year-old, Omar Hammami had remarkable charisma (Elliott 2010, 1). He was elected sophomore class president, dated a pretty cheerleader, and was a star in the gifted-student program in Daphne, Alabama. Hammami acquired his name from his Syrian-born father Shafik. Omar's mother is a warm, plainspoken woman who brought up her son as a Southern Baptist. She is reported to sprinkle her speech with plentiful "sugars" and "darlings." Omar went to Bible camps and sang "Away in a Manger" on Christmas Eve (Elliott 2010, 2). In high school, Hammami's strong interests included Shakespeare, soccer, Nintendo, and Kurt Cobain (Elliott 2010, 2).

Other than giving Omar his name, it is not clear what influence his father had on Hammami. At an interview with Eric Dolan for *The Raw Story* magazine on May 17, 2012, Omar's father, Shafik Hammami, broke into tears saying that he scoured the Internet constantly for a word of his son. Shafik said that as long as he knows Omar is alive that is good enough for him. Omar's father went on to say that Omar's mind is made up. In his mind Omar is following God's guidance, and no one can dissuade him. The author assumes that would include his father Shafik (Dolan 2012, 1)! The author speculates that Omar rebelled against what he experienced as his mother's syrupy Baptist religion. His father probably did not provide any strong religious, spiritual, or mentoring presence. The bright, charismatic Omar experienced underlying father hunger and longing. He probably struck out on his own to be like Jim Jones, David Koresh, or Charlie Manson, a strong leader and father figure himself (Olsson 2005, 33).

Omar's adolescent compatriots describe Omar as raucously funny, rebellious, contrarian, and fearless. A good friend said, "You knew Omar was going to be a leader" (Elliott 2010, 2).

Omar Hammami joined Al Shabaab in 2007. He turned his in-betweener situation in Alabama to be a grandiose father figure to at least 20 Al Qaeda franchise fighters in Al Shabaab. His young followers are Somali-Americans from a gritty part of Minneapolis. Omar Hammami has put a modern American face on Al Shabaab's medieval terror tactics (Elliott 2010, 2).

Thus after a decade, Hammami had become a key figure in Al Shabaab's ruthless Islamist insurgency in Somalia. Omar and more than 20 other Somali-Americans practice beheadings, stoning of adulterous women, and the chopping off of thieves' hands. He went by the name Abu Mansoor Al-Amriki. He had become a jihadist icon in the recruitment campaign. Omar claimed that the Western troops in Iraq and Afghanistan led himself and his colleagues to say about Osama bin Laden: All of us are ready and willing to obey all his commands (Elliott 2010, 2).

According to *The Huffington Post* reporters Guled and Straziuso, on September 13, 2013, Omar Hammami died in an ambush in Somalia. Omar Hammami was apparently killed not by an American missile attack like Anwar al-Awlaki, but in a shootout ambush by Al Shabaab warlord Ahmed Abdi Godane. In March 2012, Omar had posted a You-Tube video saying he feared for his life and made extensive criticism of Al Shabaab because they it Muslims in their attacks as well as doing assassinations of critics and character smears of Hammami. Godane even allegedly jailed Omar's wives (Dixon 2013, A5)! Dixon located tweets from Omar that reflect the polarities of late or delayed adolescent bravado. Hammami said his former colleagues in Al-Shabab planned to kill him and his close pal a Pakistan-born Briton called Osama al-Britani. Omar expressed no regrets saying:

> It's all good. Got kids and did the family thing. Who wants to be grey, achey, and wrinkley? Go out while you can still do it with a bang. (Dixon 2013, A5)

Then, however, with some nostalgia Omar said, "I'm a conservative hippie at heart—The south is still in me . . . I still go deer huntin" (Dixon 2013, A5).

Until the end, Omar seemed to be trying to resolve his inner self via the sweet Baptist mom and his effort to be a strong father-himself. Omar joined his mentors Anwar-al-Awlaki and Osama bin Laden in their legacy of Al Qaeda martyrdom.

The network of Al Qaeda's company of Robin Hood–like figures is a burgeoning recruitment business in Pakistan, Afghanistan, Somalia, and Osama Bin Laden's father's home country, Yemen. These foreign training camps link up with radical imams here in America via the Internet and wayward mosques in America.

HOMEGROWN TERRORISTS AND PRISON COMRADERY

Not unlike Al Qaeda franchise cells, enclaves of radical right wing conservative neo-Nazis, Aryan Brotherhood, or Christian Identity radicals have taken root in America.

In her timely article, Jennifer Carlile (2006) quotes from the work of Michael Radu, who is a terrorism analyst at the Foreign Policy Research Institute. Radu states, "Every (terrorist) attack has converts, and most of them have criminal records, and were converted within prisons" (Carlile 2006, 1).

Radu noted that the British Shoe Bomber Richard Reid and Jose Emilio Suarez Trashorras, the Spaniard who supplied the explosives used in the 2004 Madrid bombings, had converted while incarcerated (Carlile 2006, 1). The Carlile report goes on to note that Trashorras and Jamal Ahmidan (a nonobservant Muslim) were both brain washed into radical Islam in prison and participated with an Al Qaeda Moroccan group that made use of drug money to fund terrorist activities. These two prison converts to radical Islam took lead roles in the deadly Madrid train bombings.

As opposed to France, where Muslims tend to live in poor ghetto areas, American Muslims tend to be middle class, educated, and not often involved in crime. But American prison authorities and our politicians cannot afford to be complacent. Radical Islamist imams could quite easily seek appointments as chaplains in American prisons and spread their gospel of hatred of America among angry prisoners. Angry "skinhead" and Aryan Nation gangs have formed in U.S. prisons for decades. These young rebels in search of a cause are already bitter at law enforcement and authority (see Chapter 13 for further detail).

12

Aafia Siddiqui and Colleen LaRose: Female Homegrown Terrorists

AAFIA SIDDIQUI, PHD: BRILLIANT BUT MURDEROUS GRAY LADY OF TERROR

Aafia Siddiqui has a complex, elusive, and troubling, bewildering life story. Her history is sad, tragic, and terrifying. Born March 2, 1972, in Karachi, Pakistan, Dr. Siddiqui is an American-educated cognitive neuroscientist. She was convicted in 2010, by a U.S. jury in a federal court of assault with intent to murder her U.S. interrogators in Afghanistan. Siddiqui has persistently denied a role as the aggressor. She was sentenced to 86 years in prison and is now incarcerated in the Federal Correctional Center in Fort Worth, Texas (Hughes 2010, 1–3).

Siddiqui's supporters and some international human rights organizations claim that Aafia was not a terrorist or an extremist. They see her as a heroine who was illegally detained, interrogated, and tortured along with her children by U.S. and Pakistani authorities. The Pakistan and U.S. governments deny such claims. Siddiqui's elaborate six-month trial and extensive psychological/psychiatric evaluations raise a host of Rashomon effect–like questions. Siddiqui's case, as Bartosiewicz cogently explores and describes, poses difficult questions for legal, diplomatic, journalistic, and psychiatric experts (Bartosiewicz 2009, 42–28). These issues have profound implications for the U.S.-Pakistan political relationship. America's moral integrity and leadership in the free world is at stake in the *Brave New World* of asymmetrical warfare found in the so-called war on Islamofascist terrorism.

Aafia Siddiqui was born in Karachi, Pakistan. Her father Muhammad Salay Siddiqui was a British-educated neurosurgeon who is deceased. Her mother Ismet Faroochi is retired but was an Islamic teacher, social worker, and charity volunteer. Ismet Faroochi was active in Pakistani politics and religious circles. She had been a member of Pakistan's parliament. Deborah Scroggins, a biographer of Aafia Siddiqui, describes Ismet Faroochi as tiny in frame like her daughter, but restless, ambitious, and a dominant organizer (Scroggins 2012, 3–8). Ismet had raised Aafia to be a heroine of Islam and ever mindful of the Koran's message to go learn even if it took a Muslim to China (Scroggins 2012, 25). Aafia's scholarly retiring father wanted her to be a doctor (Scroggins 2012, 25). Ismet and Aafia, like many educated Pakistani women, admired Benazir Bhutto's success and her Harvard and Oxford education; MIT would eventually make do. Soaring ambition and profound religious ardor are a powerful combination (Scroggins 2012, 25), especially in most homegrown terrorists.

Aafia is the youngest of three siblings. Her brother is an architect in Sugarland, Texas. Her sister is a Harvard-trained neurologist who returned to Pakistan after working at Sinai Hospital in Baltimore and teaching at Johns Hopkins. Aafia Siddiqui went to school in Zambia until age eight and then finished primary and secondary school in Karachi (Saathoff 2009, 1). Siddiqui moved to Houston on a student visa in 1990 (Scroggins 2012, 35–38). She went to the University of Houston for three semesters before transferring to MIT with a full scholarship. In 1992, Siddiqui received the Carroll L. Wilson Award for her research on "Islamization in Pakistan and Its Effects on Women."

In 1993, Siddiqui received a $1,200 City Days fellowship through MIT's program to clean up Cambridge elementary school playgrounds. She graduated from MIT in 1995 with a BS in biology. Siddiqui is described by MIT schoolmates as soft-spoken, unassertive, and moderately religious (Ozment 2004, 1). She joined the Muslim Students Association (MSA) and did recruiting for MSA. Deborah Scroggins, a biographer of Siddiqui, thinks that MSA contacts may have been an important factor in drawing Aafia ever deeper into Islamic terrorism (Scroggins 2005, 35, 70). Several of MSA's most active members had been mesmerized by the charismatic Abdullah Azzam, who was Osama bin Laden's mentor (Scroggins 2005, 105–10). Azzam had established the Al Kifah Refugee Center. The center served as a worldwide recruiting post, propaganda office, and fund-raising center for the *mujahideen* fighters in Afghanistan. Al Kifah Center would become one of the nuclei for Al Qaeda. Siddiqui solicited money for the center, which, in addition to charity, advocated armed violence. One of the Al Kifah Center members had killed radical Rabbi Meir Kahane in 1990.

The Al Kifah Center was tied to the 1993 World Trade Center bombing (Scroggins 2005, 77–79).

Siddiqui met several dedicated Islamists through MSA, including its imam, Suheil Laher. Laher publically advocated Islamization and jihad before 9/11. In 1995 when Pakistan asked the United States for help in combating religious extremism, Siddiqui, in an announcement from the Kifah Center, scornfully derided Pakistan for joining what she labeled the gang of Muslim U.S. puppet governments. She quoted from the Koran urging Muslims to not take Jews and Christians as friends (Scroggins 2005, 95–97). Aafia expressed hope that more and more people would turn to Allah until America becomes a Muslim land (Scroggins 2012, 96–97). She also took a 12-hour pistol training course at the Braintree Rifle and Pistol Club (Stockman 2010, 1).

In 1995, Aafia Siddiqui had entered sight unseen into an arranged marriage to Amjad Mohammed Khan, an anesthesiologist just out of medical school in Karachi. The marriage ceremony was conducted over the telephone. The couple lived in Lexington and later Roxbury, Massachusetts. Amjad worked at Brigham and Women's Hospital. Aafia gave birth to their two older children—a boy and a girl. In 1995 Siddiqui founded the nonprofit Institute of Islamic Research and Teaching. She was its president, her husband was the treasurer, and her sister was the resident agent (Stockman 2004, 1). She attended a mosque outside Boston and helped establish the Dawa Resource Center. The center gave out Korans and offered active Islam-based advice to prisoners (Scroggins 2010, 95–96).

Siddiqui studied neuroscience at Brandeis University and received her PhD in 2001. Brandeis was a paradoxical place for Siddiqui. Brandeis retained a Jewish character and conflicted with Aafia's crescendoing Islamist beliefs. Her professors were shocked when Aafia concluded that the data on fetal alcohol syndrome showed why God had forbidden alcohol use in the Koran (Scroggins, 120). She was outspoken about science being a way of celebrating her religion often versus science, which increasingly annoyed her professors (Scroggins 2012, 120–21). Siddiqui's dissertation was on learning through imitation, titled "Separating the Components of Imitation." Her thesis advisor said that she wore a head scarf and thanked Allah when an experiment went successfully. Aafia coauthored a published article about selective learning in 2003 (Scroggins 2012, 123–24).

Shortly before 9/11, Siddiqui was accused of using an alias of Fahrem Shahin to join six alleged Al Qaeda members in obtaining $19 million worth of Liberian blood diamonds (Scroggins 2005, 273). The diamonds were alleged to be used as untraceable assets to fund Al Qaeda. Siddiqui's attorney disputed the accusation with evidence that Aafia was in Boston, not Liberia, at the time. She did remain a suspect for money laundering (at every twist and contradictory turn of Aafia's life story, there are many alternative scenarios that challenge U.S. and international law experts, not to mention the journalists, psychiatrists, and psychologists seeking psychological truth about her) (Bartosiewicz 2009, 41–51).

In 2001, Aafia's husband Amjad Khan said that his wife felt unsafe about her and her children. Khan said she wanted to move to Afghanistan to be a medic for the mujahideen. In May 2002, the FBI questioned Siddiqui and her husband about their purchase over the Internet of $10,000 worth of night vision equipment, body armor, and military manuals, including *The Anarchist's Arsenal*, *Fugitive*, *Advanced Fugitive*, and *How to Make C-4*. The couple claimed that these materials were for camping trips (Scroggins 2005, 187–89). On June 26, 2002, the couple and their children returned to Pakistan.

In August 2002, Khan claimed Aafia had been abusive, manipulative, and extremist in her thinking throughout their seven-year marriage. Khan went to Aafia's parents' home and indicated his intention to get a divorce. He argued intensely with her father, who died of a heart attack on August 15, 2002.

The author speculates that Aafia's marriages represent searches for strong father/parental substitutes, with whom to share bold action plans and deeds. Aafia's husbands and marriages also may have served as linking objects to assuage separation-loss of her father (Volkan 2004, 23) and both parents' falls from Aafia's idealizing pedestals.

Aafia never clearly explained what happened to her two missing children prior to and during her arrest in Afghanistan. Aafia apparently told one FBI agent that sometimes a person has to take up a cause that is more important than one's children (Neumeister 2009, 1–2). This could represent an unconscious wish to outdo her highly educated parents who she may have thought talked devoutly but never actually walked the walk. The author believes that Eric Shaw's concept holds true about Aafia. Shaw described a telling conflict in many future terrorists. Severe disappointment occurs when they realize that there are glaring inconsistencies between their parents' and/or families of origin's political, religious, and philosophical beliefs, and their parents' impotence in terms of actual effective social or moral action that brings authentic and effective change.

In September 2002, Siddiqui gave birth to Suleman, the last of their three children. Khan and Siddiqui's divorce was finalized on October 21, 2002. Subsequently, Siddiqui's travels and whereabouts grew murky for five years.

In 2003, the FBI alleged that she was linked to Al Qaeda–planned attacks on U.S. gas stations and underground fuel-storage tanks in the Baltimore/Washington region. Majid Khan and Uzair Paracha, known Al Qaeda operatives, were linked to Siddiqui, though her participation with them was not definitively proven (Scroggins 2012, 233–35).

In February 2003, Siddiqui married Ammar al-Baluchi in Karachi (Stockman 2010, 1). Al-Baluchi is also known as Ali Abdul Aziz Ali, a nephew of infamous Al Qaeda leader Khalid Sheikh Mohammed (KSM) (a new even more powerful linking-object husband?) Al-Baluchi is also a cousin of Ramzi Yousef, who was convicted of the 1993 bombing of the World Trade Center. The marriage to Baluchi was denied by Siddiqui's family but confirmed by Pakistani and U.S. intelligence. Al-Baluchi was arrested on April 29, 2003, and taken to Guantanamo where he was incarcerated.

Aafia Siddiqui's Psychiatric Diagnosis and Psychodynamics

The author has not examined Aafia Siddiqui but has reviewed summaries of the findings of several forensic psychiatrists and psychologists. Three of four examining psychiatrists concluded that Siddiqui was malingering (faking symptoms of mental illness).

From a psychodynamic viewpoint, it is difficult to discover her unconscious motivations via forensic psychiatric reports. Forensic psychiatric interviews assemble a different kind of data. Intrapsychic emotional content, conflict, and motivation are best obtained by voluntarily, freely, and spontaneously offered free associations; dream reports; and transference fantasies about the therapist and other people. Such data shared by a person in psychotherapy is merely data from a very different clinical domain than forensic interview data. Not better, not worse, not more important or less important, merely different.

Certainly, Aafia Siddiqui was and probably is depressed. No matter what the legal truth is about events, Aafia is likely to have posttraumatic stress disorder. Siddiqui's courtroom verbal behavior seemed to reflect severe ambivalence and possibly borderline and histrionic behavior.

The recent Boston Marathon bombers like Aafia studied in fine Boston schools. Tragically, intelligent young minds' potentials got destroyed by grandiose radical fundamentalist thinking run amok. Such are the tragic consequences of terrible human choices, as youths like Aafia and the Tsarnaev brothers grappled with awful extremes of freedom, spiritual searching, and personal responsibility.

COLLEEN LAROSE: JIHAD JANE

Colleen LaRose, a 46-year-old Pennsylvania housewife called herself "Jihad Jane." On February 1, 2011, Colleen pleaded guilty to trying to recruit Islamic terrorists to wage violent jihad and plotting to murder the Swedish artist Lars Vilks, who had drawn a cartoon of the prophet Muhammad. LaRose married at age 16 and never finished high school. She soon divorced and married again at age 24.

Colleen's marriage to "Rudy" Cavazos lasted 10 years (divorced 1998). Cavazos said that Colleen was a good woman, a bible-carrying woman (Thomas, Krolowitz, and Clarke 2010, 1–2). In 2004 Colleen moved to Philadelphia with a boyfriend. She helped Kurt Gorman care for his aging father. Colleen stayed with Gorman for five years, during which time she converted to Islam. She had been so distressed by the sudden deaths of her father and brother in 2005 that she made a suicide gesture (Thomas et al. 2010, 2).

Colleen not only got comfort from her new faith, but also became distressed and angry about Internet scenes of bloodshed in the Middle East. Her Myspace profile reflected this and her strong support for the Palestinian cause and suffering Muslims in general. This apparently progressed further to participation in violent plans of her own preparation to kill and terrorize (Thomas et al. 2010, 2).

There is meager data to speculate about Colleen's psychodynamics definitively. However, grief, loss, and depression very likely were factors. Perhaps her marriages and even her radical turn within her new Islamic faith reflected linking phenomenon and unresolved grief issues. She never talked to Gorman about any of these domains. She probably identified with radical aggressors as an acting-out and projection of her pain and loss. Colleen misperceived unfair treatment of Muslims as merged with her own pain and rather than finding words to contain and control her feelings, she sought to act out as a defense.

APPENDIX

A Concise History of Pakistan in the Context of Understanding Its Vulnerability to Homegrown Terrorism

The country that has garnered much attention due to its role in the War on Terror is Pakistan. Pakistan is a very important ally to the United States, but at many points in its cooperation, Pakistan seems to have a conflict of interest. While it cooperates with the United States, schools and important religious institutions in Pakistan advocate a radical, fundamentalist message that contradicts the government's compliance. The instability that has and currently plagues Pakistan stems from the combination of several factors: military conflicts with India and Bangladesh (formerly East Pakistan), a political system that has permanently been on the verge of change through coups and military dominance, and poor educational systems that enhance ignorance and jihadist recruitment.

When Pakistan and India obtained independence in 1947 from the British, the process of creating the two states was based on religion. The territory comprising modern-day Pakistan was drawn from the western region of the British Raj, which included Balochistan, Sindh, West Punjab, and the Northwest Frontier Province. East Pakistan was included after the region of Bengal was divided into the Indian region of West Bengal, predominantly Hindu, and East Pakistan, which was Muslim majority. The purpose of the British division was to make India the Hindu state, with Pakistan appealing to Muslims.

When the British divided the Raj into Pakistan and India, the process was far from perfect. Many Muslims scrambled to move into Pakistan, vice versa for Hindus looking to move into Indian territory. Tensions erupted into violence in Bengal, Punjab, and Sindh as the population transfer unsettled these regions. The mess that came with the partition of India resulted in boundaries that were highly uncertain, with two new governments responsible for finalizing these borders that were destined to be rivals.

The government of Pakistan was initially tied to Great Britain in that its official title was the Dominion of Pakistan and the country was a member of the Commonwealth. After partition, the first conflict between Pakistan and India occurred in 1947 when both sides failed to negotiate how the formerly independent princely state of Jammu and Kashmir would be divided. Two years later, Pakistan faced its first coup when its first prime minister, Liaquat Ali Khan, narrowly avoided being toppled by a conspiracy led by Major General Akbar Khan (Gill 2010). This coup marked the first visible sign of political instability in Pakistan, and Great Britain cut its ties when Pakistan officially became an Islamic Republic in 1956 (Pakistan would rejoin the Commonwealth eventually).

Pakistan's coups would become a defining characteristic of its politics, and the first successful coup came again through the initiative of General Khan, this time in 1958. A new constitution was adopted when Pakistan became an Islamic Republic in 1956, but the two years leading up to the coup featured four different prime ministers and a parliamentary government that was weak. President Iskander Mirza declared martial law in 1958 and dissolved the government, appointing General Khan as the overseer of order during the governmental transition in a move designed to help Mirza consolidate power. However, Khan, a powerful figure within the army, took control and declared himself president and prime minister with a cabinet of officers. This event transformed Pakistan's government into one that, for most of its existence, was entirely run by the army.

Reasons for the Pakistani government's instability extend beyond the military presence. A major issue that has persisted is the constant disagreement on what role the state should have. After partition, the reoccurring question was, "Was it to be a pluralistic, democratic country for Muslims and other religious minorities or a theocratic Islamic state?" (Rashid 2008). While religion motivated the partition, one of the fathers of the nation, Mohammed Ali Jinnah, clearly stated his intention that Pakistan respect other religions, and that religion should not be the primary factor in decision making. In reality, after Jinnah's death in 1948, Pakistan has gone in the opposite direction, where Jinnah's legacy has been distorted by an education system that is entirely based on a system that is dominated by Islam. According to Pakistani writer Ahmed Rashid, who writes for several prominent Western publications, the goal of the Pakistani Army today is to defend Islam by protecting Pakistan's "territorial and ideological (Islamic) frontiers" (Rashid 2008).

While conflict with India was the primary feature of Pakistan's early political history, Pakistan became the focus of international attention for all the wrong reasons by 1971, when the Bangladesh Liberation

War came to a head. The modern-day country known as Bangladesh was assigned to Pakistan in the partition of India due to its Muslim majority, being known as East Bengal, and, eventually, East Pakistan. With the large country of India separating Pakistan and East Pakistan, equal government administration turned out to be a difficult proposition. The Bengali people in East Pakistan had many grievances against the Pakistanis, the main one being that from the beginning of Pakistani independence, government leaders were not accepting of Bengali culture and banning the Bengali language while promoting Urdu. Bengalis also decried the government's unequal spending on main Pakistan while East Pakistan was underfunded and underrepresented. Eventually a large-scale liberation war erupted in 1971, and after a protracted struggle, East Pakistan obtained independence as Bangladesh when India joined its side.

Pakistan's defeat in Bangladesh was devastating on the country's world standing. The army committed horrible offenses as a result of the counterrevolutionary measures, with widespread rape and killings that have been placed in the context of genocide. International support for Pakistan was nonexistent at this point, making the nation desperate for foreign aid. This desperation emerged into the relationship with the United States that has extended into today. By 1957, Pakistan was receiving $500 million from the United States in return for being a U.S ally during the Cold War (Rashid 2008). By the end of the Bangladesh Liberation War, the relationship was locked in, with a CIA base established in Karachi. The United States was notably one of the last countries to recognize Bangladesh as a country when it applied for international membership.

India has been a thorn in the side of Pakistan's political aspirations since partition, but Pakistan's growth was stunted by its own failures in administration, as well as the lack of a clear national identity. Activities revolve around the main province of Punjab, which accounts for 65 percent of the nation's population (Rashid 2008). The focus on Punjab has affected the rest of Pakistan's administrative divisions, with East Pakistan the most notable victim, and regional movements have formed aiming to obtain independence for the other administrative states, such as Balochistan and Sindh. The FATA (Federally Administered Tribal Areas) have been the center of Islamist movements that are a thorn in the central government's side today.

For the first time since independence, popular elections were held in 1970, but the results did not come into realization because of the outbreak of the Bangladesh Liberation War. After the war, Zulfiqar Ali Bhutto became the first president in some time who was not in the army. Bhutto was charismatic and compelling, and helped bring money to the government by helping Pakistan to be more involved in the Arab world, where several states found large amounts of wealth through the oil trade (Rashid 2008). Pakistan's nuclear program began under Bhutto, and the constitution written in 1973 brought a structure to abide by in the government. However, in 1977 Bhutto and his Pakistan People's Party were found to have rigged the election, and in the disorder created, another military coup brought the army back to power under General Zia-ul-Haq.

Pakistan changed into the military-based state that it is today because of the reign of Zia-ul-Haq. Rashid cites the epithet that came to define Pakistani politics: "All countries have armies, but in Pakistan the army has a country" (Rashid 2008). Zia saw himself as the man to bring order to Pakistan through Islam, which meant a dictatorial-style rule that put down political dissent and instituted the most conservative and restrictive government possible. Pakistan's relationship with the United States reached its most fruitful point for Zia, with his government receiving over $4 billion worth of aid from Ronald Reagan's administration (Rashid 2008). American aid money strengthened and modernized Pakistan's army and Inter-Services Intelligence (ISI), while these military bodies provided the link for American support of the Mujahideen in Afghanistan. Essentially, Reagan and Zia's collaboration paved the way for massive funding of jihadist warriors in Pakistan's border regions with Afghanistan. Pakistani madrassahs (religious schools) were given additional funding to perform training, and the ISI's leaders and agents were enriched to great ends with American money being put into the illicit drug trade and funneled out to those in the army with the most power. Zia's rule and understanding with the United States made Pakistan the center of jihadist training and education that it is today (Rashid 2008).

The evidence from Pakistan's turbulent history gives sight to the conditions that are prevalent today in the Pakistan–Afghanistan border area. With Pakistan's military and political history well documented, it is necessary to focus on the conditions that create jihadist terrorists, which is best understood by looking at the impact the Zia regime's collaboration with the United States had. Pakistan was greatly improved when it came to military resources and regime stability, but the social situation became a scene of decay.

Pakistani society, expediently under Zia, found itself the victim of government corruption and a military-run government. Politicians in Pakistan have historically found the army a necessary institution to gain favor with to advance the interests of themselves. When the military finds itself at the center of every political discourse, eventually the military becomes the ultimate judge, which leads to an imbalance of power (Gill 2010). Being an Islamic republic like Pakistan is, religious leaders find the military to be the best instrument of power, so many powerful leaders, religious or otherwise, enjoy the unrestricted power of the military to prevent democratic processes from undermining alternative interests. With political power distributed between few parties, military leaders can fit their interests within the confines of the political party they ally themselves with.

The foreign influence on Pakistan has been instrumental in maintaining corruption as well. U.S. collaboration with the Pakistani Army and ISI has placed these organizations at the highest of power. American intervention has been shown to favor a military-based government, as it is easier to influence than a country that follows democratic principles (Gill 2010).

Another factor to consider when looking at the role of the military is just how involved they are in day-to-day Pakistani society. Officers run many important private industries, ranging from dairy farms to cement and even cornflakes (Gill 2010). Industry in Pakistan is divided between five major corporations (known as "welfare foundations") that feature state-owned businesses all across Pakistani cities. The military controls one-third of heavy manufacturing and 7 percent of private assets (Gill 2010). Therefore, the military has investments in all aspects of Pakistani society, with profits going directly to the military government. In addition, there is no reliable way to monitor how money is used in Pakistan. The manner in which Pakistan uses its massive amounts of foreign aid from the United States is not transparent.

One of the most important factors in Pakistan that contributes to the growing number of jihadists is the very poor educational systems. There is no national curriculum in Pakistan, so different provinces have differing standards. In the province known as Khyber Pakhtunkhwa, for example, where there have been many propositions in 2013 to change what is taught, the provincial Minister of Information and Culture, Shah Farman, stated:

What kind of sovereignty, freedom, and Islamic values is this when Islamic teachings, jihad, and national heroes are removed from textbooks?" . . . "Jihad is part of our faith. We will not back down [from our decision]. (Bezhan 2013)

It is easy to see how the Khyber Province has become a hotbed for Taliban training and other jihadist influence. Pakistan's literacy rate is a dismal 54 percent, and female literacy is under 30 percent (Rashid 2008). Ahmed Rashid cited a prominent Pakistani educator who stated that "this generation of Pakistanis is intellectually handicapped" (2008).

When it comes to education in Pakistan, the most important institute to examine is the madrassah system. Madrassahs are religious schools that teach with an Islamic influence on its curriculum. The rise of the madrassah has been exponential since there were 137 of them in 1947, rising up to over 40,000 according to *The News International*, the largest English-language newspaper in Pakistan. Initially a school system that was designed to provide education for future priests and Islamic judges, the madrassah system became manipulated by each of the government regimes that came to power, and now serves the purpose of spreading radical Islamic beliefs, especially jihad (Rashid 2008). With a lack of regulation and registration for all the madrassahs that have popped up throughout the country, these schools advocate for the most extreme of Muslim parties, and purposefully revise Pakistan's history to serve the national Muslim identity.

Since the Iranian Revolution in 1979, Pakistan has been at the center of an ideological battle between Saudi Arabia and Iran, who have invested large amounts in madrassahs to propagate their messages (Mirahmadi et al. 2012). Saudi Arabia invests in Sunni madrassahs that espouse fundamentalist views, while Iran's support goes toward Shia political movements and teachings. These schools have been responsible for the development of the mujahideen in Afghanistan to fight the Soviets, and today serve as the breeding ground for jihadists who wish to fight against Western interests. In one example cited, Arab gulf states were responsible for over $100 million being funneled into fundamentalist madrassahs based on a WikiLeaks report (Mirahmadi et al. 2012).

The Saudi presence in Pakistani education has been in effect since the Soviet war in Afghanistan, with the majority of madrassahs, around 65 percent, being controlled by the Deobandi sect (Rashid 2008). Madrassahs are not entirely funded by the competing Saudis and Iranians, as Pakistanis contribute financially to the madrassahs through the Muslim practice of *zakat*, a 2.5 percent of annual income given to the poor. According to Ahmed Rashid, out of the money dedicated to *zakat*, 94 percent of the money went to madrassahs (Rashid 2008). With the influence of radical Islam widespread among wealthy members of the army and many political movements, the madrassah system is much endorsed by Pakistanis themselves despite the troubling violence produced by the system.

Reforms have been proposed to take radical teaching out of the schools since 2000, but heavy opposition from Islamic political parties has prevented reforms from being put into practice. Under President Pervez Musharraf and his close relationship with the United States, a 2008 proposal finally found ground, encouraging more communication between the government and the madrassahs regarding their teachings and banning messages of jihad and extremism (Mirahmadi et al. 2012). However, many bureaucratic and political obstacles remain to keep all the madrassahs registered, much less regulating what their message is.

In conclusion, Pakistan is a country that has been plagued by the constant debate over the role of the government and the resulting lack of administration, creating unsupervised territories that have become a hotbed of jihadism. The army's constant presence as the policymaking arm and power of the government from Pakistan's early days created a persistent state of martial law, in turn promoting slack administration at the expense of spending on nuclear programs and the appearance of military might against India. Since partition, Pakistan has never been in a position where the government can reform and properly prepare its population for success. This is the result of military desperation that led to lucrative partnerships with the United States that were spent on military advancement rather than on education and other important projects that can garner the faith of its citizens.

Pakistani wasteful spending on military projects, in a sense of irony, prevents it from combating terrorism because the lack of educational spending and investment promotes ignorance and illiteracy. When the population is unable to think at an adequate intellectual level, radical thinking finds fertile ground for manipulation and the advocation of violence. With this trend becoming the norm, particularly picking up speed under the regime of General Zia, Pakistan is fighting a long battle to reverse the course of the damage the madrassah system has committed. Once again, military spending led to this system, where the emergence of madrassahs as the main vehicle of education has been the unintended result.

13

Right Wing Ideology and Its Violent Fringe[1]

TERMS AND CONCEPTS

(1) Identity theology is a form of radical religious conservatism constructed to support the ideology of the extreme right.

History—The roots of identity theology go back to the late 1800s with the rise of Anglo-Israelism, which postulated that the lost tribes of Israel had settled the British Isles. In the 1930s, Wesley Swift founded a church in California based on the tenets of Anglo-Israelism. William Gale, more radical and conservative than Swift, became minister after Swift and the church retreated from the mainstream. By the 1950s, the church's militant ideology was entrenched. In 1961, Richard Butler rose as its leader and applied the ideology to social issues. In the last two decades, the most important vehicles of identity theology—Aryan Nations—claim far in excess of 50,000 members.

Belief system—The primary values of identity theology are twofold: racial identity and national identity. In terms of racial values, identity theology posits four classes of beings: (1) Enosh—people of African origin are believed to be descended from animals. (2) Man, (3) Jews—are believed to be descendants of Cain who they believe to be a product of Eve and Satan. (4) Mongrels—are people of mixed racial background.

Man—are believed to be the descendants of Adam and Eve and are essentially people of Western European origin. In terms of national values, identity theology distinguishes between Jews and Israelites. They believe that the lost tribes of Israel resettled in Western Europe and the United States. William Gale taught that the Bible predicted that these tribes would reappear as a nation on July 4, 1776. Thus, the United States is made to be the promised land and must be cleansed in preparation for the Second Coming of Jesus Christ. As such, identity theology is a "postmillennial" religion, that is, the Second Coming will not take place until the promised land has been cleansed. Cleansing by implication means the liquidation of Enosh, Jews, and Mongrels.

A third aspect of identity theology's value system is "Christian" identity. Richard Kelly Hoskins uses a story in the biblical book of numbers to call for what he calls a "Phineas Priesthood." It essentially amounts to vigilantes meting out putative justice in the name of Christianity. This Phineas Priesthood is similar to the leaderless resistance cells of the neo-Nazis and the KKK's "Texas Guard."

What is the appeal of identity theology? To many it seems as reprehensible as Al Qaeda's Holy War on Western infidels. However, it fulfills the need for identity in those who perceive themselves as having none, for example, white men of lower socioeconomic status. It fulfills the need for action, and attracts "in-betweeners" or goalless people—often uneducated young men in search of identity and resentful of educated Jews, blacks, Asians, and Hispanics who are more competitive in getting jobs. There are thousands of churches that preach forms of identity theology but these churches do not use "identity" in their titles or on their church billboards.

The psychological power of the religious or quasi-religious symbolism of right wing groups is often overlooked by law enforcement and counterterrorism experts. This same psychological power is contained in the appeal of Al Qaeda as it mesmerizes recruits with its distorted use of the Koran.

(2) *White supremacy* is the secular belief in the supremacy of whites. The real basis of white supremacy is the economic well-being of its constituents. Membership in these groups correlates with times of economic hardship and rising numbers of immigrant populations. White supremacist groups include the KKK, neo-Nazi groups, Aryan Nations, and the skinheads. The skinhead movement originated in the United Kingdom as adherents to a particular type of music but later expanded to include violence toward immigrants. In the United States, the first skinhead group was in Boston, BASH. It included racism and homophobia as raison d'etre. Subsequently, "to bash" became a term to describe these racially motivated violent assaults. The skinhead groups can be found in widespread places such as Japan and on the Internet under the keyword "hammerskins."

(3) *Survivalists* originated as a reaction to fear of communism but more recently urban racial tension and fear of U.S. government gun control are seen as the new enemies. Survivalists believe that eventually minorities will control the cities and that cities will eventually fail to remain self-sufficient due to the minorities' incompetence. Cities will then attack the rural areas of the country. Survivalists believe

they must be able to protect themselves when this happens. They engage in paramilitary training with real guns and ammunition.

Conspiracy theories abound among survivalist groups. Common ones have to do with the fear of the "New World Order," that is, a single world government. Survivalists abhor the U.N. They also deny the jurisdiction of the federal government and speak of themselves as sovereign, for example, the "Republic of Texas," or the "Sovereign State of Arkansas."

They also believe in a "Zionist monetary conspiracy" and condemn the Federal Reserve. This denial of a central organ for regulating money allows them to print their own money. This is what the Freemen did and eventually led to the Clark ranch standoff. At that point, they had printed $300 million worth of counterfeit money.

Survivalists also deny what is known as "admiralty law" and espouse a return to common law. They refuse to acknowledge rulings made in admiralty court that can be recognized according to them by the gold fringe on the American flag.

(4) *Militia* are groups that center around protection of the right to bear arms. They organize around the Second Amendment protection but most are not usually involved in terrorism.

It is important to understand the difference between "survivalists" and "militia" groups. Militia groups are basically supporters of the Second Amendment. The Second Amendment was written to allow states to have their own militia, separate from the federal government. But these groups interpret the law as citizens' rights to own guns and organize militia. Survivalists are more extreme and believe essentially in a coming race war, against which they must prepare to defend themselves.

These groups have a typical predictable cyclical evolution in which there is recruitment, drop-off of members for whom the group becomes too radical, planning of action, drop-off again, carrying out of action, and further drop-off, which leave a radical, hard-core center, which either becomes more radical or takes on a more mainstream rhetoric and goes back to recruitment again.

Some experts think American society is particularly vulnerable to the development of radical right wing groups. The presumption they make is that the history of the U.S. involves a founding on rebellion and an associated lower tolerance for rules. So in terms of group dynamics, they function as a projection of a collective unconscious vehicle for feelings that occur in all the people in our society, but are unacceptable to the mainstream.

An additional discussion can be stirred by a focus on the importance of ritual in human behavior as a form of regression. Ritual allows individuals to regress to a point where they can feel they belong to something larger than themselves. After the 9/11 attacks on New York and the recent horror bombing in Boston, even very partisan politicians emphasized that all Americans become supportive of Bostonians. Perhaps members of the right wing groups are seeking ritual for this reason, albeit in a destructive way. Sapp noted that the most violent members of right wing groups are those on the fringe. They desperately want to be members but are not seen as such by the leaders. They exhibit what could be termed "reverse paranoia," the belief that they are being monitored and erroneously assume that they are assigned to follow someone. They then resort to violence as a means to prove the sincerity and strength of their allegiance to the group and leader.

In the future, as the population of the right wing ages, it may be replaced by younger, more violent groups, for example, skinheads. It is possible that decreased economic and job opportunity and decreased quality of attachments (childcare, ghettos, videogame world, and the absolute individualism of Generation X) create an ability to victimize more easily.

Dilemmas Involved with Monitoring and Prognosticating about Right Wing Groups

Law enforcement authorities have significant limitations about monitoring potential individual and group terrorist activities at churches, synagogues, and mosques. Similarly, law enforcement authorities have restrictions about monitoring right wing groups. In America the First Amendment strongly protects freedom of speech, religion, and the right to assemble. The Second Amendment protects the right for a militia and an individual to bear arms. The law states that these groups cannot be directly monitored by the government unless there is convincing evidence that criminal activity is occurring, and then only for 30 days.

Thus, the FBI, for example, uses informants, the Internet, and source material from the groups themselves. The biographical information about group leaders is particularly sketchy because the biographies provided by the groups themselves are often idealized or fictionalized.

Nevertheless, some important observations have accumulated. Stages of right wing groups are described by Sapp as follows: Recruiting, rhetoric, retrench, and revolt. During the phase of rhetoric is when the group may be very visible and drawing a lot of publicity. Paradoxically, authorities have less concern about dangerous behavior because they are more focused on publicity than action. The groups become quiet during the retrenching phase. They seek more mainstream names and images. This is worrisome for authorities because it is often premonitory to revolt and terrorist events.

A Magical Date?

For right wing groups, April 19 has symbolic significance. This is considered "minuteman day." It is the anniversary of Paul Revere's ride. Many paramilitary events have occurred on this day, including Ruby Ridge, the Oklahoma City bombing, and Waco.

On April 19, 1995, Timothy McVeigh destroyed the Alfred P. Murrah Federal Building in Oklahoma City. The truck bomb killed 168 people and wounded hundreds more. First guesses were that a foreign terrorist had struck. McVeigh was a hometown upstate New York young man and a decorated U.S. Army veteran. No American wanted to believe he had done such evil.

Michel and Herbeck have written a carefully researched and thorough biography of Timothy McVeigh titled *American Terrorist*. Important information about McVeigh's developmental psychology and motivation can be found in the depth and density of solid information Michel and Herbeck present.

TIMOTHY MCVEIGH: THE OKLAHOMA CITY BOMBER

McVeigh, like the majority of the homegrown terrorists described in this book, experienced significant conflicts about and disappointments in his parents. Michel and Herbeck present a poignant and pithy quote from McVeigh:

> I struggle with the question: Do I love my parents? . . . I have very few memories of my childhood, of interaction with my parents. I can't blame them for anything that's happened to me. I was often by myself or with neighbors. Most of my memories focus on that. (Michel and Herbeck 2001, 7).

It is clear that McVeigh was truly loved and cared for by his parents, grandfather, and siblings. But his parents' conflicted marital relationship brought a lot of psychological pain to their family and themselves. In those days, divorce was particularly taboo and it took many years for Bill and Mickey to finally divorce. Timothy McVeigh seemed to use extensive neurotic repression and denial in many areas of his emotional life. This seemed particularly true about his parents and like many men with anger toward their mothers, Timothy carried his unconscious maternal transference anger over into unsuccessful efforts to connect intimately with women. Tim opened up to Andrea Peters, a woman with whom he tried to get very close. During lengthy evening phone calls, McVeigh let glimpses of his anger peek through as he called his mother a "whore" and a "bitch." He blamed her for breaking up their family and hurting his dad (Michel and Herbeck 2001, 126). He wanted to impress Andrea but she only wanted a friendship. Tim's first serious girlfriend Sarah felt that his parent's divorce had left Tim feeling "lost." Sarah's intuition was that Tim held anger toward his mother (Michel and Herbeck 2001, 40). Not long after his high school graduation, Tim abruptly broke up with Sarah.

After high school, McVeigh turned down a college scholarship and entered a long spell of reflection. Such a moratorium is common among adolescents. He had always loved guns and this fascination grew more intense as he studied the Second Amendment thoroughly. He decided to become a survivalist. He latched on to *The Turner Diaries* as a kind of his bible for his identity formation (Michel and Herbeck 2001, 45). The novel is the story of Earl Turner who as an avid gun aficionado reacts to tighter gun laws by making a truck bomb and destroying FBI headquarters.

McVeigh had been a valued soldier as he served with distinction in Operation Desert Storm. Upon his return, Tim aspired to join the elite Green Berets of Special Forces. McVeigh did not make it to the Special Forces. Tim used denial as he told friends that he was not destroyed by failure but clearly his army life would never be the same (Michel and Herbeck 2001, 103). McVeigh experienced cumulative and escalating further disappointments and narcissistic wounds as he struggled to find meaningful work in the civilian world. He grew bitter and depressed, and he considered suicide (Michel and Herbeck 2001, 113, 121). McVeigh grew progressively disgusted with the government.

Like many other homegrown terrorists-to-be, Tim's fierce authority conflict focused exponentially on the U.S. government. Events at Ruby Ridge and Waco were like gasoline poured on the inner fire of his hatred (Michel and Herbeck 2001, 128–29). Bill McVeigh had no empathy for his son's anti-government views (Michel and Herbeck 2001, 129). Tim's father hunger led him to old war buddies and gun lover friends he met at gun shows he attended compulsively. On Christmas Eve 1993, McVeigh shared shocking and ominous thoughts with his youngest sister Jennifer. He told her that the federal government was the real criminal who he would get even with like Robin Hood against the evil king (Michel and Herbeck 2001, 179). The relentless progression of McVeigh's descent into the hell he created in Oklahoma City is now history. Insecurity, stubborn authority conflicts, progressive fanaticism, and paranoia are often deadly companions.

TED KACZYNSKI: THE BRILLIANT UNABOMBER, A PARADOXICAL SOUL

Tim McVeigh and Ted Kaczynski were on the same cell block at a Colorado prison and had significant contact. In their thorough and perceptive biography of Timothy McVeigh, Michel and Herbeck include in their Appendix B the April 25, 2000, letter about Tim McVeigh sent to them by Ted Kaczynski (491–96). McVeigh and Kaczynski never discussed the Oklahoma bombing; they did have many other conversations. Ted makes the interesting and perceptive observation that when a person is confined with other persons in the conditions they were in, one develops a sense of solidarity regardless of any differences or misgivings about others. Kaczynski's letter has an eerie doppelganger-like tone. It is as if Kaczynski and McVeigh became twins or alter-egos in their boiling narcissistic rage against "the system." Kaczynski described McVeigh as basically rational, perceptive, and having good social skills (Michel and Herbeck 2001, 491–92). Ted Kaczynski said that McVeigh showed no racism at that time and treated black inmates respectfully at their maximum security death row. Kaczynski provides an interesting account of McVeigh's classification of far right groups as follows: the fascist racist branch and the individualist freedom-loving branch (Michel and Herbeck 2001, 493). McVeigh said that the far left in America dislikes firearms and that the far right is attracted to firearms. Kaczynski thought that McVeigh like many on the right was attracted to powerful weapons regardless of any pressing likelihood of using a firearm. Kaczynski talked like McVeigh's doppelganger when he angrily derided the American government and its hypocritical "system," that is, of the misuse for McVeigh of legal authority, and for Kaczynski of the impersonal automatizing technology of the American political-economic system (Michel and Herbeck 2001, 495–96). The ultimate use of Kaczynski's brilliant mind in writing this letter was to rationalize and intellectualize McVeigh's and his own evil acting-out through terrorist behavior, assuming the social-political ends (system change) justify the terrorist's evil means.

Theodore John Kaczynski, PhD, labeled "the Unabomber" by the media, was born on May 22, 1942, in Chicago, Illinois. From 1978 to 1995, Kaczynski performed a nationwide bombing campaign against modern technology, its scientists, and administrative promoters as Kaczynski defined them. His planted and mailed homemade bombs killed three people and injured 23 others (Chase 2003, 11; Perez-Pena 1996, 1).

Ted Kaczynski was a child prodigy who was accepted at Harvard at the age of 16 and got a PhD in mathematics from the University of Michigan. He became the youngest (25 years old) assistant professor at the University of California at Berkley in 1967. The undergraduate students Ted taught at Berkley complained that he was highly anxious, stuttered, and mumbled during his lectures (McFadden 1996, 7–8). The author speculates that these behaviors, among other cognates, represented unconscious neurotic conflicts, social anxiety, obsessions, and phobias that were evident during his childhood. Kaczynski resigned from the University of California at Berkeley in 1969. In 1971, Ted moved to a remote cabin located in Lincoln Montana, which was without electricity or running water. He lived there as a recluse and taught himself survival skills (Chase 2003, 21; Perez-Pena 1996, 2).

According to an interview that appeared in London-based *Green Anarchist*, Kaczynski grew enraged as he observed the wilderness around his cabin being destroyed by developers. Ted's favorite spot at a two-day hike from his home had ravines and a waterfall that he loved. That special place was cut through by a road. At that moment in 1983, Ted further crystallized and intensified his long-standing resolution and tangible plans to kill and get violent revenge toward "the system."

Later in this chapter, we will return to Kaczynski's traumatic experiences at Harvard. Chase thinks Ted's Harvard experience and especially the stress of Henry Murray's stressful experiments on Kaczynski were earlier derivative roots of Ted's unrelenting and accumulating murderous rage. The author thinks Ted's rage at his father was yet an even earlier source of his projected rage at society's scientific father figures of "the system" and its technological evils. To the latter point, Perez-Pena says that the Kaczynski family's neighbors reported that when Ted's father was dying of cancer, he committed suicide and Ted did not attend the funeral in 1990 (Perez-Pena 1996, 2).

Kaczynski has been, among other things, labeled a neo-Luddite. Neo-Luddism is a philosophy opposing many forms of modern technology (Chase 2003, 97–100). The name is derived historically from the thinking of the British Luddites (1811–1816). These groups sometimes destroyed or abandoned modern equipment as well as favored a simple life away from modern technology. Luddites and neo-Luddites fear current or future negative effects on individuals, communities, or the environment by modern technology. They propose the dismantling of potentially destructive nuclear technologies, chemical technologies that create synthetic often poisonous chemicals, genetic engineering, television, electromagnetic technologies, and computer technologies (Glendinning 1990, 1).

Even President Dwight D. Eisenhower in his January 17, 1961, farewell address warned America of the dangers of the burgeoning "military-industrial complex," which can be described as the policy and monetary relationship between legislators, the armed forces, and the industrial base in a society that supports them. It is interesting to note that Eisenhower raised this complex, an emotionally charged issue as he was saying farewell, and not at his inaugural (Eisenhower 1961).

Neo-Luddites like Glendinning are highly rational and nonviolent but rigorously favor the search for new technological forms that are local and promote social justice and freedom (Glendinning 1990). Modern Neo-Luddites connect with anti-consumerism, the antiglobalization movement, anarcho-primitivism, radical environmentalism, and deep ecology. Most but not all modern Neo-Luddites would reject the raw violent tactics of Ted Kaczynski, but embrace many of the concerns expressed in his 1995 manifesto, *Industrial Society and Its Future*.

Ted Kaczynski as Exiled Radical Secular "True" Patriot

Alston Chase suggests that the imprisoned Kaczynski continues to attract large numbers of followers. Chase says that Kaczynski is an inspirational leader-in-exile of the violent green anarchist movement. Chase cites Kaczynski's letters from prison in support of violent environmentalist radicals such as the Earth Liberation Front (Chase 2000,

3). These groups destroyed $12 million worth of property in the Vail ski resort via arson and conducted violent riots during the World Trade Organization meetings in Seattle (Chase 2000, 3–4)!

It seems to the author that Kaczynski is filling a similar role to the martyred Osama bin Laden and bin Laden's mentor hero, the now-imprisoned radical Islamist "Blind Sheik" Omar Abdel Rahman. Omar Abdel Rahman was born in Egypt in 1938. This 58-year-old radical firebrand cleric was blinded by diabetes when he was 10 months old (Meredith 2005, 444). As he studied for a doctorate at Cairo's University of al-Azhar, he was moved like so many others toward becoming a militant activist by the humiliating Arab defeat in the Six-Day War of 1967. He promoted the writings of Sayyid Qtub and he traveled from mosque to mosque giving fiery sermons about jihad and martyrdom. He was imprisoned for eight months in 1970. This prison experience added a further element to the disability of his blindness. Shaw's "Personal Pathway Model" of terrorist formation is supported by Rahman's prison experiences. Homegrown terrorists often find social networks and radicalization in prisons. Cruelty and torture by prison guards and oppressive governments often add fuel to the fires of radical Islamism. Rahman's status as a professor of theology at the University of Asyut in 1973 added another credential to his charismatic spiritual mentoring for the underground network of underground revolutionary organizations like Gamma Islamiyya and Jamaat al-Jihad (Meredith 2005, 445).

The Blind Sheik's fervor became exposed blatantly in his inspiration of the first effort to blow up the World Trade Center in New York in 1993. Now he is in an American prison and has been silenced via isolation because it was found that he was recording radical sermons over the telephone from prison for distribution in American mosques! His American lawyer was convicted of taking illegal messages to his colleagues from her visits with him at the prison (Olsson 2007, 32). Pied piper terror cult music has many forms, and the fiery sermons of the Blind Sheik are prominent ones.

Rather than inspiring radical Islamists and their recruits, however, Kaczynski inspires violent environmentalist radicals and anarchists from their perception of his martyred status in prison. So, Kaczynski is difficult to categorize in the sense that he does not draw inspiration from so-called right wing Christian Identity applied theology as the basis for his homegrown terrorism. Kaczynski more closely resembles a lone wolf figure like Norwegian bomber/assassin radical secular social Darwinian Anders Behring Breivik. Breivik and Kaczynski's violent homegrown terror acts spring from a tragic and chillingly deluded individualism. Their violent premeditated murders were intended to radically change their countries' social, economic, and political structure through intimidation and fear. Implied in the motivation for such heinous crimes is an arrogant, omnipotent, and strangely omniscient distrust of their countries' existing political systems. This is a both a textbook definition of terrorism, and demonstrates a form of fundamentalist mentality. (Utopianist ethnic cleansers and religious or atheistic antigovernment fanatics all worship at the altar of the fantasy of the omnipotence of their own thoughts, words, and actions.)

Alston Chase (2000 and 2003, 69, 70), has done a thorough and data-dense study of Ted Kaczynski called *Harvard and the Unabomber: The Education of an American Terrorist.* Chase documents in detail the notion that Kaczynski had begun forming elements of his plans for a violent antitechnological and antiscientific revolution even when he was at Harvard. Chase offers an excellent and concise history of Harvard's general education philosophy and concludes that Kaczynski and his cohorts were swept up in a culture of despair, anger, nihilism, and alienation rather than a solid Judeo-Christian base of ethical and moral thought. Chase cogently observes that Kaczynski's "Unabomber Manifesto" has striking resemblance to Harvard's general education syllabus during Ted's Harvard years (Chase 2003, 185–89)!

The Murray Experiment

When Ted Kaczynski was a sophomore at Harvard, he was a paid participant in the unethical and traumatic psychological stress experiments of professor and distinguished psychologist Dr. Henry Murray. The experiments were conducted at the Murray Research Center at Harvard. Murray had taught at Harvard for over 30 years and directed the Harvard Psychological Clinic at the School of Arts and Sciences. Murray is famous for co-developing the Thematic Apperception Test (TAT) with his colleague and lover Christiana Morgan. During World War II, Murray worked for the Office of Strategic Services (OSS), where he had developed "situation tests" used to assess and select potential officers. Unlike the officers tested at OSS, the Harvard student subjects were not informed proactively about the stress interviews they would be exposed to by Murray's research team. Murray himself spoke of the interrogations as "vehement, sweeping, and personally abusive" (Chase 2003, 251). Ted and his fellow subjects were verbally assaulted, and their egos, most cherished ideals, and beliefs were challenged (Chase 2003, 288–90). Murray's interest in brainwashing was clearly connected to the stress studies and his other studies under sponsorship of the CIA. Some of such work was done in collaboration with Timothy Leary. Murray even took Psilocybin himself and published an account of his experience (Chase 2003, 274). Chase, after a thorough investigation, concluded that no LSD or hallucinogens were given to Kaczynski (Chase 2000). Kaczynski's research code name for the experiments was "Lawful." Ted probably participated in the studies for the money but did say he felt pressured to join them (Chase 2000, 1). Though Kaczynski's records were sealed, Chase documented the traumatic and frightening experiences described by Ted's cohorts in the Murray research study (Chase 2003, 282–88).

Chase says that Ted's medical and psychological exam reports early on at Harvard were good. Chase cites psychiatrist Sally Johnson's clinical interview conclusion that during Kaczynski's later Harvard years, he began to seethe with anger, worry about his health, and began to have vivid fantasies about revenge against a society he viewed as evil (Chase 2003, 19). The American "system" he thought was extracting conformity through psychological controls (Chase 2003, 267).

Chase concludes, and the author agrees, that there is one likely strand of connection between Murray's reckless and wrong-headed research ethics and Kaczynski's crystallizing hatred of "the system." The ethics of Murray's day, though not violated at that time, were nevertheless wrong and led to harm! Murray's research ethics would be denounced by serious scientists today. The Murray experiments at least played into Kaczynski's thoughts and convictions that the university, psychology, and psychiatry were compromised servants of a corrupt "system" (Chase 2003, 291–94).

Certainly by 1971, Kaczynski wrote an essay containing most of the ideas that later appeared in his infamous 1995 *Manifesto* (Chase 2003, 85). Kaczynski argued that ongoing scientific and technological "progress" would eventually lead to loss of individual liberty. The remedy espoused by Ted even back then was not merely promoting a libertarian philosophy and environmentalism, but by a resort to concrete and violent action (Chase 2000, part III). Chase cites the observation of Sally Johnson, the forensic psychiatrist who examined Kaczynski, that Ted 's acceptance of the teaching position at Berkeley (1967) was primarily to grubstake his bucolic dream of taking off in the wild woods of Canada and to eventually return to kill someone he hated (Chase 2000, part III; 2003, 304–6).

The wording and style of Ted's 1995 *Manifesto* enabled his brother David and David's wife to identify Ted as the Unabomber, and turn him in to the FBI (Booth 1998, 1–2).

Psychodynamic Data from Ted Kaczynski's Childhood and Life History

When Ted Kaczynski was six months of age, he was hospitalized because his entire body was covered in hives. He was placed in isolation because doctors were unsure of the cause. They permitted Ted no visitors, and he was hospitalized several times over the subsequent eight-month period. In March 1943, Ted's mother said that he was left emotionally unresponsive after that experience (McFadden 1996, 1–3). The author believes this was an important observation and expressed concern by Ted's mother. Some crucial psychological milestones occur during the first 16 months of life. The preverbal period is difficult to assess in terms of the long-term impact on personality. But we know that at five to six months stranger anxiety emerges. This developmental phenomenon helps the developing infant begin differentiating self from others. The primary caretakers are distinguished from strangers. The toddler builds on this process as early experiences of social relationships ensue—later, friendships with playmates and schoolmates follow. The author feels that Ted Kaczynski's mother's concerns about his socialization were warranted. As a child, Ted was observed to have a fear of buildings and played in parallel with other children rather than playing with them interactively (Chase citing Johnson 2000, parts II–III). These cumulative conflicts and problems seem to the author to have led to Ted's gradually, but steadily escalating, social anxiety, phobias, obsessions, and eventual paranoia with intense anxiety about intimacy with his family and his schoolmates.

Chase clearly describes how by 1982–1984 Kaczynski's narcissistic rage and paranoia had grown vicious toward his parents and brother (Chase 2003, 349). His mother would send him food, which enraged him. He would demand apologies from his parents for the psychological abuse he alleged they had committed toward him when he was a teenager. Ted's father Turk stayed silent, and nothing his mother Wanda said lovingly satisfied Ted.

(By age 42, Kaczynski was showing such unresolved transference toward his own parents. This clinical phenomenon in the author's experience is only occasionally seen in very neurotic or borderline children.) Ted seemed to want to make a clean break with his family at such an advanced life stage, but his unresolved ambivalence was so intense and he needed their money for his bomb making as Chase points out (Chase 2003, 349). In addition, as Alston Chase aptly observes, Ted Kaczynski despite hating psychology constantly blamed his parents for their verbal abuse like a petulant teenager or an over-psychologizing adult. Ted seemed to have conflated, fused, and confused his desire for revenge against his parents and family and his rage at "the system," with which he equated them psychologically (Chase 2003, 341).

Ted's superior intellect was always a two-edged sword. In Ted's social domain, Chase has it well summarized when he says that Ted experienced acrimony at home and social rejection/bullying at school (Chase 2000, part I). And we know now the extreme to which Ted the bullied and rejected teenager became the ultimate bombing bully.

In the fifth grade, Ted was found on testing to have an IQ of 167 and was permitted to skip the sixth grade. Ted felt this was a key event in his life. He was the smallest in his class and remembered feeling that he did not fit in with the older kids who bullied him. He was fearful about people and buildings. He played in parallel with other kids without interacting. His mother was so worried that she considered entering him in a study of autistic children run by Bruno Bettelheim (Johnson 1998, 1).

The Kaczynski family had moved to Evergreen Park, Illinois, to provide their children with a better group of friends. In the Catholic working class community, Ted's parents who were atheists told their kids to say they were Unitarians. Ted's father, Theodore "Turk" Kaczynski, took news of his son's 167 IQ as a trophy (when Ted was accepted at Harvard, it was "an ego trip for Turk") (Chase 2000, part II). Wanda, and particularly Turk, pushed Ted hard academically. Ted increasingly experienced his father as cold, critical, and distant (Chase 2000, part II). Ted skipped his junior year in high school against the advice of a teacher to whom he was close. Ted was bullied and called a "little freak" (Chase 2000, part II). In the author's opinion, Ted's relationship with his father seems to fit a neurotic pattern of rejection, rather than that of a serial killer or mass murderer. In the author's clinical experience, serial killers commonly experience early remorseless brutality from their fathers—not academic pressure and vicarious emotional overinvestment.

Diagnostic Speculations about Ted Kaczynski

Ted Kaczynski has been diagnosed with paranoid schizophrenia by Sally Johnson, a qualified forensic psychiatrist who spent time at thorough forensic interviews with Ted Kaczynski. However, Bertram Karon, a psychologist very familiar with schizophrenic persons, reviewed Kaczynski's TAT protocols from Murray's experiments and found no schizophrenic signs and only mild signs of psychopathy (Chase 2000, part III).

The author speculates that Kaczynski has a severe personality disorder with obsessional, narcissistic, and severe paranoid traits. Kaczynski's experience of severe total body hives at six months of age and lengthy isolation experiences in the hospital over the subsequent eight months could have been a factor in his tendency toward significant social anxiety, attachment/intimacy problems, and paranoia. Ted's mother seemed to have tuned in appropriately to this factor. That tuning in and concern from his mother was a plus in his developmental history.

In the area of Kaczynski's obsessions and paranoia about "the system," he does manifest symptoms of a delusional disorder (nonschizophrenic, in earlier nomenclatures called "true paranoia"). Such patients do not hallucinate and they are not delusional in other areas of their mental life (i.e., monodelusional). In the author's clinical experience, persons with delusional disorder do not respond symptomatically to antipsychotic medications in the way schizophrenic patients do, although such medications might reduce their anxiety slightly. They tend to be lonely, socially awkward, shy, and intensely ambivalent about intimate relationships. They have a strong need for an intimate relationship, yet they are anxious about and fear all forms of intimacy. Ted described to Sally Johnson how in a state of intense despair about not being able to find a woman to touch that he seriously contemplated a sex change operation so that he might hope to touch someone (Chase 2003, 305). Kaczynski's love affair with the wild woods and wilderness probably was in part a symbolic domain representing his yearning for affection, touching, and un-conflicted empathic attachment.

Some experts would argue that to commit murder at a distance with bombs is by definition psychotic. The author cannot disagree with that thinking but also agrees with Chase's summary of important psychodynamic factors whose cumulative psychosocial effects transformed Ted Kaczynski into the evil genius, that is, the Unabomber. These psychologically causal factors are:

(1) Ted's neurotic anger at his family, particularly his hypercritical father who seemed overinvested in Ted as a "trophy" for Turk Kaczynski's vicarious ambitions. In 1952 psychiatrists Adelaide Johnson and Stanley Szurek wrote a classic paper called "The Genesis of Antisocial Acting Out in Children and Adults" (1952, 323). Johnson was a child analyst who saw a delinquent child or teenager in psychotherapy. Szurek was an adult analyst who saw the child's parent(s) in analysis or psychotherapy. With their patients' permission, they shared and compared the parallel therapies. Basically they concluded that the overt areas of acting-out (antisocial) behavior in the child were the same areas of unconscious conflict, preoccupation, and fascination of their parent(s). The parents participated vigorously and vicariously in their child's symptomatic acting-out behaviors.) Ted's father Turk in particular seemed so focused on Ted's genius IQ as Turk's ticket to prestige that Turk neglected the role of a supportive dad. Kaczynski had additional cumulative anger at those who hurt, bullied, and slighted Ted in high school and college. Those narcissistic wounds led cumulatively and relentlessly to severe narcissistic rage, of which many murderers are made.
(2) The culture of despair Chase described at Harvard helped transform Kaczynski's early intellectual pleasure at Harvard into alienation, nihilism, and frustrated father hunger.
(3) The Murray experiment fed into the malignant frustration of Ted's father longings. When a noted healer like Murray disappointed Kaczynski and ended up traumatizing him, it fed the fires of Ted's narcissistic rage. The malignant epiphany surrounding Murray's ethical flaws compounded Kaczynski's relentlessly bitter hatred of American society and our imperfect institutions. It built up exponentially to unredeemable and monstrous proportions. If Kaczynski had found an ethical, well-trained, and effective psychotherapist during his Harvard years or before, his negative Unabomber identity might have been averted. The author wishes that Ted had encountered and worked in therapy with talented psychotherapist psychiatrists like Leston Havens, John Gunderson, Joan Wheelis, or John Nemiah.

TERRORISM, MARTYR PSYCHOLOGY, AND FUNDAMENTALIST MENTALITY

A young Palestinian walks into a crowded shopping mall in Israel. Before a suspicious security guard can confront him, the powerful bomb explodes. The martyr/murderer dies instantly, and many innocent people in the area are killed or injured. Tears of anguish, grief, and rage flow from the eyes of the families of victims.

At the bomber's home in Gaza, his family rejoices and offers prayers of affirmation and pride for their son's entry into paradise to be with Allah. The bomber is a hero-martyr in his home community.

Is the suicide bomber psychotic (deluded), naive, or made of loftier moral and spiritual fabric than the rest of us?

If Arafat and Sharon and other world leaders had mustered the wisdom, political vision, and spiritual courage of men like Sadat or Rabin, would suicide bomber martyrs have gained so much spurious ascendancy? I think not. Would there be fewer terror bombers? Fewer perhaps; yet evil still finds many dark lairs, as illustrated by the following poem:

Mid East Peace Dreams Dying
Old terrorists always make bad peacemakers.
Arafat and Sharon, brothers in spiritual poverty.
Failed saviors of fragile now dashed hopes.
Coward's rockets, rocks, and suicide bombs are,
crude scepters of painful wounds perpetuated.
Cursed by futile, fuming, endless revenge cycles
Warriors of hate and horror grimly spawned.
Rage run-wild, in Nightmare Rivers of blood . . .
Shed on the hands, of History's wrong-turn.
Peace so close, lost in the dust of dead dreams.
Can children's sobs, stop perpetual new Holocausts?

Political Religious Power and *The Denial of Death*

The social psychological framework offered by Ernest Becker can help us begin to understand suicide bombers, terrorists, and martyrs:

> The social hero-system into which we are born marks out paths for our heroism, paths to which we conform, to which we shape ourselves so that we can please others, become what they expect us to be. (Becker 1973, 82)

Becker goes on to observe that the cultural hero system, as he calls it, can be religious, spiritual, magical, primitive, even secular, scientific, and civilized. It serves to earn a feeling of value, specialness, and ultimate enduring meaning for an individual or group: perhaps, even providing a feeling of triumph over death (Becker 1973, 5).

Many suicide bombers, martyrs, and terrorists appear to be participating in a social hero system as described by Becker. They seem to think that they are building a spiritual edifice for their families' futures, and a paradise for themselves: all this with God's blessing in eternity. They are grandiose mythical hero legends in their own minds. Many actively seek a martyr's death.

> MARTYR, 1. A person who willingly suffers death rather than renounce his or her religion. 2. A person who is put to death or who suffers on behalf of a cause. 3. A person who undergoes severe or constant suffering. (*Random House Webster's*, 2001, 815)

If anyone on earth should understand how oppression, economic marginalization, and political persecution in refugee camps could empower and create suicide bomber martyrs, it is the Jews and Israelis. The new ghettos in Gaza and the West Bank should stir collective Holocaust memories and empathy. Throughout history, there has been no better psychosocial soil for the growth and development of recruits for martyrdom and terrorists, than among young people who witness the daily devaluation, despair, and persecution of their parents. Young people in these ghettos of group woundedness and narcissistic injury are ripe for the seductions of terror cult recruiters and folk heroes like Osama bin Laden, Hamas leaders, and fundamentalist Islamic clerics preaching sacred hatred and vengeance. Offers of U.S. economic and educational aid after a fair Middle East peace settlement are drowned out by new violence/counterviolence cycles of blood for blood. Let us meet three Middle East teenagers in the dust of dead peace dreams. Each suffers or feels triumphant in their adolescent context and psychodynamics.

SCHLOMO, SHIRA, AND ISMAIL

Schlomo

> When the rock hit my face it hurt like Hell! That Palestinian kid had a strong arm and was a good shot. Blood poured down my face. I raised my rifle but I did not have plastic bullets, so I held my fire. I am a good shot. But, I trained to defend my country, not shoot kids who throw rocks. Another soldier shot the kid. The boy screamed and fell. I gasped, but the Palestinian boy got up and ran. Plastic bullets hurt, but usually don't kill.

My name is Schlomo and I am eighteen. My home is Tel-Aviv. When I got out of high school, I chose the Army for my mandatory years of service for my country. I love my country. But, I wish I had tried to work in a hospital rather than in this street war. It is like me and these kids have hero-role-reversal problems. They are little Palestinian David's, and I am a Philistine Jew giant Goliath. Damn, I see those kids grabbing up more rocks. Some might have guns. I hope I don't have to die today. If I die, will Sharon care?

Shira

My name is Shira. I am sixteen. I live with my family in Gaza. My ugly, dumb brother is Mohammed. He is fifteen and goes to school taught by Mullahs who are very strong and strict. Mohammed and I were very close when we were little. Now I don't like him anymore because he acts like he is more important than me. My fathers smile shines all over my brother. Father seems to not pay as much attention to me anymore. Mohammed prays every morning and every evening. He rocks back and forth like a rocking chair when he prays. I think he is hypnotized. Mohammed says the Koran tells him special things when he reads it. I wish I were special too. The Mullah at Mohammed's school loves him so much that he thinks he will be chosen to be a martyr-bomber of Israelis. My mother and father have already built a shrine to Mohammed's memory after he blows up. Our parents' act so proud of Mohammed's study about how to use the bomb-belt. It takes a lot of prayer and study to be a bomber. The prayer is just as important as the special bomb-belt.

My parents and the Mullah don't know that I know as much as Mohammed does about bombs, prayer and dying with dignity. Tomorrow, before they all wake up—I will be gone to Israel with the bomb belt on. Allah will make me one of his favorite wives because so many Jews will die tomorrow. I feel Arafat and Allah's smile glowing beyond my morning sky explosion coming soon. I win Mohammed!!
Love, Shira
(Shira is a depiction of the first woman Palestinian suicide bomber.)

Ismail

My name is Ismail. I am so scared. I know I will pee my pants before I die. The bomb men of Emir Zarqawi checked my bomb carefully. It will go off when I crash this van into the police station. The bomb men are duct-taping my feet to the accelerator of the van. That will help me keep my promise to Allah and the honor of my family. My mother can now easily feed my little brothers and sisters. The Imam will smile when he hears how many American and Iraqi infidel soldiers have died from my big bomb blast. My bomb will help get the American soldiers out of my country. I will be a hero. Now I go faster, faster—I will never stop or slow down. Don't pee, don't pee. I picture Allah's smile in my mind now.

BOOOOOM!

TRAGIC FLAWS IN THINKING OF FUNDAMENTALISTS AND TERRORIST SUICIDE BOMBER MARTYRS

Fundamentalists, terrorists, and suicide bomber-martyrs are their own gods unto themselves. Whether Christians, Jews, Muslims, Sikhs, Hindus, or secular, fundamentalists see their way of thinking and believing as the one and only way. It is "their way or the highway," as that saying goes. The fundamentalist, no matter how sweet, kind, or pious he or she acts on the surface, is convinced that they have *the* superior moral, ethical, theological, epistemological and spiritual *truth*. There is no room for doubt, debate, or dialectic. The radical fundamentalist is willing to condemn to hell, or even kill, those who do not believe as they believe. The radical fundamentalist is *the* final judge, jury, and executioner. He even declares the content of heaven and hell.

This fundamentalist, devastatingly concrete, and grandiose way of thinking is more readily embraced at times of severe social turmoil, rapid social change, and economic suffering. Experiences of oppression, such as in refugee camps, provide potential psychosocial soil and roots for fundamentalist mentality. Often, fundamentalist mentality can gain momentum in an atmosphere of ignorance, arrogance, fear, hatred, insecurity, or bigotry. Fundamentalist thinking actually ignores the core meaning of what faith is really about. In Kierkegaard's terms (Kierkegaard 1843, 1940, 271), faith involves "immediacy," a "leap." Faith respects mystery. Genuine faith requires humility, reverence for life, and a realization of mankind's smallness in a big universe. Faith seeks God and his meaning in the world, in worship and never takes over God's role.

> What is faith? It is the confident assurance that what we hope for is waiting for us, even though we cannot see it up ahead. Men of God in days of old were famous for their faith.

> We know that the world and the stars—in fact, all things—were made at God's command; and that they were made from things that can't be seen. (Hebrews 11:1–3)

"Thou shall not kill" is embraced by all legitimate world religions. Killing in God's name is the ultimate in blasphemy, arrogance, and evil. Those who choose this action, and especially those "leaders" who use their "God-given" charisma or political instincts to influence vulnerable youths to devote their spiritual destiny to these evil suicidal/homicidal acts, blaspheme the core values of the religion cause or noble ideal in which they claim to believe.

NOTE

1. The author is indebted to, and appreciative of, Dr. Allen Sapp's consultation at the Group for the Advancement of Psychiatry (GAP)'s May 1997 think tank presentation/discussion, held at the GAP Committee on International Relations. Notes from Dr. Sapp's presentation were heuristically helpful in writing this chapter.

14

A Left Wing Homegrown
Terrorist: Bill Ayers

BILL AYERS AND HIS WEATHER UNDERGROUND

In this chapter, the author uses Bill Ayers's memoir *Fugitive Days* to form speculations about the psychosocial soil and roots involved in the process of his becoming a homegrown terrorist prior to and during his role as a leader in the Weather Underground's activities toward trying to end the Vietnam War. It is unethical for a psychiatrist and psychoanalyst to make a medical psychiatric diagnosis or recommend treatment without face-to-face consultation meetings. The limitations of the author's psychobiographical approach needs to be noted at the outset of this chapter.

> The U.S. created an elaborate environment for terror in Vietnam, and terrorism became the way of the war every day. (Ayers 2001, 272)
> I went for days on end with nothing to eat, no money of my own, no change in my pocket, thinking only of how to stop the war (Viet-Nam), how to make the price for continuing the war great, how to reach out to the victims of the war and stand alongside them and experience something of what they were experiencing. I wanted intimate knowledge of their situation, of their suffering. (Ayers 2001, 266)

A *counterpoint* to Ayers's view of the United States as a monolithic terror source for Vietnam can be made. Terror of various forms and ghastly extremes, despite the Geneva Convention, is a part of every war. Terror throbs in declared or undeclared wars, symmetrical or unsymmetrical wars, well-chosen wars, poorly chosen wars, or foolishly chosen wars. It is sadly true from the Battle of Brittan to Dresden, from Pearl Harbor to Hiroshima, from the Trail of Tears to Little Big Horn, and from Normandy to the ultimate horror at My Lai. War is hell and always will be. It seems a tragic fact of human nature that humans are creative in finding ways to terrorize and kill each other, and some men are also majestically creative in peace seeking and peacemaking. For every Sadat, Begin, and Rabin who genuinely personally changed from terrorist warrior to peace-seeker, there always seem to be Pol Pots, Joseph Stalins, and Idi Amins.

The Vietnam War caused vicious divisions and painful conflicts within American society, politics, and culture. In the author's opinion, only our American Civil War compared to the Vietnam War in its splitting and demoralization of our American identity and group self. The splitting process struck individual minds, families, and the group selves of whole churches and communities.

Our American struggle to heal our fragmented group self after Vietnam and three additional wars continues as reflected in not only a chronic war weariness, but a greatly lessened confidence in all three branches of our American government. There is a healthy skepticism about presidential war decision making and the choice of military solutions to world problems in general. This is true even about genuinely glaring injustices, genocide, atrocities, and brutal behavior of clearly evil world leaders. Hopefully we as a country can stay strong but wiser about what is truly our national interest and the limits of any country's economic, political, and military power.

THE POWER AND TERROR IN THE WORDS OF BILL AYERS

Bill Ayers in his memoir *Fugitive Days* uses eloquent, vivid, evocative, provocative, flamboyant, and dramatic prose. Ayers captures not only the rage, outrage, and moral anguish of himself and his violent anti-war radical colleagues, but also the strikingly similar feelings among the host of committed, civilly disobedient, and nonviolent protestors and other vigorous critics of the Vietnam War.

Bill Ayers in his *Fugitive Days* vigorously states that he and his Weather Underground were not terrorists. Yet, Ayers writes:

> We came close, it's true—whenever there are guns and bombs, the line narrows between politics and terror, between rebellion and gangsterism. We were part of a movement, and then a tendency toward armed struggle. We crossed the line and came back. Everyone wasn't so lucky. I'd hoped we learned some things. (Ayers 2001, 271)

Ayers declares that terrorists intimidate and kill innocent civilians and destroy randomly, but his Weather Underground did not intimidate but sought only to educate (Ayers 2001, 271).

In the 2009 afterword of his 2001 memoir, Ayers is careful to say about himself,

> I killed no one, and I harmed no one, and I didn't regret for a minute resisting the murderous assault on Viet Nam with every ounce of my being. (Ayers 2001, 2009, 311)

In his memoir, Ayers is poignant in his expression of affection, loyalty, and intimacy even what appears to be an emotionally intense merger/fusion with his beloved colleagues in his Weather Underground. Ayers describes in vivid detail the "Bomb for Peace" that his beloved Diana and her partner in bomb making, Terry, were making. Diana and Terry were killed in a massive explosion at the townhouse where they were preparing a bomb.

Ayers writes about the "peace bomb,"

> It was primed with heavy cotton, packed with screws and nails that would do some serious work beyond the blast, tearing through windows and walls, and, yes, people too. (Ayers 2001, 281)

The author disagrees with Ayers's contention that he and his Weather Underground were not terrorists who used violence, killing, and intimidation. It is clear to the author from Ayers's description of the symbolic and tangible purposes of his bombing of the Pentagon, for example, that powerful and effective tactics of intimidation and fear were employed. Ayers clearly experienced himself and his group as guerrilla warriors against the U.S. government and its authorities (Ayers 2001, 154). Their intention clearly was to terrorize, intimidate, and create fear in the U.S. government, police authorities, and the general public (Ayers 2001, 265–66).

Much of American public opinion was already shifting in a negative direction about the Vietnam War, and Ayers and his Weather Underground were putting the shock and awe of terror bombs as dramatic punctuations of protest to the massive U.S. war bombings in Vietnam (Ayers 2001, 152–54). In the author's opinion, such is part of the definition of terrorism regardless of Ayers's and his colleagues' conscientious efforts to rationalize and justify their actions. They did definitely make extensive efforts to do no harm to innocents during their self-appointed roles as tribes of guerrilla warriors against the U.S. government and the American political and economic "system." Ayers and his Weatherpersons should, however, have known as all Americans should have learned from our bombings in Vietnam, Cambodia, Iraq, Afghanistan, and now our drones with Hellfire missiles in Pakistan and Yemen, that collateral damage to innocents is practically impossible to prevent. Was Ayers's beloved Diana's death "collateral damage"? The unexploded ordnance and mines left behind in all wars leave tragic legacies of collateral damage to be experienced by innocents long after peace treaties have been signed and soldiers have been long gone. Ayers quotes one of his close associates,

> Our actions should speak for themselves, Rose said. They should be immediately understood and timely, fire the imagination of young people, inspire the movement, and make anyone of goodwill secretly smile—even if they denounce our tactics. (Ayers 2001, 234)

Given how many Americans were increasingly angered at our war policies in Vietnam and sympathetic to powerful anti-war sentiments, the genius and pure power of this propaganda formulation and rationalization by Rose is impressive. This tactic reminds the author of the impact of Osama bin Laden's and other Al Qaeda recruiters' way of appealing to idealistic young Muslim youths and their communities. Osama and others would appeal to Muslims' empathy and compassion for innocent Muslim brothers and sisters who have been the terrible victims of Western and U.S. invasions, bombs, and drone strikes. One country's or group's terrorist becomes another group's vicariously valued avenging rebellious hero.

BILL AYERS'S VINTAGE OF "WAR ON THE SYSTEM(S)"

The use of the metaphor of a "war on the system" to describe Bill Ayers's efforts is reminiscent of homegrown terrorists Timothy McVeigh and Ted Kaczynski. For such homegrown terrorists, there are always many kernels of truth in their verbal attacks on America. The U.S. government has always been imperfect, unwieldy, flawed, and requiring frequent checks and balances to survive and even at times to prosper. In Ayers's war against "the system" (Ayers 2001, 227), he, the author notes, is like McVeigh and Kaczynski who mingled genuine kernels of truth about the "system" with inner personal and sexual identity struggles and unresolved conflicts they felt with their parents. In Ayers's case, painful truths about the ghastly and foolish war in Vietnam appear to reverberate with, and echo his, inner personal and sexual identity struggles and efforts to resolve conflicts with his parents seemingly regardless of the war. (See the next section for psychodynamic details about these connections for Ayers, and Chapter 13 for information about similar themes for McVeigh and Kaczynski.)

Ayers's "war on the system" about the Vietnam War seems often conflated with radical antiracism; radical feminism (Ayers 2001, 107–10), radical pro-unionism (Ayers 2001, 315–16), radical anti-abuse of native Americans (Ayers 2001, 243), and radical abuse of any political power with which Ayers disagreed (Ayers 2001, 198, 239). Those many protest issues seem condensed in Ayers's memoir. Ayers's emotions soar as he describes his spiritual embrace of black leader Bob Moses of SNCC (Student Nonviolent Coordinating Committee),

> Justice and peace are twins, he said quietly that night, borne of the same desire, just as war is the twin of racism. To win peace you've got to fight for justice. He said that his war was not against the Vietnamese people but against a whole system that waged war on the people of Viet Nam and another kind of war against his own people in Mississippi. I was high, it's true, but hearing Moses cemented a connection for me. (Ayers 2001, 60)

Ayers asks himself about a American system he thinks grabs the destiny of the Vietnamese, which disenfranchises black Americans and in its cold American materialism leaves millions in poverty and labels itself free to dominate and police the world (Ayers 2001, 61).

AYERS'S PALEOLOGIC

The author thinks that in the midst of Ayers's intense emotions apparent in his writing there is at times a predicate logic, a **paleologic** as described by von Domarus. (von Domarus 1944, 104–15; Meloy 2004, 48–55). Von Domarus's principle explains the phenomenon of **condensation** wherein the part symbolizes the whole in the **unconscious**/primary process. Although predicates (racism and illegally waged war) in Aristotelian logic are employed to denote similarity between objects or concepts, in paleologic they denote identification or equivalence. The common element predicate (hated oppressing "system") is the dominant focus of attention. Other characteristics of the concept become irrelevant and are ignored, particularly ones that would contradict the identification or condensation (Meloy 2004, 52). For example, some people might agree with Ayers that racism is bad anywhere it occurs but perhaps a totally different and separate issue from disdain for a perceived illegal war.

Overinclusive writing and thinking occurs in acute schizophrenics, manics, and completely normal persons who are emotionally overwrought. Clearly Ayers is not schizophrenic or manic, and his eloquent capturing of emotions with words is a literary gift despite where his conclusions arrive and with which some of us might disagree.

PSYCHOSOCIAL AND PSYCHODYNAMIC INFORMATION REGARDING BILL AYERS

William Charles "Bill" Ayers was born on December 26, 1944, and, as previously mentioned, co-founded the Weather Underground in 1969. The Weather Underground was a self-described communist revolutionary group that conducted a campaign of bombing public buildings that expressed opposition to the Vietnam War. The bombings involved police stations (1970), the U.S. Capitol building (1971), and the Pentagon (1972). Ayers was in hiding from 1973 to 1980 when charges against him and the Weather Underground were dropped because the FBI had used illegal surveillance techniques.

Ayers is currently a retired professor in the University of Illinois College of Education, where he formerly held the titles of Distinguished Professor of Education and Senior University Scholar. His wife Bernardine Dohrn was also a passionate and articulate leader in the Weather Underground organization. Dorn was finally fined $1,500 and given three years' probation.

Bill Ayers grew up in Glen Ellyn, Illinois, where he attended public schools until his second year in high school when he transferred to a prep school called Lake Forest Academy. Ayers received a BA in American studies from the University of Michigan in 1968. His father, mother, and older brother had preceded Bill at the University of Michigan. Ayers's father Thomas G. Ayers became the CEO and chairman of Commonwealth Edison (1963–1980). Northwestern University's Thomas G. Ayers College of Commerce and Industry was named after Bill Ayers's father. It is highly psychodynamically relevant that Bill

Ayers's father was the head of one of cornerstones of the military industrial complex, that is, in "the system"! "the system" with which Thomas Ayers's son Bill and his Weather Underground would literally and figuratively go to war.

"Mom and Marx"—"Everything will be fine." (Ayers 2001, 25, 36)

In his memoir, Bill Ayers says the following about his mother,

Mom's excessive joy, unbounded optimism, generous good cheer, and surplus happiness were gift and curse. (Ayers 2001, 25)

Later in the same paragraph, Ayers says,

She never let up, and sometimes the cheeriness felt forced, a kind of willful naivete. (Ayers 2001, 25)

Ayers describes his home as a world of privilege from which he ran away early into deliverance, escape, and reinvention through reading. ("The Runaway Bunnie," "Oliver Twist," Huckleberry Finn," "A Farewell to Arms," "The Catcher in the Rye," "The Invisible Man," "On the Road"). Bill Ayers, like many imaginative preteenagers, "leapt over the wall of confinement" through books and war movies, which he also relished (Ayers 2001, 25–27).

Ayers and his siblings kidded their mother about being Pollyanna but he also credits her with being good to them and insisting on their being good to others. In an interesting paradoxical way, Ayers latched on to Karl Marx during a world civilizations course taught by an ambivalently regarded teacher/dean named Sigfried Friend. Ayers intuited immediately,

Marx and Mom would agree on one thing: "everything will be fine." The leap from Pollyanna to historical determinism wasn't all that wide. (Ayers 2001, 36)

The "Marx and Mom" theme persisted as Ayers wrote a fascinating paper for Dean Friend called "The History of Mankind Is the Relentless Search for Freedom." Ayers notes that he was confused by how Marx seemed to love capitalism and also hate it (Ayers 2001, 36–37).

Practically all of we flawed humans have love/hate experiences with our parents, our children, and ourselves, that is, ambivalence.

Over time, most of us work through and resolve our ambivalent feelings toward our loved ones and intimates. In some more tender passages at the end of Ayers's memoir, especially in his 2009 afterword, he touches on the issue his frail aging parents (Ayers 2001, 303, 312)—his mother ravaged by Alzheimer's and dying. No more Pollyanna. Ayers seems to feel resolved of his angry transference to his own father by perceiving his father as at last agreeing with Bill and supporting him.

AYERS'S SEARCH TO FIND SUPERIOR MOTHERS

It seems clear to the author that Bill Ayers benefited greatly psychologically from the love, affection, and support he experienced with women at the Children's Freedom School, the founding mothers!" in Ann Arbor; and women intimates in the Weather Underground (Ayers 2001, 76, 81). These women with strong personalities, and some with powerful sexual connections, seemed to help Ayers transcend the Pollyanna-ness he described in his childhood experience of his mother.

BACK TO AYERS'S PAPER AT LAKE FOREST ACADEMY

Unfortunately for young Bill Ayers, father-figure teacher Sigfried Friend was inappropriately nasty toward Ayers's interesting paper. The Marx and Mom ambivalent theme continued to play out as Ayers comments sardonically about his paper getting a C from Dean Friend. Unfriendly Friend apparently wrote things like "Idiot! Wrong! Moronic," and "Marx was a liar and fool" in red pencil on young Ayers's paper. In the author's opinion, Ayers's parents could have appropriately confronted Mr. Friend's unfriendliness and unprofessionalism! It is truly soul-saddening how often teachers at every level fail to grasp their crucial mentoring role beyond merely teaching the academic material!

Ayers tells the reader,

I should have footnoted Mom, but it was already so deeply woven into the fabric of my own being that it felt authentic and original. Man's search for freedom, *(And Mom)*, I wrote, was a rosy path winding its way toward sharing the wealth. (Ayers 2001, 37; emphasis added)

Unsurprisingly, Ayers grew to hate his prep school and grew disgusted with his classmates saying,

> We were mostly conformist bores, I thought, unadventurous in most things, acting out scripts already written, destined for conventional lives of canned happiness just as dull as our parents. (Ayers 2001, 37–38)

Ayers seemed to be framing, anticipating, and setting up a context for his rebellion toward his parents and his exciting acting-out to come. After an initial attempt at college, Ayers dropped out. His mother cried and his father thought it was OK as long as he did something productive and gathered "life lessons" (Ayers 2001, 41). If Ayers's mother seemed Pollyanna, his father seems to come across as woodenly practical and overcontrolled as described by Bill Ayers. Ayers certainly gained many life lessons his own way.

In the context described earlier, Ayers can be seen as an in-betweener. He was in-between his parents nest and his own place. He was in-between being a student and an overstimulating brave new world as an antiwar radical. Later as an underground guerilla warrior, Ayers described himself as "born again" into the world of an underground radical (Ayers 2001, 242). Ayers's in-betweener situation was both deeply personal in his identity striving and in the broader in-betweener state of turmoil, rage, and despair in America. In this context, Ayers later described eloquently the emergence of his "exile identity" (Ayers 2001, 226)—a new form or variation of negative identity.

A CON EDISON FATHER AND AYERS'S FATHER SURROGATES

In describing his childhood, Ayers said that his mother called him Billy or Little Bill. Con Edison's logo and mascot back then was a little animated bird in the form of a light bulb whose name was Little Bill. Ayers and his friends believed for years that Con Edison's famous ad campaign was named for Bill. Ayers said that his family fed into this illusion (Ayers 2001, 22–23). Ayers does not describe many shared father–son times during his boyhood. When Ayers was jailed during the antiwar protests, his mother cried over the phone and his father flew to Ann Arbor to counsel Bill. Ayers described his father as focused on his not tarnishing Bill's prospects for the future. Ayers felt contempt for his father saying,

What are you doing to end the war? I challenged. We may not be doing everything right, but at least we are against the war, and we are acting on our beliefs, which puts us light years ahead of Commonwealth Edison. (Ayers 2001, 72)

Bill Ayers's dad grew defensive and down-putting of Students for a Democratic Society (SDS). Bill responded by saying there is no real wealth in Commonwealth Edison. Ayers said that all his conversations with his dad were like hurling little bombs back and forth (Ayers 2001, 73)! Later in his memoir, Ayers mentions a radical colleague and his discussing a plan to burn down the First National Bank building in Chicago where Commonwealth Edison leased several floors (Ayers 2001, 174). Ayers's vivid descriptions of these father–son emotional bomb-throwing is consistent with one of Shaw's notions about personal pathways to terrorism. When a parent talks the talk of uprightness and goodness but does not walk the walk, that can open the door for a youth to launch a negative identity as a terrorist and swirl in the tides of father hunger.

In the author's opinion, Bill Ayers also, like most all of the homegrown terrorists in this study, experienced significant psychological father hunger and made use of important charismatic literary, political, and antiwar leaders as surrogate fathers and mentors: Stan Nadir, Norman Mailer, James Baldwin, Ron St. Ron, Robert Moses (SNCC), Paul Potter (SDS), Tom Hayden, Ho Chi Min (grandfather figure?), Che Guevara, Timothy Leary, Fred Hampton, Bobby Rush, Rev. Stan Gabriel, to name just a few. Marijuana lubricated the atmosphere of Ayers's new "life-lesson" campus of groups of hundreds of anarchists, street people, radicals, and rockers (Ayers 2001, 58–59).

A key inspiring mentor for Ayers's radicalization and recruitment was Paul Potter, president of SDS. Potter gave his famous speech in front of the Washington Monument to the 25,000 who marched on Washington. Many feel it is as relevant today as it was on April 17, 1965. Bill Ayers was there and heard and reacted to Potter's provocative questions. Ayers said of Potter's questions:

His questions reached out at me with the urgency of a slap. 'How will you live your life so that it doesn't make a mockery of your values? That question set me afire—it rattled in my heart and my head for years to come—and at that moment, I was recruited. (Ayers 2001, 62)

"THE FELLOWSHIP OF THE STOCKADE"

Like many homegrown terrorists, Bill Ayers found the jail environment and experience life-changing. He embraced the school of action and felt the status of what he called "the fellowship of the stockade" (Ayers, 73). Ayers alluded to the explosive launch of his career as a terrorist,

> It was illegal, yes, and dangerous, and the plans for the stuff apocalyptic. But we were freedom fighters, and we came to it in the spirit of John Brown and Nat Turner, in the name of liberty. (Ayers 2001, 198)

AYERS'S ELOQUENT DESCRIPTION OF HIS/THEIR FORM OF "NEGATIVE IDENTITY"

Bill Ayers vividly describes their lives in the "Weathermyth" of their Weather Underground life. Ayers's account gives deeper meaning to Erikson's notion of negative identity. He describes their rarely acknowledged homesickness, feeling of belonging and not belonging, loss combined with fear and anger in the exile of their underground life. Yet they felt a heightened sense of purpose. Yet, Ayers says,

> We were evicted, and we felt we never could go home." (Ayers 2001, 226)

Ayers goes on about their underground identity in a way that reminds the author of a definition of the unconscious mind:

> We disappeared then not *from* the world, but into a world, a world of invention and improvisation, a romance of space and distance and time, an outpost on the horizon of our imaginations. (Ayers 2001, 216)

Ayers later concludes the paragraph with this defining point:

> The underground was without borders or a point on a map, it's true, and it was as close to magic as I would ever come. (Ayers 2001, 216)

JUST WAR THEORY AND HOLY OR PREEMPTIVE WARS

Bill Ayers eloquently and dramatically challenged and condemned President Johnson's decision to irretrievably deepen U.S. involvement in the Vietnam War. U.S. president George W. Bush's decision to launch the preemptive "Iraqi 'Freedom' War" had stirred profound worldwide tensions, conflicts, and debate about the nature of war and its conduct. President Barack Obama's war decision to protect Libyan "innocents" and his collateral damage–laden drone attacks in Pakistan and Yemen have appropriately renewed and deepened the debate about so called just war. The U.S. Congress's reluctance or refusal to declare war for clearly stated reasons has shifted enormous war power to the U.S. president. The instantaneous worldwide reverberating mirror of TV media, the Internet, and social media dramatically focus scrutiny on war decisions.

HUMAN NATURE AND "RATIONAL" APPROACHES TO THE CONDUCT OF WAR

Rational and pragmatic men try to discuss avoidance of war and define "just war." Sigmund Freud (1930) felt that there was a parallel process between the development of civilization and the development of a superego or conscience in individual development. He felt that the personalities of great leaders were of crucial influence on the group conscience (Freud, 1933, 171). We could possibly cite in this regard— Gandhi? Christ? Mohammed? Buddha? Moses? or even Machiavelli? Sun-Tsu? Tiberius? Churchill? or Ataturk?

On this topic of a worldwide superego (conscience), the United Nations General Assembly adopted Resolution 217A (III) on December 10, 1948. This document titled "Universal Declaration of Human Rights" is an elegant, profoundly ethical and, one could say, rationally majestic statement for all members of the human family. This document, if carefully read, studied, and carefully applied, could form an effective ego ideal for the international community. It certainly offers far more hope for the future of humanity than many judgmental, fundamentalist interpretations of the Koran or the Bible. However, there are profound problems with the "Golden Rule." There are contradictions to it in human nature.

Freud felt that the commandment "to love thy neighbor as thyself" is impossible to follow. The person who inflates the idea of such ideal love of his neighbor in present-day civilization is put to dangerous disadvantage in face of a neighbor who disregards the rule (Freud 1930, 171).

Freud did hold out some hope that human reason/intellect and the scientific spirit could struggle to defeat what he called "the religious inhibition of thought" (fundamentalist mentality?) and other forms of dangerous superstitions (Freud 1933, 1720).

SOME CONFLICTING VIEWS OF WAR

Now let us examine some prevailing views about war ethics or the lack of them.

Pacifism

All over the world, millions of people march in antiwar demonstrations against war, and even the very notion of war itself. Pacifists would have everyone believe that war is always bad, whatever the context. Volkan (1988) says:

> The idea that something in the human mind and in human development causes man to make war is usually denied as vigorously as the idea that human beings are endowed with aggressive drives. (1988, 125)

Pacifism and the antiwar movement have a great appeal to many intellectuals, idealists, and "Liberal-Humanists." Pacifists see war as inherently irrational, abnormal, and evil. Humanists believe that the freedom and inner potential of all human beings can be fully realized through reason and nonviolent benevolent political-social processes. They are often, in the author's opinion, in romanticized denial about human nature.

Critics of the pacifist view of war come from many different theological and philosophical persuasions. These thinkers point out that human nature involves strong aggressive drives that are capable of malignant expression that involves cruelty, criminality, murder, and other forms of evil. These pragmatists say that good people sometimes must confront evil forcefully. C. S. Lewis (1952), a thoughtful gentle Christian writer, says:

> If one had committed a murder, the right Christian thing to do would be to give yourself up to the police and be hanged. It is therefore perfectly right for a Christian judge to sentence a man to death or a Christian to kill an enemy. (Lewis 1952, 118–19)

In this same discussion, Lewis adds:

> The idea of the knight—the Christian in arms for the defense of a good cause—is one of the great Christian ideas. War is a dreadful thing, and I can respect an honest pacifist, though I think he is entirely mistaken. (Lewis, 118–19)

This argument can lead us to a discussion of "just war" and "just war theory."

"Just War" Theory

"Just war" theory (Mosely 2001) finds its origins in Saint Thomas Aquinas's Summa Theologica, from the mid-1200s AD. Thomas Aquinas discusses the justification for war and the kinds of behavior and activity that are permissible in war. We now list the "Principles of the 'Just War'."

(1) A just war can only be waged as a "LAST RESORT." All non-violent options must be exhausted before the use of force can be justified. [The author agrees with Bill Ayers that the Vietnam War was not chosen as a last resort!]

(2) A war is just if it is waged by a "PROPER AUTHORITY." (The author again agrees with Bill Ayers that the Vietnam War was not chosen with proper authority beyond a flimsy war powers vote. Just wars in the author's opinion must be declared by Congress with the reasons for war and its end clearly stated.)

(3) A just war can only be fought to "REDRESS A WRONG" and "WITH RIGHT INTENTIONS." The cause must be for justice and not self-interest. (The majority of American decision makers in support of the war in Vietnam were sincerely convinced of the danger of the spread of worldwide communism and felt South Vietnam was a "domino" to fall. They, as Ayers concludes, were in hindsight wrong.)

(4) A just war must have a reasonable chance of success. (Several American presidents and their advisors expressed belief that the United States would prevail. They were wrong and we lost the war literally and figuratively.)

(5) The ultimate goal of just war is to reestablish peace and the violence used must be proportional to the injury suffered. (Bill Ayers eloquently expresses what many others of us concluded and deeply felt about American defeat in Vietnam. The violence and terrorism used by every warrior group and their leaders in the ill-fated Vietnam resulted in horrible, slow, still healing wounds and scars in the fabric of the search for peace.)

Just war theory, like all theories, is a helpful intellectual and philosophical process that should more often be used vigorously by politicians, military minds, and citizen voters but provides no ultimate answers.

Preemptive and "Holy" Wars

In 1998, Osama bin Laden wrote a book called *America and the Third World War*. In his book Bin Laden extends items from earlier fatwas and expounds on a global war that could be seen as analogous to the "preemptive war" policy statement of the conservative Bush administration after 9/11. The "shock and awe" of 9/11 was a defining moment for Bush as president and America as his country. The "preemptive war" policy had been gradually forming in the minds of Under Secretary of Defense Wolfowitz, Secretary Rumsfeld, and Security Advisor Rice. But, after 9/11, "preemption" reached ascendancy as a way to get the terrorists and their sponsoring states before they get us. It became a jihad or "Crusade" of powerful but fearful America. Islamists and Americans each have their plans for "preemptive war."

After careful study and vast detail of documentation, Bodansky (1999) concludes:

> Bin Laden in essence called on the entire Muslim world to rise up against the existing world order to fight for the right to live as Muslims—rights he states, which are being trampled by America's intentional spreading of Westernization. For the Islamists there can be no compromise or coexistence with Western civilization.(Bodanski 1999, 388)

Metaphorically and rhetorically, declarations of jihad against "crusaders" and preemptive wars against "the axis of evil" terror states or groups get blurry in meaning at times. It becomes dependent upon which man or woman on which street in the world it is discussed. Bush's "Orwellian" slip about an American "crusade," and the implications of Bin Laden's terror cult's jihad, are chilling.

If World War III is really a war on terrorism, it will not be won by "smart" bombs, drones, missiles, and bullets. It will be won by effective political, diplomatic, and foreign aid policymaking.

15

The Boston Marathon Bombers, Chechnya's History, and Spiritual Heirs of Osama bin Laden and Anwar al-Awlaki

THE TSARNAEV BROTHERS' TERROR BOMBS IN BOSTON

On April 15, 2013, Tamerlan and Dzhokhar Tsarnaev placed two pressure cooker bombs at the finish line area of the 2013 Boston Marathon. Three people were killed and 264 injured.

The two Boston Marathon bomber brothers are of Chechnyan descent and can be considered homegrown terrorists. A question is, In what home was their terror grown and nurtured? Is the Tsarnaev home in Chechnya, Russia, or Boston? There clearly was additional thought-reform or brainwashing done via an Internet self-radicalization process? The Internet's world of jihadist websites has blurred the distinction as to whether radicalization occurs via personal contacts with radical charismatic imams, or purely by lone wolf or wolf pack self or group self-radicalization. Hopefully the FBI investigation will reveal the extent that Tamerlan Tsarnaev was influenced by radical jihadists during his six-month stay in Russia and Chechnya/Dagestan.

In addition, Tamerlan Tsarnaev and Dzhokhar Tsarnaev's mother Zubeidat Tsarnaev has made statements to the media that raise questions about her behavior, integrity, and as to whether she may even have helped brainwash herself and her sons toward radical Islamist jihad (Caryl 2013, 3, 5, 9) Many psychiatrists and psychologists would argue that there is no more powerful a radicalizing tool than a *jihadi's* own mother.

THE ROLE OF WOMEN IN ISLAM AND THE MOTHERING
OF BOYS IN FUNDAMENTALIST FAMILIES

Here lies a crucial issue in any in-depth effort to understand the minds of so many fundamentalist Arab and Muslim men and women. Every one of us resides in our mother's body for nine months. We depend on our mother in our childhood for food and comfort. Each of us is also under her or her surrogate's authority in our childhood. Most men and women eventually gradually push away from their mother's authority. Young men often seem to push away harder.

Fundamentalist men have a particularly powerful way of reversing the power and control their mothers hold over them. Many fundamentalist religious men (Muslim, Jew, or Christian) have a deep, unconscious gynophobia. They push away from their mothers and sometimes become asexual. They learn domineering behaviors toward women. Their religious teachers give support for this dominating role.

The pervasive hostility toward woman, found in fundamentalist men of all ilk (Christian, Jewish, and Muslim), is based on profound **reaction formation** couched in religious dogma. This is true, even though outward behaviors seem affectionate or "devoted." Osama bin Laden's affection for the gynophobic and women-debasing Taliban is well known. Mullah Omar, the fugitive leader of the Taliban, took one of Osama's daughters as one of his wives. The author assumes this daughter had little conscious choice in the matter.

Let us detour briefly into the topic of Islamists' attitudes about women, because it is another unconscious dynamic within the minds of all Islamist terrorists and their potential recruits. This is a difficult issue to confront about Christian, Jewish, Islamic, or any radical fundamentalist, without sounding judgmental, but the author will try. Literally, the future of the world may depend on a neutral understanding of this dynamic and how it might be changed or modified.

Dr. Althea Horner has observed that it is likely that the mothering behavior of a woman with negative attitudes toward males will be tinged with envy and resentment, if not downright hostility, toward a son (2006, 2–6). Strict fundamentalist Islamic law gives fathers and brothers and husbands and sons the right and duty even to kill a woman if she wounds their narcissism or the group narcissism of tribe, family, and community. Especially if a male is embarrassed in a public way, a so-called honor killing is deemed appropriate and good.

Since the Koran and Islam in this sense view woman as essentially the possessions of men, this becomes the cultural background for the rearing of male children. It is likely that the mothering of boys, by more women than not, will carry overtones of the envy and resentment and even fear they feel toward the domineering male—be it their fathers or their husbands or their sons (Horner 1992, 599–610).

Defective mothering occurs as a result of these deeply embedded cultural and religious childrearing attitudes. The attendant emotional atmospheres, and the related unconscious level of maternal rejection, cause the sons to grow up with a reservoir of primitive insecurity and rage. This anger will find its outlet in rigid detachment, hostility, condescension, and domineering behavior toward women. Such immature men turn sheepishly with devotion toward older bearded imams and other male Muslim clerics for succor and direction. Mohammad Atta, the alleged 9/11 attack leader, left careful notes about how his dead body should be handled, and he rigidly stated that no woman was to touch or see him. Atta was overprotected by his mother (Sageman 2004, 86). Maternal overprotection is another source of grandiosity and subtle pathological narcissism in men. If the mother of Osama bin Laden or Mohammad Atta had begged her son to halt 9/11 plans, it seems unlikely that either of them would have taken the request seriously. The psychological reality is that many strict Muslim men like Osama and their recruits like Atta cannot be comfortably intimate with women; they fear sexuality and look to virgins in the next world for delusion-based pleasures that will sadly never come to fruition.

Peter Bergen begins his absorbing book *The Osama Bin Laden I Know* with a section called Dramatis Personae. It is, unsurprising but revealingly, an annotated list of 58 people. Only one, Alia Ghanem, Osama's Syrian-born mother, is a woman! Bergen mentions that she visited Osama several times in the mid-1990s to try to persuade him to return to Saudi Arabia. She also attended Osama's son Mohammed's wedding in Afghanistan in 2001.

Bergen quotes Mohammed Atef (Al Qaeda's former military commander, now deceased):

Sheikh bin Laden—he is always very, very careful for his mother and he is in constant touch with his mother. I was present in that meeting in Khartoum: Sheikh bin Laden told his mother, "I can sacrifice my life for you, but right now what you are talking to me is against Islam. I'm fighting against the enemies of Islam and you want that I should announce a cease-fire with the enemies of Islam." (Bergen 2006, 151)

Osama's mother said she would stop her demands. Soon after his mother's return to Saudi Arabia with his answer, Osama's citizenship was canceled. His black sheep/Robin Hood status in Saudi Arabia was assured. And his mother's pleas for moderation were ignored.

Horner hypothesizes, and the author agrees, that the promised polygamous group of virgins waiting for the (male) suicide bomber in heaven can be seen as a sexualized, idealized, fantasized/magical repair of a lifelong defective view and experience of women by these radical Arab and Muslim men. These sadly misguided terrorists believe they will finally be rewarded in the next life with a combination of an idealized, perfect, and guilt-free, but sexually gratifying, Oedipal mother that only Sophocles and Freud could fully appreciate (2006, 2–3).

With such empathic deficiencies running rampant in the fundamentalist Muslim childrearing cultural atmosphere, ego maturation and development in its fullest sense is compromised. Life and character structures thus become dominated by a brittle, rigid gender identity, with lessened capacity for empathy in crucial aspects of marriage and family relationships. And also, in the tragic disregard that Osama and Al Qaeda have had for the innocent women and children that their suicide bombers kill. Beneath the surface of espoused respect and affection for women by fundamentalist men lies an unconscious discounting, devaluing, and condescending attitude toward women. Jewish, Muslim, or Christian women who tolerate and stay subservient toward this situation stay undeveloped spiritually, intellectually, and psychologically.

FATHER HUNGER AND PSEUDOHOMOSEXUAL DYNAMICS IN RADICAL ISLAMIST YOUNG MEN

A corollary of the radical Muslim man's view of women just described is the intensification of father-hunger in these men (Herzog 2001). The latent homosexual, really *pseudohomosexual*, issues described by Lionel Ovesey prevail in father-hungry, unconsciously women-mother disrespecting lonely young Muslim men. Ovesey (1969) described that men attracted to men out of dependency and power-submission needs, rather than sexual gratification per se. Radical clerics tend to dominate young Arab/Muslim men at mosques. When these imams preach radical hatred of the United States and the West, a destructive, culturally ignorant chemistry prevails. Apparently few to no Muslim young men stand up in mosques to question or challenge any teachings of these biased Islamists, even when they preach the advocacy of murder in God's name! Such radical Islamist fundamentalist propaganda feeds the rigid, insecure mother-father hungry Muslim boys a diet of terror and hate. The angry enemy within becomes projected onto the American, British, and Israeli enemies "out there."

BACK TO THE TSARNAEV BROTHERS OF THE BOSTON MARATHON BOMBING

The Tsarnaev brothers' father, Anzor Tsarnaev, has made conflicting comments to the Russian media, at one point praising his son Dzhokhar as a "true angel," a star student. Anzor and Zubeidat Tsarnaev have at time claimed that their sons have been framed by the FBI and their son Tamerlan murdered by the FBI. Then, on other occasions, Anzor has urged his younger son to tell the truth. Anzor had said that he was coming to the United States immediately and then said that his health prevented a trip. Hardly a strong reliable father figure? Yet, Anzor Tsarnaev was seen as a tough guy by his sons as he was trained in law in Russia. After the family's asylum seeking in Boston, Anzor was reduced to fixing cars in a parking lot (Wines and Lovett 2013, 3; Remnick 2013, 19).

A point can be made that both Tsarnaev brothers fit eight of the dozen typical symptoms of attachment disorders of adults as commonly described by clinicians (Lalwani 2011): (1) *Impulsiveness* (which they may or not regret later); (2) *Negative and provocative behavior* (the Tsarnaev brothers committed an extreme form); (3) *Obsession with control* (using lying, cheating, and stealing); (4) *Lack of trust* (on the surface, Dzhokhar seemed popular, friendly, and close/engaging but in the long run, not so much); (5) *Anger and agitation* (the brothers held their anger at bay with wrestling, boxing, and academics but these sublimations gave way for their extremely cruel, destructive, and hostile behavior); (6) *Superficial positive traits* (Dzhokhar in particular could be a charmer and good conversationalist); (7) *Addictions* (Tamerlan's strict Muslim beliefs apparently held his tendency in check, but Dzhokhar was a frequent pot smoker); (8) *Lack of responsibility* (the brothers flaunted authority to the extreme of murder, including a police officer).

Such symptom check lists as cited earlier are not definitive but the author believes provide some preliminary help in the difficult domain of diagnosis of the Tsarnaev brothers. Dzhokhar and Tamerlan very likely had unconscious conflicts around their parents' divorce in 2012, their immigrant status, and the separations from their parents and homeland. Tamerlan had taken on the role as head of the family after Anzor had returned to Russia seeking money in 2011. Dzhokhar said in a tweet that he missed his father (Wines and Lovett 2013). Tamerlan was increasingly devout but rigid and authoritarian with Dzhokhar (Wines and Lovett 2013; Caryl 2013, 6; Remnick 2013, 20). However, at the special wrestling team senior ceremony, a coach stood by Dzhokhar, in the absence of a brother or father's presence.

Wines and Lovett (2013) describe Dzhokhar Tsarnaev as a master of concealment. The cool, athletic, outgoing, gregarious, and nonviolent persona known to social acquaintances and classmates had a darker private side. Dzhokhar placed raunchy jokes and posts about girls on Twitter (Remnick 2013, 20). He described terrifying nightmares about murder and destruction. He had begun to express disaffection with America and its ethos. In college Dzhokhar's grades had dropped and he skipped classes (Wines and Lovett 2013). Though excited at first about his new U.S. citizenship (September 11, 2012), he ambivalently spoke of missing Dagestan and Chechnya, saying that after a decade in America he wanted out (Remnick 2013, 20)!

PROBABLE MOTIVES OF THE TSARNAEV BROTHERS

According to a CBS news report (May 16, 2013), Dzhokhar Tsarnaev left a note in the boat he was hiding in when he was captured. Dzhokhar scrawled the note with a pen on the inside wall of the boat that was in the backyard of a home in Watertown, Massachusetts. Dzhokhar called his brother Tamerlan a martyr. He said their bombing was retribution for the U.S. crimes against Muslims in Iraq and Afghanistan. He also wrote that the victims of the Boston Marathon bombing were "collateral damage" (CBS News 2013).

Some reports emphasize that Tamerlan Tsarnaev had right-wing extremist, white supremacy, and U.S. government conspiracy literature (Anderson 2013, 1). The author thinks that radical Islamism or Islamofascism and Nazi fascism are very similar in many domains of their destructive utopianism. Lonely, disaffected in-betweeners can readily grasp spurious inspiration from right-wing or left-wing radicalism.

TSARNAEV SUMMARY

The preliminary information suggests that the Tsarnaev brothers had significant defects in empathy, authority conflicts, and ambivalent, though dutiful relationships with both their mother and father. The idealizing of both their sons by Anzor and Zubeidat Tsarnaev suggest that such idealizing by the parents may have led to inflated narcissism of both young men—particularly Tamerlan. Zubeidat Tsarnaev adored Tamerlan with a pathological sounding intensity. She at one point compared the beauty of his physique to Hercules. Both parents saw Tamerlan as their greatest legacy in the world. The father, Anzor, who had been a boxer himself, pushed Tamerlan hard to be a famous boxer (Caryl 2013, 5). Such parental adoration can be the foundation of pathological narcissism.

The cruel violence toward police suggests that they both had severe authority conflicts and rage. With eerie echoes of Dostoyevsky's *Brothers Karamazov*, there may have been Totem and Taboo in Chechnya? Did the Tsarnaev brothers display more mojo for radical action than their father? Yes, but in such massively destructive ways. And tragically, blasphemously, in the name of Allah.

Finally, Eric Shaw's concept is applicable to the Tsarnaev brothers, that is, ambivalence toward and conflict with authority—fear of authority, hate of authority, yet unconscious longing for effective authority. The author applies Shaw's notion about a telling contradiction in future terrorists' family of origin experiences. Such powerful **ambivalence** occurs when they realize that there are glaring inconsistencies in their parents' and/or families of origin's political philosophy, religion, and beliefs. Actually, their parents are impotent in terms of actual effective social or moral action. Young men like the Tsarnaev brothers become aware that their parents talk the talk of jihadist action and social change but the parents do not walk the effective walk. The degree to which Zubeidat Tsarnaev was unconsciously and vicariously invested in her sons' acting-out is as yet to be determined, but is likely the case. She certainly hysterically protested much (*Catholic Online* 2013).

HEIRS APPARENT TO OSAMA BIN LADEN AND ANWAR AL-AWLAKI

I—Feiz Mohammad

Feiz Mohammad is a 43-year-old Australian Muslim preacher of Lebanese descent. He is noted for his Islamic fundamentalism and powerful charismatic sermons. Feiz Mohammad appeared on a YouTube account held by Tamerlan Tsarnaev, and Hunt (2013) reports that Mohammad's sermons could have played a part in motivating Tamerlan Tsarnaev.

Though hardly causal, moderate Muslims in Boston and elsewhere fear such associated links with violent militant Islam. Feiz Mohammad, an ex-boxer, has drawn large crowds and has given lectures where he implied rape victims deserved rape for wearing sexy clothing. He has urged Muslim parents to have their children die as jihadist martyrs, and advocated the killing of infidel nonbelievers. He has called Jews "pigs" to be killed (Webb 2007) and called for the beheading of a Dutch politician (*The Australian* 2010). Not much is known about the details of Feiz's childhood, object relations, or adolescence to speculate about his psychodynamics. His boxing prowess celebrity would have certainly impressed Tamerlan and Dzhokhar Tsarnaev, in addition to Feiz's radical jihadi words and image over the Internet. Many homegrown terrorists have had interest in boxing, wrestling, and/or martial arts.

Former U.S. senator Joseph Lieberman in his book *Ticking Time Bomb* (2011) says that Feiz Mohammad was an example of a "virtual spiritual sanctioner." Such persons provide inspiration and provide some level of religious justification for Islamist terror violence. He rightly compares them to Anwar al-Awlaki, Abdullah el-Faisal, and Samir Khan. Killing such malignant Pied Pipers with Hellfire drones provides only temporary relief. Terror groups need, seek, and find leaders, and violent jihadist leaders need the adoration and admiration of their followers (Olsson 2005, 13). Early spotting of destructive leaders and vulnerable potential followers is most important. Exposure to the light of effective, truthful, and accurate investigative journalism leads to increased public awareness and empowerment. Community awareness proved very valuable in Boston after the bombing. It might have occurred long before the terror event. That sort of heads-up would have helped as much as any drone strike as effective terror prevention. Political correctness, secrecy, protecting of political turf, passivity, and parsing of words are not productive.

II—Adnan Gulshair el Shukrijumah

Adnan Gulshair el Shukrijumah born on August 4, 1975, in Saudi Arabia and grew up in the United States is a member of Al Qaeda. In September 2003, the FBI sent out an alert about four people they thought were a grave threat to U.S. citizens. These four included Shukrijumah, Abderraouf Jdey, Zubayr al-Rimi, and Karim el-Mejjati. Shukrjumah is wanted as a terrorist posing a grave danger to gas stations, fuel trucks, subway systems, trains, or bridges (USNews, 1).

Anderson (2010, 1) noted that 35-year-old Adnan Shukrijumah who has taken over Khalid Sheikh Mohammed's role as mastermind attack planner for Al Qaeda is the most familiar with the United States because he lived here for 15 years before fleeing. Shukrijumah was indicted in 2009 for plotting bomb attacks on the New York subway system (Anderson 2010, 1). He had done research on possible bomb attacks in Norway and the United Kingdom, and sinking a freighter in the Panama Canal (Anderson 2010, 2).

In the late 1990s, Shukrijumah trained in the Al Qaeda Afghanistan training camps and in 2004 he was declared a severe danger to the United States by then-attorney general John Ashcroft. A $5 million reward was offered for information leading to his capture (Anderson 2010, 2).

Shukrijumah's mother Zurah Adbu Ahmed was interviewed at her home in Florida. She said that Adnan talked frequently about his view that American society was crumbling from alcohol, drug abuse, and woman wearing sexually seductive clothing. His mother, like most parents and families of homegrown terrorists, said that he did not believe in violence. She claimed that he loved America and would never do "evil stuff" toward the United States (Anderson 2010, 2).

Prior to his turn toward radical Islam, Shukrijumah lived with his mother and five siblings in Miramar, Florida. At community college, he did well in chemistry and computer sciences (Anderson 2010, 2–3). He had come to South Florida when his father, a Muslim cleric and missionary trained in Saudi Arabia, moved from Brooklyn to Florida. His father died in 2004. Shukrijumah had grown steadily and fiercely convinced that he must join the holy war because of the persecution of Muslims in places like Chechnya and Bosnia (Anderson 2010, 3). Experts think that he is particularly dangerous because he has thorough knowledge of our security and has keen insights into using smaller-scale attacks outside Washington D.C., and New York City—but that maximize terror (Anderson 2010, 3).

Shukrijumah, though born in Saudi Arabia, is a citizen of Guyana, South America, where his father was born. In Afghanistan, he met Jose Padilla (the Dirty Bomber) but their mutual planning for U.S. attacks was disrupted because he and Padilla clashed and could not get along. Padilla complained to Mohammed Atef about the situation (Anderson 2010, 3). Under water-board interrogation, Padilla revealed the frightening information that he and Shukrijumah had learned how to seal up natural gas lines in apartment complexes and then detonate huge explosions. Wisely, the extensive search for Shukrijumah continues relentlessly because of his troubling expertise and ability to disguise himself and his whereabouts. The author concludes that he has outstripped his father as a new form of missionary, a malignant missionary of jihad.

APPENDIX

A Brief History of Chechnya

Chechnya has come to the attention of the world following its recent string of conflicts in a struggle to achieve independence from the Russian Federation. Chechnya is a small, mountainous region in the Caucasus, and the Chechens are a proud people who have been at odds with, and subjugated by, the Russians dating back to Tsarist times in the 16th century. While the Chechens had staged many insurrections since the 16th century, the process of Russification and Sovietization set the stage for the fierce stage of conflict that has been seen in recent times. Along with the Chechens' lifelong desire for independence, the rivalry with Russia, and their distinct regional traits, the Chechen resolve has only been strengthened by a history of conflict (Knezys and Sedlickas 1999, 10).

In a region with many diverse peoples, the Chechens have always stood out for their unique lifestyle. Divided into a clan-like system, with kinship groups known as teips, Chechens could trace their family origins through a grandfather or great-grandfather that allowed them to be knowledgeable of multiple generations of their family. Around 165 to 170 of these teips exist today. Known primarily as a mountain dwelling people, Chechens were and still are raised to be fierce fighters and tough under the social conditions they have been subjected to. A popular Chechen saying regarding the raising of their youth sums it up:

> Do not fear the enemy because he may not have a weapon. Even if he does have a weapon, it may not be cocked. But even if it is cocked, it

may not fire, and even if it is fired, it may not hit its target. But even if the bullet strikes you, the wound may be only superficial. And even if you die, you will then gain Allah's eternal grace. (Knezys and Sedlickas 1999, 14)

This attitude has continued on to the present, with every Chechen pledging to fight to the end to preserve their people and right to autonomy.

To better understand the Chechens' fierce approach to resistance and upbringing, it is necessary to mention the enduring history of conflict that Chechens have been through, particularly their history with the Russians. Beginning in the latter part of the 17th century, the Russians looked to expand their Tsarist empire in all directions, and the Chechens were seen as a group to be subjugated. By the early part of the 18th century, the Russians succeeded in taking over Chechnya, but this event only served to spark further resistance.

Starting in the mid and latter part of the century, insurrections were led starting with Sheikh Mansur, but the most successful resistance was led in the early 19th century by a man known as Imam Shamil. Through mountain fighting and guerilla warfare, the Russians were cast off by Shamil's forces, after which he formed a combined Chechen and Dagestinian Emirate revolving around Sufi Islam, whose decentralized government and small amount of obligations highly appealed to the Chechens. For 30 years, this Imamate existed until a concentrated Russian effort took back the region, with mass deportations occurring by 1863, during which 700,000 Chechens and Ingushians were expelled. However, the legacy of independence was further ingrained in the Chechen mentality.

By the late 19th century, the Russians found a new value in Chechnya that caused it to be a hot commodity. The region turned out to be a huge source of the black gold, oil, with stories of people being able to gather oil by buckets in the territory. With the establishment of the first drilling in the region by 1893, Chechnya was a region that had major political implications. By the turn of the century, it became necessary for the Tsars, and eventually the Soviets that succeeded them, to Russify Chechnya.

The Russification of Chechnya became a process that proved to be almost impossible. One of the first obstacles for the Russians and Soviets was that Chechens were a unique brand of people even within their widely diverse area. The most significant aspect of Chechen culture was its embrace of Islam. Islam had found its way into the area by the ninth century after its rapid spread from Arabia and the Islamic empire that came to be formed (Knezys and Sedlickas 1999, 12). What was unique about Islam, the Sufi branch of which came to be the dominant religion in Chechnya by the 18th century, was that it was a religion that was popular among a Caucasus region that was mainly Orthodox Christian. The practice of Sufi Islam was very popular because it did not carry the obligations that a Christian community might, which suited the Chechen preference for a more decentralized religion, as seen in the Imamate under Imam Shamil. By the 1920s, 2,675 mosques had been established, along with 140 religious schools and 850 mullahs (Gall and de Waal 1998, 33).

After the Soviets came to power, whose struggle against the Whites in the Russian Civil War was supported by the Chechens, the process of Sovietization forgot this aid. The next 40 years saw the Soviets attempting to erase entirely the role of Islam in Chechen society. By 1961, an extensive clampdown saw the Soviets close down all mosques and religious schools (Gall and de Waal 1998, 33). What aided this effort extensively was the mass deportation of Chechens in 1944, where just about every Chechen was expelled, most of whom to Uzbekistan, among other regions in the Soviet Union. Under Stalin, the Chechens were not to return as a result of their continued resistance and obstinate response to Sovietization. As under the tsars, the Chechens continued to fight bitterly, with several small-scale insurrections being suppressed by the Soviets. With its political value regarding the oil trade, combined with a full-scale Soviet war effort against the Germans, who specifically targeted the Caucasus region for its vital oil potential, the Chechens were seen as a threat. When a revolt was attempted during the high point of the war, Stalin saw to it their expulsion, and Chechens did not begin returning to Chechnya until 1961, when Nikita Khrushchev provided amnesty in the post-Stalin era.

The memory that has inspired the Chechen resistance most seen today was the deportation mentioned in 1944. Initially there was apparent harmony between the Muslim Chechens and the Bolsheviks, as the Chechens played a significant role in resisting the Whites during the civil war. Lenin's policies involved letting the regions of the Soviet Union have a relative sense of identity.

In 1921, Stalin presided over a Bolshevik Commissar on Nationalities, where he allowed the creation of a state called the Mountainous Autonomous Republic in the Caucasus. The Chechens were permitted to continue practicing Islam and even use sharia, or Islamic law, as a constitutional basis as long as they recognized the Soviets as the power holders (Gall and de Waal 1998, 53). However, this state would last only for five years, as the death of Lenin and the emergence of Stalin's power began to take hold.

Stalin's policies of agricultural collectivization were extremely taxing on the Chechens, and were met with significant resistance. Conditions under the Soviets turned out to be more of the same for the Chechens as under Tsarist Russia. This time, the Soviet focus was on eliminating the presence of Islam, and the Chechens murdered those who tried to enforce the new policies, including the local head of the secret police in 1930. An ethnic Russian named Chernoglaz, who was the new party secretary at the time, was met by an old man when touring Ingushetia, who famously compared him to a former Tsarist governor:

> "Mitnik (the Tsarist governor) was a good man, but the Tsar's government was bad," the old man said. "That is why I killed him on this same spot with a dagger like this one. I was sentenced to penal servitude for life, but twelve years later the Revolution liberated me. The Soviet government is good, but you, Chernoglaz, are a bad man. I do not want to kill you. Instead, I am giving you wise advice: go away from Ingushetia while you still have a head on your shoulders. People here are furious with you. I swear they will kill you." (Gall and de Waal 1998, 53)

After this speech, Chernoglaz ordered the arrest of the old man, and that very evening was murdered and, as forewarned, decapitated.

This tension and constant resistance caused the Chechens to be regarded as a troublesome people by Stalin, and in 1944 the deportations were instituted. Over half a million people of the Caucasus, most of whom Chechens, were sent to the steppes of Central Asia, specifically to Kazakhstan and Uzbekistan during the winter, where temperatures often reached extremes of –30 degrees. These conditions, combined with sickness and hunger, killed over 100,000 (Gall and de Waal 1998, 53) Those who did survive were given the designation of "special deportees" and were denied basic rights.

The accounts of these deportations are long remembered by the Chechens. This practice proved to be commonplace with many ethnic groups in the Soviet Union, but the deportation of the Chechens was one of the more ambitious and costly ones. Organized by Stalin's infamous chief of the NKVD, Lavrentiy Beria, it was carried out on a national holiday, Red Army Day; business was conducted starting at 5 A.M.:

> The whole male population of our village above fifteen years old were invited deceitfully to one of the buildings in the village supposedly to select dancers for a party. When they had all been collected, the doors and windows were boarded up. . . . They gave us twenty-five minutes to get ready, then they loaded us up and set off. . . . School had just opened, we were sitting in class and our teachers were taken away, and as he left our teacher managed to say that we were being taken to Siberia. (Gall and de Waal 1998, 59)

After the deportations, the Soviets undertook a campaign to remove any sign of Chechen culture, by moving in Russians and other neighboring peoples such as the Dagestanis. Thousands of Chechen soldiers fighting for the Soviets in the war were even sent back to be deported, as well as the local Chechen Party leaders who had collaborated in the event. The most insulting mark left in Chechnya was the construction of a statue dedicated to General Yermolov in the capital of Grozny in 1949, with the inscription reading, "There is no people under the sun more vile and deceitful than this one" (Gall and de Waal 1998, 62).

After Stalin's death, the restrictions on Chechens were progressively lifted and slowly they began to return home. By 1957 a Chechen-Ingushetian republic was established, and the wave of Chechens increased coming back home. The return was intensely emotional for many Chechens, who could remember the day they were deported, but more significantly the day they were able to return to their homeland (Gall and de Waal 1998, 73). Many even would bring back the bones of their deceased relatives on their train rides back in order to bury them on the grounds of Chechnya. The deportations served to strengthen the Chechen identity, whereas previously Chechens associated themselves more with the teips they came from, the result of years of oppression that caused them to band together (Gall and de Waal 1998, 74).

What further caused the Chechen-Russian animosity to fester was the fact that public discussion of the deportations was prohibited, and in the 1980s, the Soviet regime of the time under Brezhnev argued that the Chechens benefited from the event with the Soviet gift of "technical education."

Brezhnev may have been right in the regard that the Chechens benefited years after, but it certainly was not in a manner that was positive for the Soviets, for the Soviet oppression only caused the Chechens to be further united in their quest for autonomy and independence. As the vice president of the Chechen Republic, Zelimkhan Yandarbiyev, stated in 1994, "Over the last two or three hundred years we have always acted on the assumption that Russia is acting out of a wish to occupy Chechnya and expel the Chechen people from its territory" (Gall and de Waal 1998, 73).

Following the collapse of the Soviet Union, the new Russian Federation had trouble establishing its power as a successor state. In Chechnya, the communists in power were ousted and a declaration of independence was established in 1991. The major issue was that it was widely speculated that the Chechens were not capable of producing an effective state. A society based on teips, with no noticeable nobility or ruling elite, or sense of class structure in general, was determined to be unfit for a democratic state (Sakwa 2005, 10). Three years of inter-faction fighting between the new government that declared independence under Dzhokhar Dudayev and factions that requested the assistance of the Russian government ensued. During these three years, there was violence against non-Chechens, particularly Russians in the area, and many of these peoples left Chechnya, many of whom were engineers, so that Chechnya was impacted economically. These developments led the Russian government under Boris Yeltsin to send troops to Chechnya to restore order by force, which led to the first war in Chechnya.

The war went disastrously for the Russians, who were unprepared for the task that awaited them in conquering a people fully capable of defending themselves, who were extremely motivated, and had extensive knowledge of the terrain. The Russians were also extremely unmotivated and atrocities were committed on both sides throughout the war. In the Russian assault on the Chechen capital at Grozny, anywhere from 25,000 to 35,000 civilians were killed, many of whom were actually ethnic Russians (Faurby and Magnussen 1999, 1). Through successful guerilla warfare and tactical terrorist acts committed in Russia, the Chechens were able to coerce the Russians to cease their offensive.

The main perpetrator and mastermind of the Chechen defense and the Budyonnovsk crisis was a man by the name of Shamil Basayev. A Chechen with personal ties to the war, through the deaths of family members by Russian air strikes, Basayev came to symbolize the

Chechen struggle. Describing his motivations for the Budyonnovsk crisis, Basayev details his motivations:

> Before, I was not a supporter of that sort of action, to go and fight in Russia, because I knew what measures and cost it would entail . . . but when last year we were thrown out of Vedeno, and they had driven us into a corner with the very savage and cruel annihilation of villages, women, children, old people, of a whole people, then we went. (Hafez 2003, 99)

Basayev took the approach of gaining international recognition of the war and the atrocities that were occurring, with a "me against the world" attitude for the lack of help that Chechnya had received.

Basayev was raised in the traditional Chechen manner. His father was exiled in the mass deportations under Stalin and had built a house right where their ancestors' house had been upon returning from exile. His inspiration from childhood is well stated by Gall and de Waal:

> Salman Basayev (Shamil's father) brought up his sons on the tales of their ancestors. Almost every generation of the family have been fighters, protecting their homeland against invaders. One ancestor fought the Mongol hordes led by Tamerlane. Salman's great-grandfather, one of Imam Shamil's deputies, died in battle against General Yermolov. His father fought the Bolsheviks, only to die of hunger and cold in the first winter of exile in Kazakhstan. He lay in the snow unburied until the spring. (Gall and de Waal 1998, 259)

There are plenty of warriors similar to Shamil Basayev, with longstanding memories through generational stories of Russian oppression and the Soviet deportations. It is these movements for independence and autonomy that give the Chechens a sense of identity that is advanced from the times when it was all about what teip or clan a person was in.

The history of the Chechen people is that of a group who has had to fight for its identity in a region with many distinct peoples and outside influences. When narrowing the Chechen history down to its interactions with the Russians, however, one sees the Chechens simply fighting for survival of their very culture. From the expansion of Tsarist Russia to the oppressing regime of the Soviet Union, the Chechen people have been fighting Russification and Sovietization, policies that attempted to cleanse them of their identity and ethnic pride. However, the legacy of the Chechens is, and will remain, of a people who, through these conflicts and attempts at outside imperialism, are willing to fight until the last Chechen dies to preserve his unique culture and people. In a broader context, the Russians have inherited the issues that the Soviets had to deal with, in that there are many ethnic peoples seeking autonomy and outright independence from century long struggles against Russification.

16

Decisions, Actions, and Responsibility of Homegrown Terrorists

Not all decisions or subsequent actions are drastically influenced by unconscious psychological factors or internal psychological conflicts. When the decision maker's internal world is "calm," there is little need to extensively probe hidden psychological elements. When the decision maker's internal world is "agitated," however, his or her decisions to a great extent can become personalized. An in-betweener's internal world is invariably vulnerable or agitated. A leader or follower in radical Islam may unconsciously equate a set of circumstances in the external world with an unresolved internal conflict, or otherwise be influenced by symbolic contaminants, strong emotions, and unconscious fantasies. Homegrown terrorist recruits, as our study indicates, often have personal life pathway issues that combine to intensify their in-betweener situation. Often one of their personal pathway issues involves intense disappointment in, or conflict with, their parents. This leads to father hunger or longing and a search for father or older brother figures in the adolescent or young adult years. Radical Islamist imams such as Anwar al-Awlaki provide a unique fit for homegrown terrorists in the making, like Nidal Hasan, the Tsarnaev brothers, and Umar Abdulmutullab.

Rangel (1971) believed that understanding the ego function of decision making would help psychoanalysts deal with the concept of responsibility. This is of course important in confronting the plans or behavior of homegrown terrorists. Using Freud's (1926) concept of signal anxiety as a starting point, Rangel developed a metapsychological explanation of the process of unconscious decision making by the ego. As a result of signal anxiety, which foreshadows intrapsychic danger, defensive operations of the **ego** are initiated. The aim of these defenses is to keep derivatives of instinctual drives, impulses, and/or painful affects from emerging into consciousness and/or action.

According to Rangel, before fully experiencing signal anxiety, the ego permits a small, controlled amount of impulse to discharge—a tiny "test" within the mind, to see whether the ego can allow the impulse full-blown expression. Homegrown terrorists-to-be often test out their angry or hateful impulses by Internet social media entries. They often seek peer support for their future terror plans. This clearly occurred with Dzhokhar Tsarnaev (Boston Marathon bomber), whose college friends Dias Kadyrbayev and Azamat Tazhayakov from University of Massachusetts, Dartmouth, have been indicted by a federal grand jury for taking evidence from Dzhokhar's dorm room and tossing some of it in the trash (Sacchetti 2013, 1–5). It is not fully clear that Dzhokhar specifically "tested" his bombing ideas and impulses with his friends. Dzhokhar had asked them to go to his dorm room where they found a laptop, backpack, fireworks torn open, and a jar of Vaseline. The retained laptop contained Dzhokhar's postings, which contained "tiny tests" and more ominous evidence of his homegrown terror inclinations (see Chapter 15).

In Rangel's theory, if such a tiny "test" happens, then one's conscience responds to the trial balloon and causes the ego to produce anxiety. Like the impulse that initiated it, the level of this anxiety is small—below the level of signal anxiety (Freud 1926). At this point, the ego must "choose" what to do next: allow the full discharge of the impulse or stop the impulse from being discharged. Rangel called this process *intrapsychic choice conflict*:

> The delineation of an intra psychic choice conflict spells out a moment in intrapsychic life in which the human psyche is confronted with the opportunity, and the necessity, to exercise its own directive potentials and to determine its own active course. . . . Taken by itself, psychic determinism is incomplete, unless it is viewed in the context of the role played by the individual himself in controlling and shaping his own destiny. (Rangel 1971, 440)

Rangel (1971, 431) then describes a "decision-making function of the ego" specifically designed to resolve the intrapsychic choice conflict, which is followed by action. The anxiety-choice-decision-action sequence he describes serves as the theoretical model for the psychoanalytic contribution to decision theory. All decision making, whether it involves engaging in an international conflict or buying a piece of land, involves planning. Rangel (1971, 439) helps us understand the planning process in which the individual unconsciously scans "memories of previous psychic traumata, by which the utility of anticipated decisions are judged. The scope and security of predictions are thus enormously amplified by bringing into play previous experience and the entire sweep of the psychogenetic past."

In the anxiety-choice-decision-action sequence that Rangel refers to, both emotional and cognitive elements operate mostly on the unconscious level. According to Rangel, uncertainty results from an incomplete or unsatisfactory cognitive search for the anticipated outcome—what would be called in today's terms the "what if" scenario. When a satisfactory "what if" outcome cannot be determined, indecision results:

> Indecision is the unwillingness or inability of the ego to commit itself to a course of action either because of this or even after the cognitive consequences are known; and doubt is the emotional state accompanying either or both of these cognitive conditions. (Rangel 1971, 439)

As a child matures into an adult, decision making obviously begins to involve increasingly sophisticated and conscious (secondary process) thinking—but some of the "problem solving" preceding it continues to take place largely on an unconscious level. Fixation and regression in the adult individual's mental life influence decision-making functions. When fixations and regressions are severe enough, the secondary process thinking involved in decision making is inhibited. This is very often the case with homegrown terrorists' recruitment decisions and actions.

SUMMARY

Psychoanalysts regularly investigate acting-out. But, psychoanalysis has yet no comprehensive theory of action. However, Rangel's ideas help us get close. The "tiny tests" or "what if" processes that Rangel describes are helpful in perhaps spotting anlages of nascent terror actions in future homegrown terrorists. Rangel helps us in refining our thinking about their actions, possible sense of responsibility, and hints about their decision-making process.

Dr. Nidal Hasan gave several glaring evidences of his inner "tiny tests" of his future terrorist inclinations in his behavior during his psychiatry residency at Walter Reed Department of Psychiatry. His grand rounds presentation was filled with hints about his anlages of radical jihadist proclivities (see Chapter 7). Naser Jason Abdo linked himself to his older brother figure Dr. Nidal Hasan (see Chapter 8).

Adam Gadahn's teenage Internet postings could have given hints of his in-betweenerism, father longings, and identity searching. Rebellious toward a religiously nomadic father and a Jewish physician grandfather, Adam was ripe for a radical jihadist recruiter's picking. Unfortunately, Adam's "tiny tests" about *jihadi* actions probably took place in the presence of his radical recruiters who exploited Adam's talents (see Chapter 5 for details).

John Walker Lindh's behaviors even as a teenager could be seen as crying out for a therapist to help him explore the "tiny tests" between the lines of his adolescent identity crisis. Later his actions and behavior grew more specific as he converted to Islam and eventually headed to Yemen to study Arabic and later to Pakistan, where his radicalization apparently deepened (see Chapter 6).

Farouk Abdulmutallab's ("the underwear bomber") Internet postings cried out about his father/big brother longings for help (see Chapter 10). The same observations can be made about the "tiny tests" leaping from between the lines of Richard Reid's ("the shoe bomber ") behaviors (see Chapter 10).

There were hints about "tiny tests" going on for Ted Kaczynski as long ago as his days at Harvard as discussed by Alston Chase (see Chapter 13). Timothy McVeigh's "tiny tests" were evident all along the way of his personal pathway toward homegrown terror. Family members apparently did not spot his "what ifs" in time to suggest therapy even when he was talking about depression and suicide (see Chapter 13).

Aafia Siddiqui's brilliant mind seemed to give evidence of a symphony of "tiny tests" as she ambitiously searched for ways to effectively perfect her education and gain social justice for fellow Muslims (see Chapter 12).

Bill Ayer's "tiny tests" were in evidence during his efforts to be true to his moral core values, even during his adolescent rebellions that seemed to not get the effective attention of his parents or teachers. These issues were alluded to constantly in his eloquently written memoir, *Fugitive Days* (see Chapter 14).

Bryant Neal Vinas presents further complexities about so-called tiny tests. Vinas met Najibullah Zazi in Pakistan in 2008. Zazi is from Queens, Long Island, and had, like Vinas, wanted to join the Taliban to fight against U.S. forces and their allies in Afghanistan. Zazi went on to attempt to perform suicide bombings in the New York subways during rush hour. He was arrested in 2009 before he could attack successfully (D'Olivio and Fitzpatrick 2010, 1).

The Vinas–Zazi association illustrates the importance of social networks and friendships in the whole domain of terrorist recruitment that is observed by Marc Sageman (2004, 82–91, 175–84). In many instances, the terror cult network is like a new and superior family. A vehicle of adventure, rebellion, and separation-individuation from conflicts and angry disappointments in parents and families, churches, and temples of origin. Vinas's "tiny tests" occurred gradually and relentlessly moved toward radical actions (see Chapter 9 for details, including his fascinating change of heart about his homegrown terrorism).

Moore and Fine (1990, 3) write that action "implies intentionality, purpose, and meaning, though the intention need not be conscious, meaning may be only latent, and the action need not be observable, nor need it involve motor activity." They differentiate between "act" and "action": "The former connotes something done or effected, whereas the latter implies a process that involves more than one step, is continuous, or is capable of repetition" (1990, 3). Adaptive (rational) action "is the result of the resolution and integration of needs, defenses, and external reality in a satisfactory compromise that leads to relative inner harmony and effective mastery. It does not imply absence of conflict; rather, it refers to effective ego functioning that integrates drive derivatives and superego influences at an optimal level of influence" (Moore and Fine 1990, 3).

Some people seem more inclined to action than others. Research into the inclination toward action versus passivity has identified a number of determinants. For example, observation of infants and children has shown inherent, temperamental differences in the degree of "motor-mindedness," the willingness to take action (Mahler 1975), or engage in "nondestructive aggression" (Parens 1979). Other observations of early decision making include the influence of traumatic events occurring before the capacity for verbal expression. Such experiences demand discharge in action as the only means of communicating frustration. Derivations of these events continue into adulthood as idiosyncratic reenactments (Dorn 1974; Volkan 1995).

As a child matures, other developmental factors influence action. Among the "nonspecific manifestations of ego weakness" (Kernberg 1975, 22) are intolerance of anxiety and poor impulse control. Both foster a propensity toward action. In addition, superego defects are associated with a propensity toward action, especially doubtful and irrational action in which the absence of an individual's inner sense of conscience or psychologically internalized moral imperatives do not prohibit action. And a host of other factors contribute to the propensity toward action, including unconscious fantasies, identifications with active or passive adults significant in childhood, and culturally accepted norms for activity and passivity.

In listing these factors that promote a greater potential for action in one individual than in another, we do not mean to imply that action is something pathological and undesirable. Every day we take many actions—they are a necessary aspect of psychic life, and the essence of being alive. The healthy ego's synthesis guides the individual to the safest instinctual drive discharge, the one that most closely approaches the ego ideal, and that causes the least conflict with internalized values. In other words, the healthy ego incorporates all factors and guides the decision maker into the best decision that person can make under all circumstances, both internal and external.

Nevertheless, there are unconscious factors that influence and interfere with an individual's decision-action sequence. When such influences are strong and constant in an individual's mind, certain behaviors may be habitually repeated. These behaviors need to be spotted before homegrown terrorist go into action. Invariably future homegrown terrorists give subtle or not so subtle hints.

CONCLUSIONS

It is important to note that the psychodynamics and personal pathways to homegrown terrorism discussed in this book, though important and necessary causal aspects of homegrown terror, are not totally sufficient to explain homegrown terrorism or terrorists. In other words, these psychodynamic factors can be found in individuals who have not turned radical or participated in any acts of terror. The psychodynamics we have explored are helpful as a part of the process of understanding and identifying individuals who very likely could convert to terrorist identities or experience malignant epiphanies of identity and radical fundamentalist mentality or thinking that can lead to recruitment to terror groups and subsequent terrorist actions. For example, when Russian counterterrorism authorities alerted the FBI about their concerns about Tamerlan Tsarnaev, the FBI interviewers might have found the psychodynamic issues presented in this book helpful at their interviews with the Tsarnaev brothers.

PSYCHODYNAMIC PATTERNS

The key psychodynamic patterns in homegrown terrorists are as follows: (1) Severe ambivalence toward or disappointment in early parental figures, often resulting in father/parental hunger or longing. (2) Ambivalence about a spouse, marriage, and intimacy. (3) The presence of adolescent or young adult life phase "in-betweener" situations and prolonged adolescent identity searching and crises. (4) Ambivalence toward and conflict with authority—fear of authority, hate of authority, yet unconscious longing for effective authority. (5) A telling contradiction in future terrorists' experiences occurs when they realize that there are glaring inconsistencies between their parents' and/or families of origin's political philosophy, religion and beliefs, and their parents' impotence in terms of actual effective social or moral action that brings authentic and effective change, that is, very influential parents who talk the talk but do not walk the walk.

A particularly important corollary of the fifth psychodynamic pattern earlier is applicable when an in-betweener shows intense conflict, anger, and/or disappointment in their parents, which overlaps with abrupt change in the family's religious/spiritual commitments or immigration status. Often this corollary's domain involves a parental divorce or marital conflicts (see sections on Naser Jason Abdo, Adam Gadahn, Bryant Neal Vinas, the Boston Marathon bombers Tamerlan and Dzhokhar Tsarnaev, John Walker Lindh, Richard Reid, Bill Ayers, Osama Bin Laden, Timothy McVeigh, and Aafia Siddiqui). These parental and religious, moral, spiritual conflicts are often entwined at a subtle level. These homegrown terrorists are/ere in many ways very sensitive individuals who showed intense moral and spiritual concerns from early in their lives. Bill Ayers was an avid reader from his childhood onward. He wrote vividly about the depth of his concerns about moral integrity and values even as he lived the daily life of a revolutionary terrorist fugitive! Osama bin Laden, while supporting radical jihadi training and horrible terror missions, wrote sensitive and emotional poetry (Olsson 2007, 49–50). Future homegrown terrorists often show sudden intense preoccupation with reading and memorizing the Koran, the Bible, or other moral, religious, or political literature. This bibliophilic proclivity readily turns towards radical Internet offerings in our contemporary culture. Timothy McVeigh became obsessed with survivalist literature, the Turner Diaries, and Second Amendment rights. Homeland security and FBI interviewers should probe these areas thoroughly, not perfunctorily when interviewing suspected homegrown terrorists. It is especially important for the interviewer to look for the convergence of several or all of the psychodynamic factors because the impact of them on vulnerability for homegrown terrorist recruitment is cumulative.

The recruitment of homegrown terrorists involves the charismatic exploitation of "in-betweener" life situations by radical imams and Internet recruiters. Terror groups and their recruiters use well-recognized mind control and thought-reform techniques. They use social group atmospheres or virtual Internet atmospheres to accomplish their ends. They exploit normal tendencies for adolescents to rebel, separate, and individuate from their family of origin and seek noble ideals and causes, that is, the spiritual/religious identity domain.

The "personal pathways" of homegrown terrorists discussed in this book highlight the extreme level of susceptibility to recruitment by radical Islamist terror groups. The key variables are:

(1) Absent, disappointing, vicariously invested, or neglectful parents (associated with father/mother hunger or longing).
(2) Significant conflicts with authority.
(3) Identity struggles.
(4) The narcissistic injury triggered by the inability to find the dignity of a job, career path, and marital partner.
(5) Exposure to radical Islamist imams or recruiters, often encountered in radical mosques, prisons, or radical Muslim ghetto social networks.

These are common and ominous findings in the histories of future homegrown terrorists.

THE INTERNET MEDIA AS MESSAGE

The Internet is a potent recruitment tool as the now-deceased al-Awlaki proved extensively and effectively with his "in-betweener" recruits. Virtual detailed terrorist training camps are burgeoning on the Internet. Such Internet offerings are effective in thought-reform and emotional brainwashing. They are a kind of online prep school.

JIHADI PRISON "MISSIONS"

Radical Islamist prison chaplain imams or prison-visiting volunteers like Aafia Siddiqui in her early years in Boston could quite easily exploit positions as educational volunteers or clergy in American prisons. There, they could spread their gospel of hatred of America among angry prisoners. These young rebels in search of a cause are already bitter at law enforcement and authority. Prisons can be fertile soil for the recruitment of homegrown terrorists.

OBSERVATIONS AND RECOMMENDATIONS

(1) The ascendancy of the Internet and social media has in many ways made distinctions about the exact location and circumstances of the psychological birth of a terrorist less relevant. Homegrown versus foreign-grown fanaticism or terror plotting is not as crucial as identifying them early and dealing with them effectively. So-called lone wolves, lone wolf packs, or idealistic rebellious youths anywhere in the world can self-recruit or be recruited easily, especially if they are at in-betweener stages of life. The more authority figures condemn and verbally insult or demean young terrorists, the more they tend to become like some Robin Hoods or stars in an old James Dean movie like *Rebel without a Cause*. In essence, the media coverage and politicians' speechifying needs to be as skillful as was accomplished in Boston recently. Steady, clear, firmness with neutrality is helpful, macho rhetoric, not so much, because it only inflames terrorists and revenge seekers.

(2) *Special foreign student programs* should be established. High grades, high IQs, and academic prowess should not be the only admission criteria, nor the only ongoing evaluation process criteria of all graduate students. Interview techniques to allow detection of early signs of radicalization and fundamentalist rigidity would be helpful. In-depth admission group interviews and ongoing peer and faculty-student discussion groups should allow for sharing of the normal anxieties of immigrants. Candid discussions about cultural adjustments are necessary for life in diverse and economically struggling modern America.

(3) *Individual, couples, and family psychotherapy* should be readily available to any foreign student new to America and needing a talking cure process. Support groups for foreign students who feel anger, pain, or conflicts about American foreign policy should be available for ventilation. What foreign students see as the implications of American foreign policies for their cultural, religious, or spiritual values should be discussed openly.

(4) *A commission to study American immigration policy* as it relates to fundamentalist mentality should be appointed, especially as it appears in radical right wing groups and radical Islam. By implication, this group would delve deeply into the Judeo-Christian values that permeate and enrich our American democracy. Such information should be plainly available (up-front) to any foreign undergraduate/graduate student so that it can be discussed during the application process or at any evaluation event thereafter. All undergraduate and graduate programs in the United States should have a thorough lecture and discussion course on the U.S. Constitution, the Federalist Papers, and our political processes.

(5) *The 9/11 Commission Report (2012)* is elegantly written and is extremely valuable. It should be reviewed frequently by the heads of all relevant government agencies and used to assess ongoing updates of the recommendations. The 9/11 report urges that "stove-piping" needs to be constantly avoided by fluid open information sharing between all anti-terrorism agencies (Kean and Hamilton 2012, 416–19). For example, the Boston police were told too late about Tamerlan Tsarnaev's ominous trip back to Chechnya the year prior to the Boston Marathon bombing (Fox News 2013).

(6) Heads of all colleges and universities should appoint representatives to a council that studies immigration, visa, and foreign student relations on American campuses. This should also include study of radical right wing and radical left wing and anarchist student groups and their campus activities and behavior. Students themselves should participate fully so that norms and standards of lively, respectful, and healthy debate can be maintained.

(7) *Aids to Understanding the Complexity of Presidential Decision Making.* The George W. Bush Presidential Library at Southern Methodist University has a special section devoted to allowing any person to face and make many of the crucial decisions that President Bush made during his presidency. It is done in an electronic virtual decision-tree format that captures the complexity and emotional atmosphere of presidential decision making. This feature could be used at American high schools, colleges, and graduate schools. All students, and especially foreign students, could learn vividly what the president's war decisions in Iraq and Afghanistan were like. Debates, respectful disagreements, and meaningful discussions would help young people understand more fully what the conundrums and paradoxes were all about for a president. President Bush's book *Decision Points* and critical reviews would be helpful resources.

(8) Thoughtful high school, college, and graduate school teachers and clergy can benefit from re-assessing teachers and professors importance as role models, mentors, and wise counselors of students. (Dr. Malik Hasan, the Fort Hood Al Qaeda terrorist attacker, said that Awlaki was his teacher, mentor, and friend!) Teaching of technical concepts and didactic lectures are important, but so is an effort to

be aware of problems, conflicts, and strong emotions in students. Coffee shop discussions after class are valuable. Foreign students in particular can be drawn out about their perceptions and misperceptions about America. If the two bombers of the Boston Marathon had been engaged by their teachers beyond grades, winning wrestling/ boxing matches, and getting scholarships, perhaps they might have been engaged in more depth. A course in comparative religion's vigorous discussions might have allowed their anger to have been shifted away from bombs or at least been spotted. TV news reports that Tamerlan Tsarnaev had to be asked to leave a mosque on Martin Luther King Day when a speaker compared MLK favorably with the prophet Muhammad. Some people had tried to talk to Tamerlan but it is not clear to what depth mosque members followed up (Tamerlan Tsarnaev Mosque Outbursts Described 2013, 1).

On many occasions, moderate Muslims are too passive about confronting potential violent Salafist ideas and actions. Teachers and campus clergy need reliable and experienced mental health consultants. Teachers and professors too uncomfortable with roles as mentors and counselors for students would best seek other professional work. Compassionate mentoring can help prevent in-betweeners from being vulnerable to terror cult recruitment.

(9) Mahmoud Muhammad Taha—A Worthy Muslim Mentor for All Americans to Study: Taha, Sudan's Remarkable and Radically Peaceful Martyr of Islam

Taha was 76 years old when he was executed by Sudan's president Gaafar Nimeiry on January 18, 1985. He was a theologian and leader in the Sudanese Republican Party, and had always advocated liberal reform in Sudan and in Islam. Taha had played a prominent role in Sudan's struggle for independence.

Mahmoud Muhammad Taha is the anti-Qtub! Taha was hanged by an Arab dictator; he was executed in 1985 after protesting the imposition of Sharia in Sudan by President Gaafar al-Nimeiry. Taha became something highly unusual in contemporary Islam: a moderate martyr. Taha reconciled Muslim belief with 20th-century values. He was a revolutionary but diametrically opposite from Qtub (Packer 2006, 62).

After 9/11, millions of people around the world have heard of Qtub, but Taha is unfortunately unknown.

Islamism for many in the West has taken on the terrifying face of the masked jihadist of full-length identity-hiding veils, the religious militia, the blurred figure in the security video, the anti-American mob burning American flags (Packer 2006, 62). Taha was born in 1909 in Rufaa, a small town on the bank of the Blue Nile in central Sudan. When he was six years old, his mother died, and he and

his three siblings worked on his father's farm until his father Muhammad Taha died in 1920. Taha's aunt supported his education,
and he went on to engineering school at Gordon Memorial College
that eventually became the University of Khartoum. He graduated
in 1936 and spoke out iconoclastically against the educated elite of
Sudan who showed far too much patronage to the colonial powers
and traditional religious leaders. Mahmoud helped form the Republican Party in 1945 and was imprisoned for a year when he refused
to stop his political activities. The British governor pardoned him
but like so many malignant radical " 'bad guys" we have discussed,
this peaceful progressive "good guy" was put in prison again for
two years for leading a revolt against the British in his hometown
of Rufaa. Taha later described the "closed space" of prison in a way
that totally contrasted with Osama bin Laden, Qtub, the Blind Sheik
Rahman, al-Zawahiri, and others:

> When I settled in prison I began to realize that I was brought
> there by my Lord and thence I started my Khalwah [night
> vigil or religious retreat from the world] with him. (The Re-
> publican Thought, 1)

Taha's seclusion continued after his release in 1948. He prayed,
fasted, and read widely (Wells, Shaw, Russell, Lenin, Marx) in a
hut near his in-laws. While in seclusion, Taha spoke to few people
and had long unruly hair and bloodshot eyes. His wife brought him
simple food but her family urged her to divorce her formerly successful professional husband who many people thought was going
psychotic; she refused. In this three-year period, Taha developed his
radically new vision of the meaning of the Koran. After this period
of seclusion (1951), he dedicated the rest of his life to teaching it
(Packer 2006, 62).

Taha in his most important book called *The Second Message of Islam*
(1967) emphasizes that the Koran was revealed to Muhammad in
two phases: first in Mecca for 13 years when Muhammad addressed
humanity in general as filled with notions of freedom, equality, sincerity, worship, kindness, and peaceful coexistence. Then, in Medina, the writings grew full of rules, coercion, threats, and "law of
the sword." Packer aptly notes:

These two seem a bit like the Christian Old Testament [law and vio-
lence] and the New Testament [Love and atonement]. (Packer 2006, 63)

The Meccan verses are the ideal Islam of freedom and equality that
will be revived when humanity has reached a stage of development
or spiritual evolution when it is capable of accepting them. (Packer
2006, 63)

Taha used the name "Republican Brothers" for his new spiritual
movement and his disciples recall him as a transformed, saintly

presence like Christ or Socrates. Taha was a valued mature teacher who welcomed argument but with honesty, serenity, intellectual vigor, and charisma. Taha is sometimes compared to Gandhi by some Sudanese, and perhaps the 20th century was not ready for "the Second Message of Islam"! Taha like Jesus was constantly condemned by Sudanese and Egyptian clerics and his movement was under attack by the fundamentalist Muslim Brotherhood (Packer 2006, 63).

Packer in his fascinating article "The Moderate Martyr" eloquently captures the profound importance of Taha's ideas, which severely threatened the Sudanese Islamist hardliners. Packer says eloquently:

> What's truly remarkable about Taha is that he existed at all. In the midst of a gathering storm of Islamist extremism, he articulated a message of liberal reform that was rigorous, coherent, and courageous. His vision asked Muslims to abandon fourteen hundred years of accepted dogma in favor of a radical and demanding new methodology that would set them free from the burdens of traditional jurisprudence" (Packer 2006, 64)

Taha argued that Islamic law had harsh punishments and repressed free thought. Taha thought that the Koran's liberating ideas from the early centuries after Muhammad got closed off to critical revision for a millennium.

> When Taha spoke of "Sharia," he meant the enlightened message of the Meccan verses, which is universal and eternal (Packer 2006, 64).

Taha's teachings, not unlike Socrates's, collided with the power politics of the establishment. Sudan's military dictator Gaafar al-Nimeiry who seized power in 1969 was an opportunistic tyrant who used one political model after another (Marxism, Arab nationalism, pro-Americanism) to justify his control of Sudan. Turabi, the brilliant political henchman and manipulator, was an enemy of Taha. Taha had once alienated Turabi with a slight by saying, "Turabi is clever but not insightful." It is very likely that Taha's execution for apostasy was bogus and engineered by Turabi. Taha was offered a way to repent under Sharia but he refused and went to his hanging with head held high. He told his Republican brothers, "You back down. As for me, I know that I'm going to be killed. If not in court, the Muslim Brotherhood will kill me in secret" (Packer, 65).

If only Muslim political thinkers could fully grasp the dialectic process of democracy that Jefferson and Adams argued from, they would have never contemplated assassination as a political tool.

In the decade after Taha's death, the slithering Turabi was the political strategist of the Islamist revolution and the reign of terror of Omar al-Bashir. Turabi even declared that women and men are equal. Turabi, stealing from Taha, eventually claimed cynically that women can lead Islamic prayers and covering their heads is not obligatory. Apostasy is not a crime for Turabi later, and Muslim women can marry Christians and Jews! In Khartoum, people were amazed that Turabi sounded exactly like Taha! Turabi seemed to be aware of his terrible failures and Sudan's mire of mass death, slavery, civil war, and genocide. Taha would likely chuckle from his grave as his old enemy slithers to try to be a newborn "Republican Brother." Taha, if like Socrates could have many Platos to expound on his ideas, could be like a breath of spiritual fresh air to the Muslim world!

(10) Homeland security and counterterrorist professionals can benefit from using the concept of in-betweeners when they interact and study in-betweener countries and in-betweener communities. When combined with the application of Shaw's concept of the Personal Pathway to terrorism, early detection of individuals and communities where terror recruitment might flourish is possible. This is true whether the in-betweener community is in Chechnya, Yemen, Somalia, Iraq, Syria, Libya, Egypt, or America. There has been a highly charged political divide in American politics in recent times. It can be argued that America is an in-betweener country with in-betweener communities, communities that are in-between economic recession and job loss, and deeper economic distress and joblessness.

Economic uncertainty, joblessness, and petty religious squabbles find many Americans in-between jobs, between marriages, between school and job-searching, and, between traditional faith and church homes and atheism, agnosticism and secular-materialism. Particularly young people, and also other jobless and faithless individuals, are vulnerable to recruitment by cults, right wing groups, radical Muslim, and anarchist groups. Such groups provide simplistic and readymade roads to identity or negative identity.

(11) *Calling Out Narrow-minded Atheists Possessing Fundamentalist Mentality.* An articulate, well-reasoned, philosophically well-founded apologetics, and compassionate teaching of Judeo-Christian values and traditions to high school, college, and graduate students helps prevent spiritual and moral vacuum in youths. This liberal education can help prevent nihilism and situations like "Harvard's Culture of Despair" that Alston Chase thought had such a profoundly negative effect on Ted Kaczynski, the Unabomber. Atheism in some of its rigid fundamentalist forms can clearly be as destructive as fundamentalist mentality is among radical Islamist terrorist

recruiters. An atheistic atmosphere of youthful existential despair or tepid perfunctory Judaism or Christianity can present more opportunity for recruitment to Islam and subsequent radicalization. Adam Gadahn, Omar Hammami, John Walker Lindh, and Colleen LaRose are probable examples. Their situations show how tepid traditional religious commitments and conflicted, dysfunctional family situations combine with in-betweener situations to form a vulnerability to homegrown terrorist recruitment.

(12) Clergy knowledgeable in comparative religions, philosophers, theologians, psychologists, and psychiatrists' knowledgeable about brainwashing and terror cult recruitment can be helpful to assist homeland security staff and foreign policy makers and implementers. They can help continually confront and correct the distorted theology that is woven into terrorist groups' recruitment techniques and propaganda.

Afterword

What We All
Can Do to Help Prevent
Homegrown Terrorism

Homeland security and law enforcement authorities frequently remind us through the media that all Americans should stay alert to unusual and suspicious activities in the environment. If we notice anything suspicious, we are urged to report it immediately to the authorities. Empathy about a friend, acquaintance, relative, or student's in-betweener stress-related issues is as important as vigilance about immediate physical danger.

The author has some suggestions for school teachers, professors, parents, and community members. In our interactions in the home, at work, school, on the Internet, with friends, acquaintances, and neighbors, we can be alert to behaviors and signs of the possibility that a person is vulnerable to homegrown terror recruitment, or showing religious or political verbal signs of radicalization.

1. A young person is vulnerable to radicalization when he or she is in-between schools, in-between high school and college, in-between se-mesters, in-between college and a job, in-between jobs, or in-between marriages or intimate relationships. An individual or family in-between religions or that has had an abrupt change in religious affiliation, such as espousing more radical fundamentalist views or declaring complete loss of religious commitment, is at risk for radicalization. Families in-between countries such as in an immigrant situation are sometimes ripe for radicalization. The Tsarnaev family's dysfunctions are a good example. They were stressed by divorce, immigrant status, and abrupt religious changes.

   To develop friendships with immigrant families and foreign students is helpful to both persons. Coaches, neighbors, and relatives of the Tsarnaev brothers and their family did reach out and try to be helpful and supportive. Retrospectively, the efforts made were too shallow. Tamerlan Tsarnaev in particular was an accomplished boxer, physically intimidating, and a narcissistic bully who assaulted his own girlfriend (Remick 2013, 19). Being a good friend and calling out Tamerlan could be a frightening and intimidating task (*POLITICO* 2013, 1). Friends of the Tsarnaev brothers had plenty of chances to spot radical hate material on their social media texting and the websites over which they got excited. If a person gets violently angry over vigorous discussion of religious convictions, it is often a sign of **fundamentalist mentality** and possibly an underlying radicalization.

2. An in-betweener who begins to spend inordinate amount of time in monolithic biblical or Koranic study, memorization, and angry/ aggressive vocalization of religious or political ideas or ideology can be of concern. This is particularly true if an angry, resentful, judgmental, or overtly hostile tone or behavior accompanies the preaching or proselytizing efforts. Most all of us enjoy a lively debate or discussion about politics or religion but we should be wary if we feel fearful of others during such discussion. Tamerlan Tsarnaev had to be quieted down and asked to leave a Boston area mosque on Martin Luther King Day when he stood up to protest a visiting imam's stating that MLK and Muhammad were alike. (*POLITICO* and AP 2013, 1) This event and several other "tiny tests" and even more overtly aggressive or assaultive behavior on Tamerlan's part were not followed up by authorities (Remick 2013, 19). Nor was the Russian security's concern about him that was reported to the FBI. Rather than pulling away from a verbally acting-out in-betweener, professors, clergy, and friends should be curious. They/we should best stay engaged with the person until it is clear what danger might be involved or not so much danger.

3. Finally, high school, college, and graduate school teachers should frequently revisit the self-examining exploration of their role as mentors, counselors, and frontline assessors of the mental stability and general level of stress of their students. Teaching involves not just the conveying of technical educational material, but also an empathetic presence and listening ear. Empathy is a key word for all of us in regard to homegrown terror prevention—not merely suspicion and vigilance about immediate danger.

Appendix I

Timeline of Homegrown Terrorist Actions

December 26–31, 1969—Bernadine Dohrn spoke truculently about forming underground collectives for an "armed struggle" and justified violence against the U.S. government.

March 6, 1970—Greenwich Village townhouse explosion. Weather Underground members were constructing a powerful nail-containing bomb intended for use at a non-commissioned officers' dance at the Fort Dix, New Jersey, U.S. Army base. The bomb exploded prematurely killing Weather Underground members Diana Oughton, Ted Gold, and Terry Robbins.

June 9, 1970—New York Police headquarters bombing. Ayers and others of Weather Underground claimed responsibility for a dynamite bombing after a six-minute warning.

September 13, 1970—Prison break of Timothy Leary, "The Old Man," out of the California prison at San Luis Obispo. Facilitated by the Weather Underground, Leary and his wife were transported to Algeria. Described in detail by Ayers in *Fugitive Days.*

May 19, 1972—Pentagon Building bombing. On Ho Chi Minh's birthday, the Weather Underground placed a bomb in a bathroom in the Air Force wing of the Pentagon.

February 26, 1993—First World Trade Center Tower truck bombing, New York City. Six persons dead, one thousand injured. Mastermind—Ramzi Yousef, financed by Khalid Sheikh Mohammed and inspired by Omar Abdel Rahman (the Blind Sheik), mentor and colleague of Osama bin Laden.

April 19, 1995—Timothy McVeigh's truck bomb destroyed the Alfred P. Murrah Federal Building in Oklahoma City, killing 168 and injuring hundreds more.

April 24, 1995—After the publication of his "Unabomber Manifesto" in *The New York Times,* Ted Kaczynski, the Unabomber, ended his 1978–1995 series of 16 bombings that killed three and injured 23.

August 7, 1998—Simultaneous Al Qaeda bombings of U.S. Embassies in Nairobi. Kenya (212 killed, 4,000 wounded), mastermind—Abdullah Mohammed who was inspired by Osama bin Laden and Ayman al-Zawahiri, and Dar es Salaam, Tanzania (11 dead and 85 wounded), done by local members of the Egyptian Islamic Jihad.

October 12, 2000—Suicide bombing of the USS *Cole* at Port of Aden, Yemen. Seventeen U.S. sailors killed, thirty-nine injured. Ahd al-Rahim al-Nashiri (homegrown Saudi terrorist), inspired by Osama bin Laden and Al Qaeda.

September 11, 2001—"9/11" Attack on the World Trade Towers in New York and the Pentagon in Washington, D.C. The Al Qaeda inspired and planned attack killed approximately 2,996 people.

November 25, 2001—John Walker Lindh was captured by Afghan Northern Alliance soldiers as he participated as a Taliban soldier. John had purportedly spent seven weeks in an Al Qaeda training camp near Kandahar, Afghanistan, where he met Osama bin Laden (Ashley 2005, 2).

December 22, 2001—The "Shoe-Bomber" Richard Reid was overpowered by passengers on Flight 63 from Paris to Miami as he tried to light a fuse connected to explosives in his shoe.

May 8, 2002—Jose Padilla, the would-be "Dirty Bomber," was arrested at Chicago's O'Hare Airport before he could pursue his bomb plan.

January 2008—Bryant Neal Vinas was captured by Pakistani forces after joining and participating with Al Qaeda in two rocket attacks on U.S. forces in Afghanistan. Vinas, a native Long Islander, had also provided Al Qaeda with information about the Long Island Rail Road for a thwarted plan for bombings.

July 2008—Aafia Siddiqui was arrested in Afghanistan and in September of 2010 she was sentenced to 86 years in prison for assault to commit murder of her interrogators. She also was implicated in other plans for bomb attacks against the United States.

November 5, 2009—Psychiatrist Nidal Malik Hasan made a solo terrorist attack at Fort Hood, Texas, murdering 13 and wounding 23. Major Hasan was significantly inspired by master homegrown American Islamist recruiter Anwar al-Awlaki.

December 25, 2009—Umar Farouk Abdulmutullab, the so-called Underwear Bomber, was thwarted by passengers aboard Flight 253 from Amsterdam to Detroit before he could detonate the plastic explosives in his underwear. The intent was to kill the 289 people on board and people below in the city.

February 1, 2011—Colleen LaRose, "Jihad Jane," pleaded guilty to charges of trying to recruit Islamist terrorists to wage violent jihad and planned murder of the Swedish artist Lars Vilks, who did a cartoon depicting Mohammad.

July 29, 2011—Pfc. Nasar Jason Abdo was arrested for planning a bomb and small arms attack on a Killeen, Texas, restaurant frequented by Fort Hood soldiers. Abdo expressed sympathy and support for Dr. Hasan.

April 15, 2013—Dzhokhar and Tamerlan Tsarnaev placed two pressure cooker bombs at the finish line area of the 2013 Boston Marathon. They killed three and injured 264 others.

Appendix II

Violent Radicalization and Homegrown Terrorism Prevention Act

110th CONGRESS
1st Session
H. R. 1955
AN ACT

To prevent homegrown terrorism, and for other purposes.

Be it enacted by the Senate and House of Representatives of the United States of America in Congress assembled,

SECTION 1. SHORT TITLE

This Act may be cited as the Violent Radicalization and Homegrown Terrorism Prevention Act of 2007'.

SEC. 2. PREVENTION OF VIOLENT RADICALIZATION AND HOMEGROWN TERRORISM

(a) In General-Title VIII of the Homeland Security Act of 2002 (6 U.S.C. 361 et seq.) is amended by adding at the end the following new subtitle:

'Subtitle J—Prevention of Violent Radicalization and Homegrown Terrorism

'SEC. 899A. DEFINITIONS

'For purposes of this subtitle:

'(1) COMMISSION—The term 'Commission' means the National Commission on the Prevention of Violent Radicalization and Homegrown Terrorism established under section 899C.

The Congressional Record of the 110th Congress of the United States House of Representatives, October 23, 2007.

'(2) VIOLENT RADICALIZATION—The term 'violent radicalization' means the process of adopting or promoting an extremist belief system for the purpose of facilitating ideologically based violence to advance political, religious, or social change.

'(3) HOMEGROWN TERRORISM—The term 'homegrown terrorism' means the use, planned use, or threatened use, of force or violence by a group or individual born, raised, or based and operating primarily within the United States or any possession of the United States to intimidate or coerce the United States government, the civilian population of the United States, or any segment thereof, in furtherance of political or social objectives.

'(4) IDEOLOGICALLY BASED VIOLENCE—The term 'ideologically based violence' means the use, planned use, or threatened use of force or violence by a group or individual to promote the group or individual's political, religious, or social beliefs.

'SEC. 899B. FINDINGS

'The Congress finds the following:

'(1) The development and implementation of methods and processes that can be utilized to prevent violent radicalization, homegrown terrorism, and ideologically based violence in the United States is critical to combating domestic terrorism.

'(2) The promotion of violent radicalization, homegrown terrorism, and ideologically based violence exists in the United States and poses a threat to homeland security.

'(3) The Internet has aided in facilitating violent radicalization, ideologically based violence, and the homegrown terrorism process in the United States by providing access to broad and constant streams of terrorist-related propaganda to United States citizens.

'(4) While the United States must continue its vigilant efforts to combat international terrorism, it must also strengthen efforts to combat the threat posed by homegrown terrorists based and operating within the United States.

'(5) Understanding the motivational factors that lead to violent radicalization, homegrown terrorism, and ideologically based violence is a vital step toward eradicating these threats in the United States.

'(6) Preventing the potential rise of self radicalized, unaffiliated terrorists domestically cannot be easily accomplished solely through traditional Federal intelligence or law enforcement efforts, and can benefit from the incorporation of State and local efforts.

'(7) Individuals prone to violent radicalization, homegrown terrorism, and ideologically based violence span all races, ethnicities, and religious beliefs, and individuals should not be targeted based solely on race, ethnicity, or religion.

'(8) Any measure taken to prevent violent radicalization, homegrown terrorism, and ideologically based violence and homegrown terrorism in the United States should not violate the constitutional rights, civil rights, or civil liberties of United States citizens or lawful permanent residents.

'(9) Certain governments, including the United Kingdom, Canada, and Australia have significant experience with homegrown terrorism and the United States can benefit from lessons learned by those nations.

'SEC. 899C. NATIONAL COMMISSION ON THE PREVENTION OF VIOLENT RADICALIZATION AND IDEOLOGICALLY BASED VIOLENCE

'(a) Establishment—There is established within the legislative branch of the Government the National Commission on the Prevention of Violent Radicalization and Homegrown Terrorism.

'(b) Purpose—The purposes of the Commission are the following:

'(1) Examine and report upon the facts and causes of violent radicalization, homegrown terrorism, and ideologically based violence in the United States, including United States connections to non-United States persons and networks, violent radicalization, homegrown terrorism, and ideologically based violence in prison, individual or 'lone wolf' violent radicalization, homegrown terrorism, and ideologically based violence, and other faces of the phenomena of violent radicalization, homegrown terrorism, and ideologically based violence that the Commission considers important.

'(2) Build upon and bring together the work of other entities and avoid unnecessary duplication, by reviewing the findings, conclusions, and recommendations of—

'(A) the Center of Excellence established or designated under section 899D, and other academic work, as appropriate;

'(B) Federal, State, local, or tribal studies of, reviews of, and experiences with violent radicalization, homegrown terrorism, and ideologically based violence; and

'(C) foreign government studies of, reviews of, and experiences with violent radicalization, homegrown terrorism, and ideologically based violence.

'(c) Composition of Commission—The Commission shall be composed of 10 members appointed for the life of the Commission, of whom—

'(1) one member shall be appointed by the President from among officers or employees of the executive branch and private citizens of the United States;

'(2) one member shall be appointed by the Secretary;

'(3) one member shall be appointed by the majority leader of the Senate;

'(4) one member shall be appointed by the minority leader of the Senate;

'(5) one member shall be appointed by the Speaker of the House of Representatives;

'(6) one member shall be appointed by the minority leader of the House of Representatives;

'(7) one member shall be appointed by the Chairman of the Committee on Homeland Security of the House of Representatives;

'(8) one member shall be appointed by the ranking minority member of the Committee on Homeland Security of the House of Representatives;

'(9) one member shall be appointed by the Chairman of the Committee on Homeland Security and Governmental Affairs of the Senate; and

'(10) one member shall be appointed by the ranking minority member of the Committee on Homeland Security and Governmental Affairs of the Senate.

'(d) Chair and Vice Chair—The Commission shall elect a Chair and a Vice Chair from among its members.

'(e) Qualifications—Individuals shall be selected for appointment to the Commission solely on the basis of their professional qualifications, achievements, public stature, experience, and expertise in relevant fields, including, but not limited to, behavioral science, constitutional law, corrections, counterterrorism, cultural anthropology, education, information technology, intelligence, juvenile justice, local law enforcement, organized crime, Islam and other world religions, sociology, or terrorism.

'(f) Deadline for Appointment—All members of the Commission shall be appointed no later than 60 days after the date of enactment of this subtitle.

'(g) Quorum and Meetings—The Commission shall meet and begin the operations of the Commission not later than 30 days after the date on which all members have been appointed or, if such meeting cannot be mutually agreed upon, on a date designated by the Speaker of the House of Representatives. Each subsequent meeting shall occur upon the call of the Chair or a majority of its members. A majority of the members of the Commission shall constitute a quorum, but a lesser number may hold meetings.

'(h) Authority of Individuals to Act for Commission—Any member of the Commission may, if authorized by the Commission, take any action that the Commission is authorized to take under this Act.

'(i) Powers of Commission—The powers of the Commission shall be as follows:

'(1) IN GENERAL—

'(A) HEARINGS AND EVIDENCE—The Commission or, on the authority of the Commission, any subcommittee or member thereof, may, for the purpose of carrying out this section, hold hearings and sit and act at such times and places, take such testimony, receive such evidence, and administer such oaths as the Commission considers advisable to carry out its duties.

'(B) CONTRACTING—The Commission may, to such extent and in such amounts as are provided in appropriation Acts, enter into contracts to enable the Commission to discharge its duties under this section.

'(2) INFORMATION FROM FEDERAL AGENCIES—

'(A) IN GENERAL—The Commission may request directly from any executive department, bureau, agency, board, commission, office, independent establishment, or instrumentality of the Government, information, suggestions, estimates, and statistics for the purposes of this section. The head of each such department, bureau, agency, board, commission, office, independent establishment, or instrumentality shall, to the extent practicable and authorized by law, furnish such information, suggestions, estimates, and statistics directly to the Commission, upon request made by the Chair of the Commission, by the chair of any subcommittee created by a majority of the Commission, or by any member designated by a majority of the Commission.

'(B) RECEIPT, HANDLING, STORAGE, AND DISSEMINATION— The Committee and its staff shall receive, handle, store, and disseminate information in a manner consistent with the operative statutes, regulations, and Executive orders that govern the handling, storage, and dissemination of such information at the department, bureau, agency, board, commission, office, independent establishment, or instrumentality that responds to the request.

'(j) Assistance from Federal Agencies—

'(1) GENERAL SERVICES ADMINISTRATION—The Administrator of General Services shall provide to the Commission on a reimbursable basis administrative support and other services for the performance of the Commission's functions.

'(2) OTHER DEPARTMENTS AND AGENCIES—In addition to the assistance required under paragraph (1), departments and agencies of the United States may provide to the Commission such services, funds, facilities, and staff as they may determine advisable and as may be authorized by law.

'(k) Postal Services—The Commission may use the United States mails in the same manner and under the same conditions as departments and agencies of the United States.

'(l) Nonapplicability of Federal Advisory Committee Act—The Federal Advisory Committee Act (5 U.S.C. App.) shall not apply to the Commission.

'(m) Public Meetings—

'(1) IN GENERAL—The Commission shall hold public hearings and meetings to the extent appropriate.

'(2) PROTECTION OF INFORMATION—Any public hearings of the Commission shall be conducted in a manner consistent with the protection of information provided to or developed for or by the Commission as required by any applicable statute, regulation, or Executive order including subsection (i)(2)(B).

'(n) Staff of Commission—

'(1) APPOINTMENT AND COMPENSATION—The Chair of the Commission, in consultation with the Vice Chair and in accordance with rules adopted by the Commission, may appoint and fix the compensation of a staff director and such other personnel as may be necessary to enable the Commission to carry out its functions, without regard to the provisions of title 5, United States Code, governing appointments in the competitive service, and without regard to the provisions of chapter 51 and subchapter III of chapter 53 of such title relating to classification and General Schedule pay rates, except that no rate of pay fixed under this subsection may exceed the maximum rate of pay for GS-15 under the General Schedule.

'(2) STAFF EXPERTISE—Individuals shall be selected for appointment as staff of the Commission on the basis of their expertise in one or more of the fields referred to in subsection (e).

'(3) PERSONNEL AS FEDERAL EMPLOYEES—

'(A) IN GENERAL—The executive director and any employees of the Commission shall be employees under section 2105 of title 5, United States Code, for purposes of chapters 63, 81, 83, 84, 85, 87, 89, and 90 of that title.

'(B) MEMBERS OF COMMISSION—Subparagraph (A) shall not be construed to apply to members of the Commission.

'(4) DETAILEES—Any Federal Government employee may be detailed to the Commission without reimbursement from the

Commission, and during such detail shall retain the rights, status, and privileges of his or her regular employment without interruption.

'(5) CONSULTANT SERVICES—The Commission may procure the services of experts and consultants in accordance with section 3109 of title 5, United States Code, but at rates not to exceed the daily rate paid a person occupying a position at level IV of the Executive Schedule under section 5315 of title 5, United States Code.

'(6) EMPHASIS ON SECURITY CLEARANCES—The Commission shall make it a priority to hire as employees and retain as contractors and detailees individuals otherwise authorized by this section who have active security clearances.

'(o) Commission Personnel Matters—

'(1) COMPENSATION OF MEMBERS—Each member of the Commission who is not an employee of the government shall be compensated at a rate not to exceed the daily equivalent of the annual rate of basic pay in effect for a position at level IV of the Executive Schedule under section 5315 of title 5, United States Code, for each day during which that member is engaged in the actual performance of the duties of the Commission.

'(2) TRAVEL EXPENSES—While away from their homes or regular places of business in the performance of services for the Commission, members of the Commission shall be allowed travel expenses, including per diem in lieu of subsistence, at rates authorized for employees of agencies under subchapter I of chapter 57 of title 5, United States Code, while away from their homes or regular places of business in the performance of services for the Commission.

'(3) TRAVEL ON ARMED FORCES CONVEYANCES—Members and personnel of the Commission may travel on aircraft, vehicles, or other conveyances of the Armed Forces of the United States when such travel is necessary in the performance of a duty of the Commission, unless the cost of commercial transportation is less expensive.

'(4) TREATMENT OF SERVICE FOR PURPOSES OF RETIREMENT BENEFITS—A member of the Commission who is an annuitant otherwise covered by section 8344 or 8468 of title 5, United States Code, by reason of membership on the Commission shall not be subject to the provisions of such section with respect to membership on the Commission.

'(5) VACANCIES—A vacancy on the Commission shall not affect its powers and shall be filled in the manner in which the original appointment was made. The appointment of the replacement member shall be made not later than 60 days after the date on which the vacancy occurs.

'(p) Security Clearances—The heads of appropriate departments and agencies of the executive branch shall cooperate with the Commission to expeditiously provide Commission members and staff with appropriate security clearances to the extent possible under applicable procedures and requirements.

'(q) Reports—

'(1) FINAL REPORT—Not later than 18 months after the date on which the Commission first meets, the Commission shall submit to the President and Congress a final report of its findings and conclusions, legislative recommendations for immediate and long-term countermeasures to violent radicalization, homegrown terrorism, and ideologically based violence, and measures that can be taken to prevent violent radicalization, homegrown terrorism, and ideologically based violence from developing and spreading within the United States, and any final recommendations for any additional grant programs to support these purposes. The report may also be accompanied by a classified annex.

'(2) INTERIM REPORTS—The Commission shall submit to the President and Congress—

'(A) by not later than 6 months after the date on which the Commission first meets, a first interim report on—

'(i) its findings and conclusions and legislative recommendations for the purposes described in paragraph (1); and

'(ii) its recommendations on the feasibility of a grant program established and administered by the Secretary for the purpose of preventing, disrupting, and mitigating the effects of violent radicalization, homegrown terrorism, and ideologically based violence and, if such a program is feasible, recommendations on how grant funds should be used and administered; and

'(B) by not later than 6 months after the date on which the Commission submits the interim report under subparagraph (A), a second interim report on such matters.

'(3) INDIVIDUAL OR DISSENTING VIEWS—Each member of the Commission may include in each report under this subsection the individual additional or dissenting views of the member.

'(4) PUBLIC AVAILABILITY—The Commission shall release a public version of each report required under this subsection.

'(r) Availability of Funding—Amounts made available to the Commission to carry out this section shall remain available until the earlier of the expenditure of the amounts or the termination of the Commission.

'(s) Termination of Commission—The Commission shall terminate 30 days after the date on which the Commission submits its final report.

'SEC. 899D. CENTER OF EXCELLENCE FOR THE STUDY OF VIOLENT RADICALIZATION AND HOMEGROWN TERRORISM IN THE UNITED STATES

'(a) Establishment—The Secretary of Homeland Security shall establish or designate a university-based Center of Excellence for the Study of Violent Radicalization and Homegrown Terrorism in the United States (hereinafter referred to as 'Center') following the merit-review processes and procedures and other limitations that have been previously established for selecting and supporting University Programs Centers of Excellence. The Center shall assist Federal, State, local and tribal homeland security officials through training, education, and research in preventing violent radicalization and homegrown terrorism in the United States. In carrying out this section, the Secretary may choose to either create a new Center designed exclusively for the purpose stated herein or identify and expand an existing Department of Homeland Security Center of Excellence so that a working group is exclusively designated within the existing Center of Excellence to achieve the purpose set forth in subsection (b).

'(b) Purpose—It shall be the purpose of the Center to study the social, criminal, political, psychological, and economic roots of violent radicalization and homegrown terrorism in the United States and methods that can be utilized by Federal, State, local, and tribal homeland security officials to mitigate violent radicalization and homegrown terrorism.

'(c) Activities—In carrying out this section, the Center shall—

'(1) contribute to the establishment of training, written materials, information, analytical assistance and professional resources to aid in combating violent radicalization and homegrown terrorism;

'(2) utilize theories, methods and data from the social and behavioral sciences to better understand the origins, dynamics, and social and psychological aspects of violent radicalization and homegrown terrorism;

'(3) conduct research on the motivational factors that lead to violent radicalization and homegrown terrorism; and

'(4) coordinate with other academic institutions studying the effects of violent radicalization and homegrown terrorism where appropriate.

'SEC. 899E. PREVENTING VIOLENT RADICALIZATION AND HOMEGROWN TERRORISM THROUGH INTERNATIONAL COOPERATIVE EFFORTS

'(a) International Effort—The Secretary shall, in cooperation with the Department of State, the Attorney General, and other Federal Government entities, as appropriate, conduct a survey of methodologies implemented by foreign nations to prevent violent radicalization and homegrown terrorism in their respective nations.

'(b) Implementation—To the extent that methodologies are permissible under the Constitution, the Secretary shall use the results of the survey as an aid in developing, in consultation with the Attorney General, a national policy in the United States on addressing radicalization and homegrown terrorism.

'(c) Reports to Congress—The Secretary shall submit a report to Congress that provides—

'(1) a brief description of the foreign partners participating in the survey; and

'(2) a description of lessons learned from the results of the survey and recommendations implemented through this international outreach.

'SEC. 899F. PROTECTING CIVIL RIGHTS AND CIVIL LIBERTIES WHILE PREVENTING IDEOLOGICALLY BASED VIOLENCE AND HOMEGROWN TERRORISM

'(a) In General—The Department of Homeland Security's efforts to prevent ideologically based violence and homegrown terrorism as described herein shall not violate the constitutional rights, civil rights, or civil liberties of United States citizens or lawful permanent residents.

'(b) Commitment to Racial Neutrality—The Secretary shall ensure that the activities and operations of the entities created by this subtitle are in compliance with the Department of Homeland Security's commitment to racial neutrality.

'(c) Auditing Mechanism—The Civil Rights and Civil Liberties Officer of the Department of Homeland Security shall develop and implement an auditing mechanism to ensure that compliance with this subtitle does not violate the constitutional rights, civil rights, or civil liberties of any racial, ethnic, or religious group, and shall include the results of audits under such mechanism in its annual report to Congress required under section 705.'

(d) Clerical Amendment—The table of contents in section 1(b) of such Act is amended by inserting at the end of the items relating to title VIII the following:

'SUBTITLE J—PREVENTION OF VIOLENT RADICALIZATION AND HOMEGROWN TERRORISM

Passed the House of Representatives October 23, 2007.

Appendix III

Recommended Reading List

American news networks tend to ignore the responses of moderate Muslims to these events sometimes, but this website provides a Muslim perspective and defense to the perception that the Muslim community forsakes these actions.

http://theamericanmuslim.org/tam.php/features/articles/al-shabab/0020052

This is a group of Somali imams' response to Al-Shabaab's actions.

http://theamericanmuslim.org/tam.php/features/articles/powerpoint_presentations/

PowerPoint presentations

http://theamericanmuslim.org/tam.php/features/articles/american_muslim_resources_collections_of_articles_and_references/

Resource Center that includes lists of Fatwas given by Muslim leaders against terrorism as well as discussions about the Koran and Hadith relating to extremism.

Ayers, Bill. (2001). *Fugitive Days: Memoirs of an Antiwar Activist*. Boston: Beacon Press.

Bergen, Peter. (2006). *The Osama bin Laden I Know: An Oral History of Al Qaeda's Leader*. New York: Free Press.

Bodansky, Yossef. (1999). *Bin Laden: The Man Who Declared War on America*. New York: Prima Publishing, Random House.

Chase, Alton. (2003). *Harvard and the Unabomber: The Education of an American Terrorist*. New York: W. Norton & Company.

Coll, Steve. (2005). "Young Osama: How He Learned Radicalism and May Have Seen

America." *The New Yorker* (December 12, 2005): 48–50 and 59–61.

Fields, Rona. (1977). *Society under Siege: A Psychology of Northern Ireland*. Philadelphia: Temple University Press.

Lifton, Robert. (1989). *Thought Reform and the Psychology of Totalism: A Study of "Brainwashing" in China.* Chapel Hill: University of North Carolina Press, 419–437. (Originally published by W.W. Norton, 1961.)

Michel, Lou., and D. Herbeck. (2001). *American Terrorist: Timothy McVeigh & the Tragedy at Oklahoma City.* New York: Regan Books/Avalon Books of HarperCollins.

Olsson, Peter. (2005). *Malignant Pied Pipers of Our Time: A Psychological Study of Destructive Cult Leaders: From the Rev. Jim Jones to Osama bin Laden.* Baltimore: PublishAmerica.

Olsson, Peter. (2007). *The Cult of Osama: Psychoanalyzing Bin Laden and His Magnetism for Muslim Youths.* Westport, CT; London: Praeger Security International of Greenwood Publishing, now ABC-CLIO.

Packer, George. (2006). Letter from Sudan, "The Moderate Martyr: A Radically Peaceful Vision of Islam." *The New Yorker* (September 11, 2006): 61–69.

Pipes, Daniel. (1983). *In the Path of God: Islam and Political Power.* New York: Basic Books. (Originally published by Transaction Publishers, New Brunswick, New Jersey, 2002)

Sageman, Marc. (2004). *Understanding Terror Networks.* Philadelphia: University of Pennsylvania Press, pp. 82–91, 175–84.

Shaw, Eric. (1986). "Political Terrorists: Dangers of Diagnosis, Alternatives to the Psychopathological Model." *International Journal of Law and Psychiatry* 8: 188–189.

Stern, Jessica. (2003). *Terror in the Name of God: Why Religious Militants Kill.* New York: Harper Collins, pp. 220–22.

Sullivan, Andrew. (2001). "This Is a Religious War." *The New York Times Magazine* (October 7, 2001): 1–5.

Wright, Lawrence. (2006). *The Looming Tower: Al-Qaeda and The Road to 9/11.* Alfred A. Knopf: New York.

Glossary

Key Concepts and Definitions

Many of the definitions in this addendum expand upon and refer to terms and concepts used within the book. Definitions are based on those in the American Psychiatric Glossary *(APG), 1975 and 1994, and Moore and Fine's* Psychoanalytic Concepts *(PC), 1990, as well as other sources cited in the glossary.*

Acting out: Expression of unconscious emotional conflicts or feelings in actions rather than words. The person is not consciously aware of the meaning of such acts (*APG* 1994).

Ambivalence: The coexistence of two opposing drives, desires, feelings, or emotions toward the same person, object, or goal. These may be conscious or partly conscious; or one side of the feelings may be unconscious. Example: Love and hate toward the same person (*APG* 1975, 13–14).

Anniversary reaction: An emotional response to a previous event occurring at the same time of year. Often the event involved a loss and the reaction involves a depressed state. The reaction can range from mild to severe and may occur at any time after the event (*APG* 1994, 10).

Applied psychoanalysis: Use of insights and concepts gained from clinical psychoanalysis to enlarge or deepen the understanding of various aspects of human nature, culture, and society. Most prominent have been studies in the fields of history, biography, literature, art, religion, mythology, and anthropology. The application of psychoanalysis to biography and history has given rise to the terms psychobiography and psychohistory, which some scholars suggest, that leads to an artificial compartmentalization in the recording of human history (*PC* 1990, 27).

Borderline personality disorder (BPD): BPD is characterized by instability of interpersonal relationships, self-image, affects, and control over impulses.

Manifestations may include frantic efforts to avoid real or imagined abandonment; unstable, intense relationships that alternate between extremes of idealization and devaluation; recurrent self-mutilation or suicidal threats; and inappropriate, intense, or uncontrolled anger (*APG* 1994, 99).

Brainwashing: A method for systematically changing attitudes or altering beliefs through psychological stress techniques (Random House College Dictionary 2001, 162).

Condensation: A psychological process often present in dreams in which two or more concepts are fused so that a single symbol represents the multiple components (*APG* 1975, 36.).

Conscious: The content of the mind or mental functioning of which one is aware (*APG* 1975, 36).

Countertransference: The psychiatrist's partly unconscious or conscious emotional reaction to his patient (*APG* 1975, 38).

Denial: A defense mechanism, operating unconsciously, used to resolve emotional conflict and allay anxiety by disavowing thoughts, feelings, needs, or external reality factors that are consciously intolerable (*APG* 1975, 41).

Displacement: A defense mechanism, operating unconsciously, in which an emotion is transferred from its original object to a more acceptable substitute used to allay anxiety. (*APG* 1975, 44).

Doppelganger: A ghostly double or counterpart of a living person (Random House Webster's New Collegiate Dictionary, 393). This notion can be associated with the concept of a twinship transference talked about in Self Psychology. See Twinship Transference.

Ego: In psychoanalytic theory, one of the three major divisions in the model of the psychic apparatus [mind]; the others being the id and the superego. The ego represents the sum of certain mental mechanisms, such as perception and memory, and specific defense mechanisms. It serves to mediate between the demands of the primitive instinctual drives (id), of internalized parental and social prohibitions (superego) and of reality. The compromises between these forces achieved by the ego tend to resolve intrapsychic conflict and serve an adaptive and executive function. [Note: Psychiatric usage of the term should not be confused with common usage, which denotes self-love or selfishness.] (*APG* 1994, 45).

Ego ideal: The part of the personality that comprises the aims and goals for the self; usually refers to the conscious or unconscious emulation of significant figures with whom one has identified. The ego ideal emphasizes what one should do or be in contrast to what one should not be or not do (*APG* 1994, 46).

Fundamentalist mentality: Olsson (2004) says, "Fundamentalists, no matter how sweet, kind, or pious they behave on the surface, are convinced that they have THE superior moral, ethical, theological, epistemological, political, and spiritual truth. Fundamentalists, (Christian, Jewish, Muslim, Sikh, Hindu, even some anti-war pacifists) experience in a delusional way their own way of thinking and believing as "THE one and only way." Fundamentalist mentality is more prevalent and seems more readily embraced at times of severe social turmoil, rapid social change, economic hardship, and related oppression of minority groups. The radical fundamentalists of any religious or political group are willing to confidently condemn to hell and or kill those who do not believe exactly as they do. They are the final judges, juries, and "holy" executioners. There is no room for honest discussion, doubt or debate. They are their own gods themselves (Olsson 2007, 152).

Group self: There is a parallel process by which an individual's sense of himself as part of a group is formed. In essence, inner representations of our self and our self-in-a-group are parallel and conjoined early developmental and maturational experiences (Olsson 2005, 150); In 1976, Heinz Kohut first described the group self (Kohut 1978).

Groupthink: Irving Janis in 1972 described the "Groupthink Hypothesis" in explaining the Bay of Pigs mistake early in John F. Kennedy's presidency. Janis said, "Members of any small cohesive group tend to maintain esprit de corps by unconsciously developing a number of shared illusions and related norms that interfere with critical thinking and reality testing." A contention of this book is that radical Islamist leaders and Western leaders can become victims of this process (Janis 1972).

Ideology: The expression of values and beliefs underlying behavior (Olsson/Sapp 1997).

In-betweeners: A term to describe Margaret Singer's observation (Singer 1995) that any normal person is vulnerable to recruitment and exploitation by a cult group during periods of rapid change in his or her life. Or, who are at "in-between times" or key transitions in their lives (Singer 1995, 21.) "In-betweeners" are in between relationships, in between divorce and remarriage, in between high school and college, in between jobs, and so on (Olsson 2007, 113). Olsson contends that nations, tribes, and societies can also become "in-betweeners" and are more vulnerable to terror cult recruitment during rapid social, economic, and political change.

Introjection: A defense mechanism, operating unconsciously, whereby loved or hated external objects are taken within oneself symbolically. The converse of projection may serve as a defense against conscious recognition of intolerable hostile impulses" (*APG* 1975, 92).

Linking object: Something actually present in the environment that is psychologically contaminated with various aspects of the dead and the self. Such objects mainly provide a locus for externalized contact between aspects of the mourner's self-representation and the aspects of the (mental) representation of the deceased" (Volkan 1981, 20, 101).

Negative identity formation: Erik Erikson (1964), who wrote so eloquently about adolescence, described young people who have lost respect for their parents' values and ethical standards as experiencing negative identity formation. They join a throng or worldwide community of adolescent rebels who in their tragic disappointment in their parents' generation mock and devalue their fallen and shallow role models. They often also limit their own potential satisfaction and accomplishments.

Object (intrapychic): The internalized representation, in the mind of one person, of another person's mind and its function in the perceived interpersonal relationship (Olsson 2007, 154).

Object relations: The emotional bonds that exist between an individual and another person, as contrasted with his interest in, and love for himself: usually described in terms of his capacity for loving and reacting appropriately to others (*APG* 1975, 110); Object relations are one of the important domains in assessing an individual's psychodynamics (Olsson 1994).

Overdetermination: The concept of multiple unconscious causes of an emotional reaction or symptom (*APG* 1994, 95).

overinclusiveness: A type of association disorder observed in some schizophrenia patients. The individual is unable to think in a precise manner because of an inability to keep irrelevant elements outside perceptual boundaries. (In the author's opinion overinclusive thinking can also occur in manic patients or normal persons who are highly anxious or stressed.) (Mosby's Medical Dictionary, 8th edition. 2009, Elsevier).

Paleologic: See VonDomarus principle and Condensation.

Preconscious: Thoughts that are not in immediate awareness but that can be recalled by conscious effort (*APG* 1975, 122).

Primary process: In psychoanalytic theory, the generally unorganized mental activity characteristic of unconscious mental life. Seen in less disguised form in infancy and in dreams. It is marked by the free discharge of energy and excitation without regard to the demands of the environment, reality, or logic. (See secondary process.) (*APG* 1975, 123).

Projection: A defense mechanism, operating unconsciously in which what is emotionally unacceptable in the self is unconsciously rejected and attributed to others (*APG* 1994, 108).

Pseudo-homosexual dynamics: Lionel Ovesey's concept that many people's participation in homosexual behavior is not connected to sexual gratification but rather is related to power, dependency, and submission.

Psychiatry: The medical specialty that studies and treats a variety of disorders that affect the mind-mental illnesses. Because our minds create our humanity and our sense of self, our specialty cares for illnesses that affect the core of our existence. The common theme that unites all mental illnesses is that they are expressed in signs that reflect the activity of the mind—memory, mood, and emotion, fear and anxiety, sensory perception, attention, impulse control, pleasure, appetitive drives, willed actions, executive functions, ability to think in representations, language, creativity and imagination, consciousness, introspection, and a host of other mental activities. Our science explores the mechanisms of these activities of the mind and the way their disruption leads to mental illness. When disruption occurs in syndromal patterns in these multiple systems in the mind, we observe disorders that we diagnose as dementias, schizophrenias, mood disorders, anxiety disorders, or other mental illnesses. Our patients, our science, and our history define our specialty, not by the form of treatment provided (e.g., psychotherapy, medications), nor by the presence or absence of known mechanisms of illness. Its province defines psychiatry: the mind. (Andreasen 1997)

Psychodynamics: The aspect of psychoanalytic theory that explains mental phenomena, such as thoughts, feelings, and behavior, as the results of interacting and opposing goal-directed or motivational forces. The theory focuses on the interplay of such forces, illuminating processes, developments, progressions, regressions, and fixations. The concept of the psychic apparatus as a tripartite structure of the mind (Ego, Id, and Superego) aids in understanding the dynamics postulated." (*PC* 1990, 152–53)

Psychogenesis: Attempts to understand "psychogenetics" are based on the premise that what happens in the mind in the present is influenced or even determined by events and processes that happened in the past (i.e., psychic determinism). Discontinuities and phenomena that appear random and unexplainable can be understood by following a chain of causation in the sequential relationship of psychic events arising from a complex interplay of conscious and unconscious forces (*PC* 1990, 153).

Rationalization: A defense mechanism, operating unconsciously, in which an individual attempts to justify or make consciously tolerable by plausible means, feelings, or behavior that otherwise would be intolerable. (Radical Islamists like Bin Laden's pronouncements about the murder of western women, children, and noncombatants during Al Qaeda's terror attacks.)

Reaction formation: A defense mechanism, operating unconsciously, wherein attitudes and behavior are adopted that are the opposites of impulses the individual harbors either consciously or unconsciously (e.g., excessive moral zeal may be a reaction to strong but repressed asocial or antisocial impulses) (*APG* 1975, 133).

Regression: Partial or symbolic return to earlier patterns of reacting or thinking (*APG* 1975, 116).

Repression: A defense mechanism, operating unconsciously, that banishes unacceptable ideas, fantasies, affects, or impulses from consciousness or that keeps out of consciousness what has never been conscious. Although not subject to voluntary recall, the repressed material may emerge in disguised form. Often confused with the conscious mechanism of suppression (*APG* 1975, 135).

Right wing ideology: An ideology that is absolute with no shades of meaning. It involves dualistic thinking, for example, "us vs them," black and white, childlike (Sapp 1997, 1).

Secondary process: In psychoanalytic theory, mental activity and thinking characteristic of the ego and influenced by the demands of the environment. Characterized by organization, systematization, intellectualization, and logical adult thought and action (*APG* 1975, 139).

Self-object/self-object transference: In the self-psychology of Kohut, a transference relationship in which the therapist serves as a therapeutic self-object for the patient by providing needed self-enhancing and self-regulatory functions and emotional stability . . . which can subsequently be internalized and transformed into the structure of the patient's self" (*APG* 1994, 136).

Self-psychology: An elaboration of the psychoanalytic concepts of narcissism and the self, developed by Heinz Kohut and his colleagues. Self-psychology is characterized by emphasis on the vicissitudes of the structure of the self; the associated subjective, conscious, preconscious, and unconscious experience of selfhood; and the self in relation to its sustaining self-objects (*PC* 1990, 174–79); "The basic premise of the psychoanalytic psychology of the self is the defining position it assigns to empathy and introspection" (Kohut 1985, 73).

Splitting: A mental mechanism in which the self or others are viewed as all good or all bad, with failure to integrate the positive and negative qualities of self and others into cohesive images. Often the person alternately idealizes and devalues the same person" (*APG* 1994, 128).

Sublimation: A defense mechanism, operating unconsciously, by which instinctual drives, consciously unacceptable, are diverted into personally and socially acceptable channels (*APG* 1994, 129).

Thanatos: (Death Instinct) In Freudian theory, the unconscious drive toward dissolution and death. Coexists with and is in opposition to the life instinct or eros" (*APG*, 34); Many modern psychoanalysts such as the author would be skeptical of Freud's strictly dualistic theory here, but some would use it to describe clinical situations where for various reasons there is excessive destructive aggression towards another person or the self (Olsson 2007, 156).

Topographic model of the mind: Freud's model of the structure of the mind, first described in terms of the conscious-preconscious-unconscious and a simple conflict theory of the conscious opposing the unconscious (*APG* 1994, 134).

Totem and taboo: Freud's 1913 allegorical essay based on anthropological sources. Freud uses psychoanalytic formulations to describe the period in primitive man's development when despotic father figures led small tribes where the leader considered all the women in the tribe his exclusive property. The young men (sons) grew jealous and rose up to kill the father and consume him in a totem feast. The sons' guilt, conflict, and remorse made them impotent with the women of the tribe. The powerful ghost of the father was displaced on to a fierce animal or totem. Freud connected these totems with primitive tribe's use of human sacrifice, cannibalism, and totemic prohibitions except for special festivals or occasions. Without effective and ethical leadership, even some modern groups and tribes can regress and resort to what the psychoanalyst Bion called basic or primitive assumption groups called (1) fight-flight, (2) dependency, (3) pairing agendas. Postwar Iraq is replete with examples of these dynamics.

Transference: The unconscious assignment to others of feelings and attitudes that were originally associated with important figures (parents, siblings, etc.) in one's life. The transference relationship follows the pattern of its prototype. The psychiatrist utilizes this phenomenon as a therapeutic tool to help the patient understand emotional problems and their origins (*APG* 1994, 135).

Twinship transference: One of the three major types of self-object transferences (mirroring, idealizing, and alter-ego[twinship]) (*APG* 1994, 136).

Umma: Islamic global community or supernation.

Unconscious: That part of the mind or mental functioning of which the content is only rarely subject to awareness. It is a repository for data that has never been conscious (primary repression) or that may have been conscious and later repressed (secondary repression) (*APG* 1975, 151).

References and Works Consulted

Adam Gadahn Fast Facts—CNN.com. Available at: http://www.cnn .com/2013/03/23/us/adam-gadahn-fast-facts/index.html. Accessed September 10, 2013.

Andreasen, N. 1997. "What Is Psychiatry?" Editorial in *The American Journal of Psychiatry* 154(5): 592.

Anderson, C. 2010. New al-Qaida Leader Knows US Well. MSNBC: AP Exclusive. Available at: http://www.msnbc.msn.com/id/38588735/ns/us_news-security?GT1=43001. Accessed August 6, 2010.

Anderson, H. 2013. BBC News, Washington. Available at: http://www.bbc .co.uk/news/world-us-canada-23541341.

Angry and Defiant Zubeidat Tsarnaeva Insists She Isn't a Radical. *Catholic Online* (News Consortium), April 29, 2013. Available at: http://www.catholic .org/printer_friendly.php?section=Cathcom&id=50712

Arieti, S. 1967. "The Intrapsychic Self." In *Feeling. Cognition. and Creativity in Health and Mental Illness*. New York: Basic Books.

Arieti, S. 1974. *Interpretation of Schizophrenia*. New York: Basic Books.

Ashley, B. 2005. "Silent Treatment: New Details Are Emerging about John Walker Lindh's Volatile Time in Afghanistan." *Marin Independent Journal*.

Ayers, B. 2001. *Fugitive Days: Memoirs of an Antiwar Activist*. Boston: Beacon Press.

Bartosiewicz, P. 2009. *The Intelligence Factory: How America Makes Its Enemies Disappear*. Report, *Harper's Magazine*: 42–51.

Becker, E. 1973. *The Denial of Death*. New York: The Free Press of Macmillan.

Bergen, P. 2001. *Holy War, Inc: Inside the Secret World of Osama bin Laden*. New York: Touchstone, Simon and Schuster.

Bergen, P. 2006. *The Osama bin Laden I Know: An Oral History of Al Qaeda's Leader*. New York: Free Press.

Berman, P. 2003. "The Philosopher of Islamic Terror." *The New York Times* (March 23).

Bernfeld, S. 1923. *Uber eine typische form de männlichen pubertät*. Imago, p. 9.

Beutel, Alejandro. "Radicalization and Homegrown Terrorism in Western Muslim Communities: Lessons Learned for America." Minaret of Freedom Institute: August 30, 2007. Available at: http://www.minaret.org/MPAC%20Backgrounder.pdf.

Bezhan, Frud. "Jihadist Teachings Drawn Back into Classroom in Pakistani Province." *Radio Free Europe Radio Liberty*, September 25, 2013. Available at: http://www.rferl.org/content/pakistan-education-jihad-islam-khyber/25092236.html.

Bodansky, Y. 1999. *Bin Laden: The Man Who Declared War on America*. New York: Prima Publishing, Random House.

Booth, W. 1998. "Kaczynski Sentenced to Four Life Terms." *Washington Post* (May 5, 1998): A02. Available at: http://www.washintonpost.com. Accessed September 21, 2013.

Burns, J. 2009. "Terror Inquiry Looks at Suspects Time in Britain." *The New York Times* (December 30). Available at: http://www.nytimes.com/2009/12/30/world/europe/30nigerian.html.

Bush, G. 2010. *Decision Points*. New York: Crown Publishers.

Carlile, J. 2006. Islamic Radicalization Feared in Europe's Jails. MSNBC, July 7. Available at: http://www.msnbc.msn.com/id/13733782/.

Caryl, Christian. "'Misha' Speaks: An Interview with the Alleged Boston Bomber's 'Svengali'." *The New York Review of Books*, April 28, 2013. Available at: http://www.nybooks.com/blogs/nyrblog/2013/apr/28/tamerlan-tsarnaev-misha-speaks/.

Chase, A. 2000. Harvard and the Making of the Unabomber. *The Atlantic Online*, Available at: http://www.theatlantic.com/past/docs/issues/2000/06/chase1-4.htm.

Chase, A. 2003. *Harvard and the Unabomber: The Education of an American Terrorist*. New York: W. Norton & Company.

Coll, Steve. 2005. "Young Osama: How He Learned Radicalism and May Have Seen America." *The New Yorker* (December 12): 48–50 and 59–61.

Dixon, Robyn. 2013. "Wanted American Militant Reported Dead in Somalia. Originally—*Los Angeles Times*. Published in *The Keene Sentinel*. World/Nation section (September 13): A5.

Dolan, Eric W. "Parents of American Jihadist Speak Out about Their Son." *The Raw Story*, May 17, 2012. Available at: http://www.rawstory.com/rs/2012/05/17/parents-of-american-jihadist-speak-out-about-their-son/.

D'Olivio, Amy, and Shane Fitzpatrick. 2010. "The Muslim-American Community's Response to Global Jihadism." Available at: http://lawenforcementtoday.com/tag/law-enforcement-community-in-the-united-states/.

Dorn, R. 1974. "The Geography of Play and the Analysis of the Adult." *International Journal of Psychoanalytic Psychotherapy* 3: 90–115.

D'Souza, D. 2009. *Life after Death: The Evidence*. Washington, DC: Regnery Publishing, Inc. *What's So Great about Christianity*. ygodinstitute.org and dineshdsouza.com.

Eisenhower, Dwight D. (1961) "Military-Industrial Complex Speech." Transcribed from *Public Papers of the Presidents*, as found in the United

States Archives. Available at: http://coursesa.matrix.msu.edu/~hst306/documents/indust.html

Elliot, M. 2004. "The Shoe Bomber's World." *TIME* (February16). Available at: http://www.time.com/time/printout/0.8816,203478,00.html.

Elliott, A. The Jihadist Next Door. Available at: http://www.nytimes .com/2010/01/31/magazine/31jihadist_t.html?_r=1&emc=eta1. Accessed September 28, 2010.

Engel, B. 2005. *Breaking the Cycle of Abuse.* New Jersey: Wiley-Blackwell.

Erikson, E. 1964. *Insight and Responsibility.* New York. Norton and Company, 99.

Faurby, Ib, and Marta-Lisa Magnussen. 1999. "The Battle(s) of Grozny." *Baltic Defence Review* 2: 75–87.

Fernandez, M, and J. James Dao. 2011. *New York Times.* Available at: http://www.nytimes.com/2011/07/30/us/30awol.html?_r=0.

Fields, R. 1986. "Psychological Profile of a Terrorist." Paper presented at the American Psychological Association Convention, Washington, DC.

Fox, Alison. 2013. "Neighbor Describes Friendly Argument on Religion, Politics," *The Wall Street Journal*: 1–3. Available at: http://online.wsj.com/article/SB10001324127887324493704578434902549213938.html.

Freud, A. 1936. *The Ego and the Mechanisms of Defense.* New York: International Universities Press, 137–38.

Freud, S. 1919. *The Uncanny. The Standard Edition of the Complete Works of Sigmund Freud,* ed. J. Strachey. Vol. 17. London: Hogarth Press.

Freud, S. 1921. *Group Psychology and the Analysis of the Ego. The Standard Edition* Vol.8. London: Hogarth Press.

Freud, S. 1926. *Inhibitions, Symptoms and Anxiety. Standard Edition* 20: 77–174.

Freud, S. 1930. *The Future of an Illusion/Civilization and Its Discontents. The Standard Edition of the Complete Psychological Works of Sigmund Freud,* ed. J. Stachey, 141–43. Vol. 21. London: Hogarth Press.

Freud, S. 1933. *New Introductory Lectures on Psychoanalysis. The Standard Edition of the Complete Psychological Works of Sigmund Freud,* ed. J. Strachey, 171. Vol. 22. London Hogarth Press.

Gall, Carlotta, and Thomas de Waal. 1988. *Chechnya: Calamity in the Caucasus.* New York: New York University Press.

Gill, Avleen. "Role of Military in Pakistan Politics." *New Delhi Television Limited,* 2010. Available at: http://www.ndtvmi.com/b4/dopesheets/avleen.pdf.

Glendinning, C. 1990. "Notes towards a Neo-Luddite manifesto" 1990, Utne Reader.

Goldberg, J. 2006. "Letter from Gaza: The Forgotten War: The Overlooked Consequences of Hamas's Actions. . *The NewYorker* (September 11). Available at: http://www.newyorker.com/archive/2006/09/11/060911fa_fact2.

Hafez, Mohammed M. 2003. *Why Muslims Rebel: Repression and Resistance in the Islamic World.* Boulder, CO: Lynne Rienner Publishers.

Herridge, C., and P. Browne. Accused Fort Hood Shooter Releases Excerpts from His Sanity Board Hearing. Available at: http://www.foxnews.com/us/2013/08/05/accused-fort-hoodshooter-releases-excerpts-from-his-sanity-board-hearing.

Herzog, James. 2001. *Father Hunger.* New York: Analytic Press.

Holliday, S. Extremist Reeducation and Rehabilitation in Saudi Arabia. Available at: www.jamestown.org/terrorism/news/article.php?articleid= 2373620. By Dr. Christopher Boucek (Princeton University), reviewed by Sam Holliday.

Holzer, H. M. Taliban John. Available at: http://www.henrymarkholzer.citymax.com/talibanjohn.html/.

Horner, A. 1992. "The Role of the Female Therapist in the Affirmation of Gender in Male Patients." *Journal of the American Academy of Psychoanalysis* 20: 599–610.

Horner, A. 2006. "Culture, Personality and the Psychodynamics of Islamic Terrorists." *The FORUM of the American Academy of Psychoanalysis and Psychodynamic Psychiatry* 51(1): 1–3.

Hunt, L. Feiz Mohammad: One Lead for the Boston Bombings. Available at: http://thediplomat.com/asean-beat/2013/04/22/feiz-muhammad-one-lead-for-the-boston-bombing/.

Hughes, C. J. 2010. "Pakistani Scientist Found Guilty of Shootings." *The New York Times* (February 4). Available at: http://www.nytimes.com/ 2010/02/04/nyregion/04siddiqui.html.

Isaacson, Walter. (2007) *Einstein: His Life and Universe.* New York: Simon and Schuster.

Janis, Irving. 1972. *Victims of Groupthink: A Psychological Study of Foreign-Policy Decisions and Fiascoes.* Boston: Houghton Mifflin, 35–36.

Johnson, A., and S. Szurek. 1952 "The Genesis of Antisocial Acting Out in Children and Adults." *The Psychoanalytic Quarterly* 21: 323.

Johnson, Kevin. 2011. "AWOL Soldier Charged in Bombing Plan on Texas Post." *USA Today.* Available at: http://www.usatoday.com/news/mil itary/2011-07-28-awol-soldier-targets-forthood.

Johnson, Sally. 1998. "Psychological Evaluation of Theodore Kaczynski" Available at: http://www.courttv.com/trials/unabomber/documents/psycho logicalhtml. Court TV. Accessed February 4, 2009.

Karoliszyn, Henrick, and John Marzulli. "Long Island-Bred Terrorist's Plea Reveals LIRR Plot." *New York Daily News* (July 24, 2009). Available at: http://www.nydailynews.com/news/crime/long-island-bred-terrorist-plea-reveals-lirr-plot-article-1.398453.

Kates, B. 2010. "Al Qaeda-Linked New Jersey Man Sharif Mobley, Arrested in Yemen, Worked in Nuclear Power Plants." *New York Daily News* (March 12).

Kean, T, and L. Hamilton. 2002. *The 9/11 Commission Report.* New York, London: W.W. Norton.

Kernberg, O. 1975. *Borderline Conditions and Pathological Narcissism.* New York: Jason Aronson.

Kernberg, O. 1984, "The Couch at Sea: Psychoanalytic Studies of Group and Organizational Leadership." *The International Journal of Group Psychotherapy* 34: 1–17.

Khatchadourian, R. 2007. "Reporter at Large: Azzam the American: The Making of an Al Qaeda Homegrown." *New Yorker* (January 22).

Kierkegaard, S. 1843, 1940. *Stages on Life's Way*, trans. W. Lowrie. New York: Schocken Books, 271.

Knezys, Stasys, and Romanas Sedlickas. 1999. *The War in Chechnya.* College Station: Texas A&M University Press.

Kohut, H. 1971. *The Analysis of the Self.* New York. International Universities Press.

Kohut, H. 1978. "Creativeness, Charisma, Group Psychology." In *Search for the Self: Selected Writings of Heinz Kohut: 1950–1978,* ed. Paul Ornstein. Vol. 2. New York: International Universities Press.

Krikorian, G., and H. G. Reza. 2006. "Orange County Man Rises in al Qaeda: "Azzam the American," or Adam Gadahn, Has Moved from Translator to Propagandist." *Los Angeles Times* (October 8), Sunday home edition.

Lalwani, P. 2011. Attachment Disorder in Adults. Available at: http://buzzle .com/articles/attachment-disorder-in-adults.html, pp. 1–2.

Lawrence, B., ed. 2005. *Messages to the World: The Statements of Osama Bin Laden.* trans. J. Howarth. London: Verso.

Levi, M. 2009. "Key Points: President Obama's Cairo Speech." *CBSNews.com* (June 4).

Lewis, C. S. 1952. *Mere Christianity,* 2001 edition. New York: Harper Collins, 118–19.

Lifton, R. 1989. *Thought Reform and the Psychology of Totalism: A Study of "Brainwashing" in China.* Chapel Hill: University of North Carolina Press. (Orig. pub. 1961, W.W. Norton, 419–37).

LINDH—*Time* Magazine, October 2002 issue. "The American Taliban." Availableathttp://www.washingtonpost.com/wp-dyn/content/gallery/2009/11/10/GA2009111000920. Accessed November 13, 2009.

LINDH Parents of American Jihadist Speak Out about Their Son. *The Raw Story.* May 17, 2012.

Mahler, M. S. 1975. "Discussion of "Healthy Parental Influences on the Earliest Development of Masculinity in Baby Boys" by R. J. Stoller, Margaret S. Mahler Symposium, Philadelphia. *Psychoanalytic Forum* 5: 244–47.

McFadden, R. 1996. *Prisoner of Rage*—A special report; From a Child of Promise to the Unabomber Suspect. *The New York Times.* Available at: http://www.nytimes.com/1996/05/26/us/prisoner-of-rage-a-special-report-from-a-child. Accessed September 21, 2013.

McKinley, J, and J. Dao. 2009. "Fort Hood Gunman Gave Signals before His Rampage." *New York Times* (November 8). Available at: http://www .nytimes.com/2009/11/09/us/09reconstruct.html.

McLuhan, M. 1964. *Understanding Media: The Extensions of Man.* New American Library, New York: McGraw-Hill Company.

Meloy, J. R. 1988. "On the Relationship between Primary Process and Thought Disorder." *Journal of the American Academy of Psychoanalysis:* 48–55. Available at: http://www.forencis.org/.

Meloy, J. R. 2004. "Indirect Personality Assessment of the Violent True Believer." *Journal of Personality Assessment.* Available at: http://www.forencis.org.

Meredith, M. 2005. *The Fate of Africa: From the Hopes of Freedom to the Heart of Despair.* New York: Public Affairs of the Perseus Books Group.

Michel L., and D. Herbeck. 2001. *American Terrorist: Timothy McVeigh & The Tragedy at Oklahoma City.* New York: Regan Books /Avalon Books of Harper Collins.

Mirahmadi, Hedieh, M. Farooq, and Waleed Ziad. "Pakistan's Civil Society: Alternative Channels to Countering Violent Extremism." *World Organization for Resource Development and Education*, October 2012. Available at: http://www.worde.org/wp-content/uploads/2012/10/WORDE-Report-Pakistan-Civil-Society-Alternative-Channels-to-CVE.pdf.

Moore. N, and B. Fine. 1990. *Psychoanalytic Terms and Concepts*. New Haven: American Psychoanalytic Association and Yale University Press.

Mosely, A. 2001 *Just War Theory. The Internet Encyclopedia of Philosophy*. Available at: http://www.utm.edu/research/iep/j/justwar.htm.

Neumeister, L. July 4, 2009. "Details Emerge on Woman Accused of al-Qaida Ties." Available at: http://www.guardian.co.uk/world/feedarticle/85921 08?FORM=ZZNR.

Olsson, P. 2005. *Malignant Pied Pipers of Our Time: A Psychological Study of Destructive Cult Leaders: From the Rev. Jim Jones to Osama bin Laden*. Baltimore: Publish America.

Olsson, P. 2007. *The Cult of Osama: Psychoanalyzing Bin Laden and His Magnetism for Muslim Youths*. Westport, CT: London: Praeger Security International of Greenwood Publishing, 20–23.

Ovesey, L. 1969. *Homosexuality and Pseudohomosexuality*. New York: Science House.

Ozment, Katherine. 2004. "Who's Afraid of Aafia Siddiqui?" *Boston Magazine* (October). Available at: http://www.bostonmagazine.com/2006/05/whos-afraid-of-aafia-siddiqui/.

Packer, G. 2006. "Letter from Sudan 'The Moderate Martyr: A radically peaceful vision of Islam.'" *The New Yorker* (September 11): 61–69.

Padilla, Jose. 2005. Profile: Jose Padilla. BBC.co.uk, November 22, 2005. Available at: http://news.bbc.co.uk/1/hi/world/americas/2037444.stm/.

Papps, N. 2005. "The Man behind the Mask: Terror Target Melbourne." *Melbourne Herald Sun* (September 13).

Parens, H. 1979. *The Development of Aggression in Early Childhood*. New York: Jason Aronson.

Perez-Pena, R. 1996. "On the Suspects Trail: The Suspect; Memories of His Brilliance, and Shyness, but Little Else." *The New York Times*. Available at: http://www.nytimes.com/1996/04/05/us/suspect-s-trail-suspect-memories-his-brilliance-sh. Accessed September 21, 2013.

Pipes, D. 1983. *In the Path of God: Islam and Political Power*. Originally published by New York: Basic Books (2002) edition by Transaction Publishers, New Brunswick, New Jersey.

Pipes, D. 2011. "Another Islamist Soldier Turns Terrorist." Available at: http://www.washingtontimes.com/news/2011/aug/1/another-islamist-soldier-turns-terrorist.

Rangel, L. 1969. "Choice-Conflict and the Decision-Making Function of the Ego—A Psychoanalytic Contribution to Decision Theory." *International Journal of Psycho-Analysis* 50: 599–602.

Rangel, L. 1971. "The Decision-Making Process: A Contribution from Psychoanalysis." *The Psychoanalytic Study of the Child* 26: 425–52.

Rangel, L. 1973. "A Psychoanalytic Perspective Leading to the Syndrome of the Compromise of Integrity." *International Journal of Psycho-Analysis* 55: 3–12.

Rangel, L. 1989. "Action Theory within the Structural View." *International Journal of Psycho-Analysis* 70: 189–203.

Rashid, Ahmed. 2002. *Taliban: Militant Islam, Oil and Fundamentalism in Central Asia.* New Haven: Note Bene Publications, Yale University Press.

Rashid, Ahmed. 2008. *Descent into Chaos: The United States and the Failure of Nation Building in Pakistan, Afghanistan, and Central Asia.* New York: Viking.

Reid, R. 2001. Who Is Richard Reid? BBC.co.uk, pp. 2–4, December 28, 2001, world edition. Available at: http://news.bbc.co.uk/2/hi/uk_news/1731568.stm/.

Remick, D. 2013. "The Culprits." *The New Yorker* (April 29): 19.

Robinson, A. 2001. *Bin Laden: Behind the Mask of the Terrorist.* New York: Arcade Publishing. 2001.

Ross, B, and R. Schwartz. 2009. "Major Hassan's E-mail: 'I Can't Wait to Join You' in Afterlife: American Official Says Accused Shooter Asked Radical Cleric When Is Jihad Appropriate, ABC News, November19, 2009. Availableat:http://abcnews.go.com/Blotter/official-nida-hasan-mail-wait-join-afterlife/story?id=9130339.

Rotella, S. and J. Meyer. "A Young American's Journey into Al Qaeda; Bryant Neal Vinas of Long Island, N.Y . . . Tells Investigators How He Trained and Fought Alongside Terrorists." Available at: http:// articles.latimes.com/2009/jul/24/nation/na-american-jihadi24 2–26–10.

Saathoff, Gregory B. 2009. "Forensic Psychiatric Evaluation; CST Aafia Siddiqui," March 15. Court document (reprinted by the NEFA Foundation).

Sacchetti, M. 2013. Dzhokhar Tsarnaev's College Friends Indicted. *The Boston Globe*, August 8, 2013. Available at: http://www.bostonglobe.com/metro/2013/08/08/dzhokhar-tzarnaev-college-friends-indicted. Accessed August 21, 2013.

Sageman, M. 2004. *Understanding Terror Networks.* Philadelphia: University of Pennsylvania Press, 82–91, 175–84.

Sakwa, Richard. 2005. *Chechnya: From Past to Future.* London: Anthem Press.

Sapp, A. "White Supremacy and Violent Right Wing Ideology." Group for the Advancement of Psychiatry: Committee on International Relations, Spring 1997—Meeting notes from Dr. Sapp's presentation and the group discussions and chairperson's research, pp. 1–5.

Scroggins, D. 2012. *Wanted Women: Faith, Lies & the War on Terror: The Lives of Ayaan Hirsi Ali & Aafia Siddiqui.* New York: Harper Collins.

Shane, S, and J. Dao. 2009. "Tangle of Clues about Suspect at Fort Hood." *New York Times* (November 14). Available at: http://www.nytimes.com/2009/11/15/us/15hasan.html.

Shaw, E. 1986. "Political Terrorists: Dangers of Diagnosis, Alternatives to the Psychopathological Model." *International Journal of Law and Psychiatry* 8: 188–89.

Siddiqui, Aafia. 2001. "Separating the Components of Imitation." PhD diss, Brandeis University. Available at: http://www.worldcat.org/title/separating-the-components-of-imitation/oclc/47642755.

Silver, C. and T. Coleman. 2013. Non-Belief in the United States. University of Tennessee at Chattanooga. Dissertation named, "Atheism, Agnosticism, and Nonbelief: A Qualitative and Quantitative Study of Type and Narrative," pp. 1–8. Available at: http://www.atheismresearch.com/.

Singer, M. 1995. *Cults in Our Midst: The Hidden Menace in Our Everyday Lives.* San Francisco: Jossey-Bass Publishers, 21, 64–69.

Stern, J. 2003. *Terror in the Name of God: Why Religious Militants Kill.* New York: Harper Collins, 220–22.

Stockman, Farah. 2004. "Roxbury Address Eyed in FBI Probe." *The Boston Globe* (April 10). Available at: http://www.boston.com/news/local/articles/2004/04/10/roxbury_address_eyed_in_fbi_probe/.

Stockman, Farah. 2010. "Scientist Decries Guilty Verdict." *The Boston Globe* (February 4). Available at: http://www.boston.com/news/nation/articles/2010/02/04/scientist_decries_guilty_verdict/.

Suddath, Claire. 2009. Bryant Neal Vinas: An American in AlQaeda. Available at: http://content.time.com/time/nation/article/0,8599,1912512,00.html.

Sullivan, A. 2001. "This Is a Religious War." *The New York Times* (October 7): 1–5.

Tamerlan Tsarnaev Mosque Outbursts Described. Associated Press-POLITICO.com. Available at: http://www.politico.com/story/2013/04/tamertan-tsarnaev-mosque-outbursts-described-9047. Accessed September 5, 2013.

Thomas, P. B. Krolowitz, and S. Clarke. 2010. ABC NEWS Exclusive: "Jihad Jane's" Ex-Husband Says Suspect (Colleen LaRose) Was Bible-Carrying Churchgoer. Available at: http://abcnews.go.com/print?id=10080443.

Tsarnaev D Left Note in Boat Explaining Motives, CBS report says. Reuters in Washington. Thursday May 16, 2013. Guardian.co.uk.

Tyrangiel, J. 2001. The Taliban Next Door. *TIME,* December 9, 2001, pp. 1–4. Available at: http://www.time.com/time/printout/0,8816,187564,00.html.

Tzarnaev, Tamerlan—"I Don't Understand Them," Bombing Suspect Said of Americans. Available at: http://www.foxnews.com/us/2013/04/19/surviving-boston-marathon-bombing-suspect-hails-from-overseas-been-in-us-for/#ixzz2Xq99wNMl.

Tzarniev, T. Boston Police Chief Says Feds Never Shared Warnings about Bomber. Fox News.com. Available at: http://foxnews.com/politics/2013/05/09/.

Umar Farouk Abdulmutallab's Online Posts Detail "Loneliness." MSNBC.COM., 2005, pp. 1–3, Available at: http://www.msnbc.msn.com/id/34618228/ns/us_news-washington_post/print/1/displaymo. Accessed December 29, 2009.

US News. A Hunt for "the Pilot." Available at: http://www.usnews.com/news/articles/030407/7terror_3htm. Accessed March 30, 2003.

Volkan, V. 1981. *Linking Objects and Linking Phenomenon.* New York: International Universities Press, Inc.

Volkan, V. 1986. *The Need to Have Enemies and Allies: From Clinical Practice to International Relationships.* Northvale, NJ: Jason Aronson.

Volkan, V. 1995. *The Infantile Psychotic Self and Its Fates: Understanding and Treating Schizophrenics and Other Difficult Patients.* Northvale, NJ: Jason Aronson.

Volkan, V. 2004. *Blind Trust: Large Groups and Their Leaders in Times of Crisis and Terror.* Charlottesville, VA. Pitchstone Publishing.

Von Domarus, E. 1944. "The Specific Laws of Logic in Schizophrenia." In *Language and Thought in Schizophrenia,* ed. A. Kasinin, 104–115. New York: Norton.

Weather Underground. 2013. "Weather Underground Organization (Weatherman)" (PDF). FBI. August 20, 1976. Archived from the original on October 31, 2008. Accessed October 18, 2008.

Webb, Carolyn. "Sheikh Sparks Outrage." *The Age* (January 19, 2007). http://www.theage.com.au/news/national/sheikh-sparks-outrage/2007/01/18/1169095914411.html?page=fullpage.

White, E. 2012. Nigerian Underwear Bomber Gets Life in Prison. *The Washington Times* (February 16). Available at: http://www.washingtontimes.com/news/2012/feb16/nigerian-underwear-bomber-faces-life.

Wines, M., and I. Lovett. 2013. The Dark Side, Carefully Masked. *The New York Times* Wines, Michael and Ian Lovett. Dzhokhar Tsarnaev's Dark Side, Carefully Masked—NYTimes.com. Available at: http://nytimes.com/2013/05/05us/dzhokhar-tsarnaevs-dark-side-carefully-masked.ht.

Wright, L. 2006. "Annals of Terrorism: The Master Plan: For the New Theorists of Jihad, Al Qaeda Is Just the Beginning." *The New Yorker* (September 11): 48–58.

Wright, Lawrence. 2006. *The Looming Tower: Al-Qaeda and the Road to 9/11.* New York: Alfred A. Knopf.

Index

psychology of, 28. *See also* Suicide bomber-martyrs

Homegrown terrorists/terrorism: acting out by, 141; bomb making, 5, 55, 99, 109; charisma and, 9–10; decisions, actions, and responsibility of, 139–41; defined, 1–2; help to prevent, 155–56; Internet media as message, 146; making of, 62; martyr psychology and fundamentalist mentality, 101–3; media as messenger, 2–3; normal and abnormal leaders/ groups, 6; observations and recommendations regarding, 147–51; Personal Pathway Model in, 32, 61, 95, 152; prison experiences of, 13, 32, 58–59, 71, 147; psychodynamic patterns, 145–46; psychology of recruiter, 4–5; rationalizations of, 14, 18, 50, 110; televised terrorist event, 3–4; tiny tests, 140–43, 156. *See also* Father hunger of homegrown terrorists; In-betweeners

Homosexual dynamics, 40, 47, 48

Horner, Althea, 123

Hoskins, Richard Kelly, 87

Hussain, Syed Qurban, 22

Identity: Christian Identity Theologies, 11; negative identity formation, 24–26, 62, 115–17, 152, 176; theology of, 86–87

In-betweeners: future terrorists, 12–14; group psychology in recruitment, 26; homegrown suicide bombers, 26; individual and group self, 24–25; internal world of, 139; leaders, self-extensions, and group power, 25; overview, 11–12, 22–24; peer pressure and, 28–30; suicide cult followers, 27–28; terror cult recruitment, 27; as useful concept, 152; the West as father figure, 30–31. *See also* Homegrown terrorists/ terrorism

India, 78, 80

Individual self-formation, 24–25

Institute of Islamic Research and Teaching, 74

Intellectual Atheists/Agnostics (IAA), 19

Internet: as Al Qaeda training camp, 32, 64, 71; brainwashing forms on, 62; Islam through chat rooms, 43, 47; *jihadi* websites, 13, 18, 51, 122, 129; media as message, 77, 142, 146; military equipment purchases on, 75; for monitoring terrorists, 89; network of holy warriors on, 36; nonexistence of God on, 19; propaganda on, 11, 26, 67; rebellious loners on, 16, 67–68; self-radicalization process, 1, 122; social media use, 3, 140, 147; terrorism and, 3–5, 147

In the Shade of the Quran (Qutb), 36, 59

Intrapsychic choice conflict, 140

Iraq: Al Qaeda training camps in, 11; in-betweener community in, 152; as in-betweener country, 26; terrorist recruiters in, 28; U.S. military action in, 2, 110; U.S. war decisions in, 148

Islamic Group (Egypt), 36

Islamic Society of Orange County, 44

Islamic terrorists: father hunger in, 125–26; fundamentalist mentality, 20–21; media technology and, 3; Moroccan Islamist militants, 60; radical imams, 13, 71, 146; Tunisian Islamist militants, 60. *See also* Al Qaeda; Jihad/jihadists; Radical Islamists; Taliban

Islamic Thinkers Society (ITS), 61

Islamist jihad. *See* Jihad/jihadists

Islamofascism, 37, 127

Israel, 14–15, 35, 86, 101, 103–4

Japan, 87

Jihad Jane. *See* LaRose, Colleen

Jihad/jihadists: American *Jihadis,* 26; declarations of, 121; Egyptian Islamic Jihad, 36, 59; establishment of, 35; Global Salafi Jihad, 24;

About the Author

PETER A. OLSSON, MD, is an assistant professor of psychiatry at Dartmouth Medical School and an adjunct professor of clinical psychiatry at Baylor College of Medicine in Houston. Dr. Olsson is a Fellow of the American Academy of Psychoanalysis. He is a distinguished life fellow of the American Psychiatric Association. Olsson retired from active clinical work to write full time in September 2011.